EDITED BY LEONARD HOLLIS

The
Rose
Annual
1971

THE ROYAL NATIONAL
ROSE SOCIETY

'ALEC'S RED' (H.T.)
'Fragrant Cloud' × *'Dame de Coeur'*
Raised by J. Cocker & Sons Ltd.
PRESIDENT'S INTERNATIONAL TROPHY AND GOLD MEDAL 1970
See page 175
(The colour illustration in the 1970 Rose Annual was not representative)

Contents

Patrons, Officers and Council   6

Presidents and Awards   8

Arrangements for 1971   9

The Society's Gardens   13

Report of the Council   15

Annual Accounts   18

The President's Page   20

Gallica Roses TESS ALLEN   22

The Class for a Stem J. L. HARKNESS   30

The Famous Fragrant Reds DERRICK EVERITT   31

The Enthusiast W. R. JOHNSON   34

William Paul—Victorian Rosarian BETTY MASSINGHAM   36

Symposium on Roses for Rainy Districts LEONARD HOLLIS, DR. A. DICK, L. POOLE, J. CRAIG WALLACE, DR J. T. WATTS, COL. W. B. WRIGHT   40

Steve's Maggot W. D. ROBERTS   58

The Rose and William Cowper DR. MICHAEL BALL   60

Rose Foliage F. FAIRBROTHER   63

Roses from Kitchen Window Cuttings F. C. H. WITCHELL   66

A Tale of Five Cuttings PATRICIA HONNOR   68

Roses from Cuttings LEONARD HOLLIS   69

Back to 1913 ARBEL M. ALDOUS   72

On Safari through Senghenydd ANON   78

The Men behind the New Roses NIGEL RABAN   80

Seasonal Notes in 1970 VERA F. P. DAY   91

The Rosarian's Year Book, 1890 J. L. HARKNESS   95

Fifty Years of Progress in Climbing and Rambling Roses E. B. LE GRICE   103

Black Spot and Overhead Irrigation PETER BEALES   110

Roses in the Gardens of The National Trust (2) GRAHAM THOMAS   112

3

CONTENTS

The Use of Urea in Black Spot Sprays   J. H. BARTRAM   121
A Motherly Touch   R. S. B. PINKS   124
Plant Breeders' Rights and Roses   128
Rose Seed Germination in relation to Stock Production
   J. B. BLUNDELL AND G. A. D. JACKSON   129
Early 19th Century Climbing Roses in New Zealand   NANCY
   STEEN   136
Pegged Down Roses   S. M. GAULT   142
An Alternative to DDT   E. V. ELWES   145
Notes From My Files   E. F. ALLEN   146
Growing Roses by the Sea   JOHN R. WINSHIP   149
The Provincial Display Gardens   S. M. GAULT   151
The Decorative Classes   JULIA CLEMENTS   155
The Summer Show   J. P. WOOD   159
The Northern Rose Show   R. C. BALFOUR   164
The Autumn Rose Show   GORDON FORSYTH   168
The Trial Ground and Display Garden 1970   L. G. TURNER   172
The Awards to New Roses in 1970   175
European Rose Trials   STELVIO COGGIATTI   178
International Awards 1970   181
Book Reviews   185
The Rose Analysis   L. G. TURNER   189
International Rose Convention—New Zealand 1971
   W. A. JAMES   198

COLOUR PLATES   *facing page*
'Alec's Red'   3
'Golden Chersonese'   14
'Chorus Girl'   15
'City of Gloucester'   32
'Charles Dickens'   33
'Picasso'   48
'Grace Abounding'   49
'Golden Times'   96

CONTENTS

facing page

'Stephen Langdon'   97
'National Trust'   112
'Rosy Mantle'   113
'Esther Ofarim'   128
'Megiddo'   129
'Lagoon'   144
'Roaming'   145
First Prize Box and Bowl 1970   160
'Lorna Doone'   161
'Dorrit'   176
'Sunday Times'   177

MONOCHROME PLATES   *facing page*

Frank M. Bowen   20
A Typical Stem as required for the Single Stem Class   28
Gallica Roses   29
R. rugosa 'Scabrosa' and 'Canary Bird'   64
R. sericea pteracantha and *R. multiflora watsoniana* 65
Wilhelm Kordes and Edward Le Grice   80
Jean Gaujard, Louis Lens and Sam McGredy   81
'Pink Perpetue' and 'Chaplin's Pink Climber'   104
'Ritter von Barmstede' and 'Schoolgirl'   104
In the garden of Old Roses at Nymans, Sussex (The National
    Trust)   105
'Mme Gregoire Staechelin' and 'Handel'   105
'Lamarque' at the rear of a yellow and white border   136
Borders at Hidcote, Glos. (The National Trust)   136
Rose Gardens at Rome and Geneva   137
'Dundee Rambler' adorns a pergola in Mrs Nancy Steen's
    garden in New Zealand   137

COMMITTEES FOR 1971

FINANCE AND GENERAL PURPOSES COMMITTEE

R. C. Balfour *ex-officio* (CHAIRMAN)

L. A. Anstiss	E. V. Elwes	J. Roscoe
H. G. Clacy	J. W. Mattock	B. W. W. Sampson
Gordon Edwards	R. L. Pallett	J. H. Shotter
	Brig. C. E. Lucas Phillips	

The President, Deputy President, Hon. Treasurer, Past-Presidents, Editor, The Chairmen of the New Seedling Judging Committee, the Gardens Management Committee, and of the Exhibitions Committee are *ex-officio* members of this Committee.

NEW SEEDLING JUDGING COMMITTEE

Maj.-Gen. R. F. B. Naylor (CHAIRMAN)

E. F. Allen	A. P. C. Dickson	E. B. Le Grice
R. C. Balfour (*ex-officio*)	Gordon Edwards	J. W. Mattock
F. M. Bowen (*ex-officio*)	F. Fairbrother	S. McGredy
W. K. Bentley	S. M. Gault	C. F. Roberts
John Clarke	C. W. Gregory	B. W. W. Sampson
A. M. Cocker	J. L. Harkness	W. E. Tysterman
	Leonard Hollis	

EXHIBITIONS COMMITTEE

H. N. Raban (CHAIRMAN)

R. C. Balfour (*ex-officio*)	John Clarke (*ex-officio*)	J. S. Mattock
F. M. Bowen (*ex-officio*)	S. M. Gault	C. F. Roberts
Mrs. H. G. Clacy	M. F. Goodchap	J. Roscoe
H. G. Clacy	W. A. James	J. H. Shotter

GARDENS MANAGEMENT COMMITTEE

J. L. Harkness (CHAIRMAN)

E. F. Allen	John Clarke (*ex-officio*)	Maj.-Gen. R. F. B. Naylor
R. C. Balfour (*ex-officio*)	S. M. Gault	(*ex-officio*)
F. M. Bowen (*ex-officio*)	J. W. Mattock	W. E. Tysterman
H. G. Clacy (*ex-officio*)		

PRESIDENTS OF THE
ROYAL NATIONAL ROSE SOCIETY

1877–1904 The Very Rev. DEAN HOLE v.m.h.

1905–06 CHARLES E. SHEA
1907–08 E. B. LINDSELL
1909–10 Rev. F. PAGE-ROBERTS
1911–12 Rev. J. H. PEMBERTON
1913–14 CHARLES E. SHEA
1915–16 EDWARD MAWLEY, v.m.h.
1917–18 Sir EDWARD HOLLAND
1919–20 H. R. DARLINGTON, v.m.h.
1921–22 Sir EDWARD HOLLAND
1923–24 SYDNEY F. JACKSON
1925–26 C. C. WILLIAMSON
1927–28 H. R. DARLINGTON, v.m.h.
1929–30 ARTHUR JOHNSON
1931–32 HERBERT OPPENHEIMER
1933–34 Dr. A. H. WILLIAMS
1935–36 Major A. D. G. SHELLEY, r.e.
1937–38 HERBERT OPPENHEIMER
1939–40 JOHN N. HART, c.b.e.

1941–42 CHARLES H. RIGG
1943–44 HERBERT OPPENHEIMER
1945–46 A. NORMAN ROGERS
1947–48 A. E. GRIFFITH
1949–50 E. J. BALDWIN, o.b.e.
1951–52 D. L. FLEXMAN
1953–54 WILLIAM E. MOORE
1955–56 OLIVER MEE, o.b.e.
1957–58 A. NORMAN
1959–60 F. FAIRBROTHER, m.sc., f.r.i.c.
1961–62 E. ROYALTON KISCH, m.c.
1963–64 Maj.–Gen. R. F. B. NAYLOR, c.b.,
          c.b.e., d.s.o., m.c.
1965–66 F. A. GIBSON
1967–68 Maj.–Gen. R. F. B. NAYLOR, c.b.,
          c.b.e., d.s.o., m.c.
1969–70 JOHN CLARKE
1971 FRANK M. BOWEN, c.eng.

THE QUEEN MARY COMMEMORATION
MEDAL AWARDS

1957 ALEX DICKSON & SONS
1957 SAMUEL McGREDY & SON
1957 E. B. Le GRICE
1957 HERBERT ROBINSON, m.b.e.

1957 OLIVER MEE, o.b.e.
1957 A. NORMAN
1964 BERTRAM PARK, o.b.e., v.m.h.

THE DEAN HOLE MEDAL AWARDS

1909 Rev. J. H. PEMBERTON
1910 EDWARD MAWLEY, v.m.h.
1912 GEORGE DICKSON, v.m.h.
1914 CHARLES E. SHEA
1917 E. B. LINDSELL
1918 Sir EDWARD HOLLAND
1919 Rev. F. PAGE-ROBERTS
1919 GEORGE PAUL
1920 H. R. DARLINGTON, v.m.h.
1921 S. McGREDY
1923 Miss E. WILLMOTT, f.l.s.
1924 SYDNEY F. JACKSON
1925 COURTNEY PAGE
1926 C. C. WILLIAMSON
1930 Dr. J. CAMPBELL HALL
1930 WILLIAM E. NICKERSON
1931 ARTHUR JOHNSON
1933 HERBERT OPPENHEIMER
1935 Dr. A. H. WILLIAMS
1935 WALTER EASLEA
1936 ALISTER CLARK
1937 Major A. D. G. SHELLEY, r.e.
1940 JOHN N. HART, c.b.e.
1942 CHARLES H. RIGG
1942 Dr. HORACE J. McFARLAND
1945 Dr. H. V. TAYLOR, c.b.e.
1947 A. NORMAN ROGERS
1948 Dr. G. E. DEACON

1949 W. E. MOORE
1949 A. E. GRIFFITH
1950 JOHN RAMSBOTTOM, o.b.e.,
          Dr.sc., m.a.
1950 F. S. HARVEY-CANT, m.b.e.
1950 E. J. BALDWIN, o.b.e.
1952 D. L. FLEXMAN
1952 BERTRAM PARK, o.b.e., v.m.h.,
          Mérite Agri.
1952 Dr. A. S. THOMAS, o.b.e., v.m.a.
1954 W. E. HARKNESS
1956 OLIVER MEE, o.b.e.
1958 A. NORMAN
1959 W. J. W. SANDAY
1960 F. FAIRBROTHER, m.sc., f.r.i.c.
1962 H. G. CLACY
1962 E. ROYALTON KISCH, m.c.
1964 G. D. BURCH
1964 Maj.–Gen. R. F. B. NAYLOR, c.b.
          c.b.e., d.s.o., m.c.
1965 H. EDLAND
1965 E. BAINES
1966 EDGAR M. ALLEN, c.m.g.
1966 F. A. GIBSON
1967 ALEX DICKSON
1967 W. KORDES
1969 J. W. MATTOCK
1970 JOHN CLARKE

8

Arrangements 1971

Amateur Spring Competition 4th and 5th May

The Amateur Spring Competition for roses under glass is to be held in conjunction with the Flower Show at The Royal Horticultural Society's Halls, Westminster. By courtesy of The Royal Horticultural Society members will be admitted to both Halls on presentation of their Membership Certificates. Payment for accompanying visitors may be made at the turnstile.

Summer Show 2nd and 3rd July

The Summer Show is to be held at the Alexandra Palace, London, N.22 and will occupy the Great Hall and Palm Court for both days.

Northern Show 20th and 21st July

The Northern Show is to be held in conjunction with the Roundhay (Leeds) Horticultural Society at Roundhay Park, Leeds. Members, who may be accompanied by one guest, will be admitted, *once only*, on presentation of their Certificate of Membership.

Autumn Show 14th and 15th September

The Autumn Show is to be held in The Royal Horticultural Society's Halls, Westminster, and will occupy the New and Old Halls for the two days.

Schedules for these Shows are available on request to The Secretary, The Royal National Rose Society, Chiswell Green Lane, St. Albans.

Admission to Shows

Members will receive a Certificate of Membership which will admit the holder to the above shows and the provincial shows listed thereon, two transferable tickets for the Summer Show and two transferable tickets for the Autumn Show.
Prices of admission to the public will be:

Summer Show 2 July 11.30 a.m. to 5 p.m. 50p, 5 p.m. to 8 p.m. 30p.
3 July 10 a.m. to 5 p.m. 30p.

Autumn Show 14 September 11 a.m. to 7 p.m. 30p.
15 September 10 a.m. to 5 p.m. 15p.

Members may purchase additional tickets for the Summer and Autumn Shows at half price. Applications accompanied by remittances must be received at the Society's office not less than three days before the respective show.

Northern Show 20 July 11 a.m. to 3 p.m. £1·25, 3 p.m. to 6 p.m. 75p, 6 p.m. to 9 p.m. 40p.
21 July 10 a.m. to 5 p.m. 30p, 5 p.m. to 8 p.m. 20p. Children under 15 15p both days. Old Age Pensioners 20p on 21 July only.

No price reductions other than the above are granted at the Northern Show.

R.N.R.S. Classes at Provincial Shows and Admission Arrangements

By the courtesy of the organisers of the following Shows, members of The Royal National Rose Society are offered special concessions in respect of exhibiting and free admission which the Council acknowledges with thanks. Unless indicated by an asterisk both concessions will apply. Details of the Shows offering free admission to R.N.R.S. members are given on the Membership Certificate:

Ashington Rose Society's Show on 10 July.

Berwick-upon-Tweed and District Rose Society's Show on 25 July.

Bexleyheath and District Rose Society's Show on 26 June.

★*Bournemouth and District Rose Society's Show* on 26 June. (No R.N.R.S. classes.)

Bramhall, Cheadle Hulme and Woodford Agricultural and Horticultural Society's Show on 21 August.

Bristol and District Group of R.N.R.S. Show on 7 July.

Bryndorion (Swansea) and District Rose Society's Show on 26 June.

Clontarf Horticultural Society's Show on 26 June.

Colchester Rose and Horticultural Society's Show on 26 June.

Congleton and District Horticultural Society's Show on 10 July.

Eastleigh and District Rose, Carnation and Sweet Pea Society's Show on 3 July.

Formby Horticultural and Agricultural Society's Show on 10 July.

Franche (Kidderminster) and District Rose Society's Show on 26 June.

Glamorgan (Vale of) Agricultural Society's Show on 18 August.

Hereford and West of England Rose Society's Show on 26 June.

★*Hitchin Horticultural Society's Show* on 26 June. (No R.N.R.S. classes.)

Ipswich and East of England Horticultural Society's Show on 10 July.

Isle of Wight Rose, Carnation and Sweet Pea Association's Show on 26 June.

Lakeland Rose Show on 2 and 3 July.

Leicester and Leicestershire Rose Society's Show on 10 July.

Manx Rose Society's Show on 10 and 11 July.

North of England Rose, Carnation and Sweet Pea Society's Show on 13 and 14 August.

North Western Group of R.N.R.S. Show on 5 September.

Nottingham Rose Society's Show on 10 and 11 July.

Reading Horticultural Federation's Show on 20 and 21 August.

Renfrew Horticultural Society's Show on 18 September.

Scottish National Sweet Pea, Rose and Carnation Society's Show on 7 and 8 August.

Southampton (Royal) Horticultural Society's Show on 9 and 10 July.

★*Southport Flower Show* in Victoria Park, Southport on 25, 26 and 27 August (10 a.m. to 9 p.m., 9 a.m. to 9 p.m. and 9 a.m. to 5.30 p.m.). R.N.R.S. Classes but *not* free admission.

West Cumberland Rose Society's Show on 10 July.

West Midlands Rose Society's Show on 17 and 18 July.

Please note that the Certificate of Membership does not admit to the Southport Flower Show or any other Show not listed.

For further details and schedules of the aforementioned Shows application should be made to The Secretary, R.N.R.S.

Display Gardens

Members and their friends are cordially invited to visit the displays of rose varieties that have received awards provided at:

Cardiff—Roath Park

Edinburgh—Saughton Park
Glasgow—Pollok Park
*Harrogate—Northern Horticultural Society's Gardens, Harlow Car
Southport—Botanic Gardens
Taunton—Vivary Park
Teesside—Borough Park, Redcar

   * At Harlow Car the rose displays occupy a small portion of the ground only and it is hoped that visitors will each be willing to contribute a donation of 10p towards general upkeep.

Rose Bulletin

The Rose Bulletin will be published in October, and all members will receive a copy free of charge. Items of news, topical rose stories and interesting reports from members will be welcomed and should be sent to the Secretary.

New Zealand—International Rose Conference

Council is endeavouring to obtain the most advantageous terms for members wishing to attend the Conference in New Zealand but, unfortunately, at the time of going to press these have not been finalized. All members interested in this tour are particularly requested to advise the Secretary irrespective of whether application has previously been made to an agent.

   Details of the Conference appear on page 198.

Lecture Aids

It is regretted that no lecturing equipment may be borrowed for private viewing.

   Film

"Focus on the Rose" is a 16-mm. colour film with sound track. It is loaded on two spools and runs for 1 hour 17 minutes. Every aspect of rose cultivation is covered and also included are beautiful views of the Society's Garden at St. Albans and shots of the Summer Show at Alexandra Palace, London.

   It is available for hire by members and Affiliated Societies for lecture purposes subject to the following conditions:

1. Borrowers shall pay a hire charge of £3 at the time of booking. The fee includes outward carriage.

2. The booking form and indemnity must be signed before any reservation is made.

3. A first-class sound projector and experienced operator must be employed for the screening.

4. A spare take-up spool and can will be provided, and these must be returned with the film.

5. The film must not be re-wound after screening.

6. Any damage must be reported on the "Damage Report" accompanying the film. Under no circumstances should any attempt be made to repair a break.
   The film must not be screened on a silent projector.
   A charge of £1 per day will be made for each day the film is retained after the day following the screening.

   Slides

There are sets of slides available covering:
   General cultivation

Bed Preparation and planting
Varieties with historical connections
Modern varieties
The Evolution of the Rose—a set prepared by Gordon Rowley of Reading University.

Film Strip

This is in two parts:
   Preparation of the soil and planting—36 frames
   Rose Pruning—37 frames
Full details of all equipment and booking form may be obtained from the Secretary.

Library

The library at St. Albans contains a comprehensive collection of books on rose growing and is open to members during office hours (Monday to Friday, 9 a.m. to 5 p.m.). Alternatively, books (not more than two at one time) will be despatched by post, subject to postage being paid by the borrower. A list of books available will be sent on application.

Sales

The following items are available from the office:

Publications

Additional copies of the current issues of:

Roses: A Selected List of Varieties	25p
Roses: The Cultivation of the Rose	25p
The Rose Annual	50p
The Rose Bulletin	15p

There is also a selection of good secondhand copies of back editions of *The Rose Annual* at 25p each.

Member's tie, made in good quality terylene and bearing a single motif of the Tudor rose on a plain background. Choice of maroon, navy blue, rifle green, medium grey, dark brown or bronze background—£1·05 each, three for £3.

Member's badge, depicting the Tudor rose worked in red and white enamel with either brooch or stud (buttonhole) fitting—30p each.

Postcard views of the gardens—2p each.

Slides—eight shots of the Shows mounted on 35 mm transparencies—65p per set.

The American Rose Society

An arrangement has been made whereby members resident in Great Britain may join the American Rose Society by remitting their subscriptions of £4·80 to The Secretary, The Royal National Rose Society, Chiswell Green Lane, St. Albans, Hertfordshire.

Subscriptions and Resignations

Members are reminded that subscriptions are due and payable on 1 January each year and it would assist the office administration if the reminder form is returned with the remittance.

Any member wishing to resign must give notice to the Secretary on or before 1 February, after which date the member will be liable for the subscription for the current year.

The Society's Gardens

The Society's Gardens at St. Albans are provided for the enjoyment of members and their friends. They are divided into two sections, the Trial Ground and Display Garden.

THE TRIAL GROUND is for new seedlings where some 750 varieties may be seen undergoing trials. Varieties are submitted before being introduced into commerce and for this reason the majority will be under number. Adjudication is carried out by the New Seedling Judging Committee and varieties are eligible for the Society's Gold Medal, Certificate of Merit and Trial Ground Certificate awards. The President's International Trophy is awarded annually to the best seedling and the Henry Edland Memorial Medal to the most fragrant variety on trial.

Varieties that have received a trial award since 1963 are planted in a bed around the perimeter of the ground.

THE DISPLAY GARDEN has been extended in recent years and now occupies approximately seven acres. Here may be found over 500 old and new varieties.

How to Get to the Gardens

The Gardens are situated approximately four miles from St. Albans Station and are off the main Watford Road (A412). Visitors using public transport may travel by the following routes:

British Rail to St. Albans City Station—London terminus St. Pancras or *Underground* (Bakerloo Line) to Watford, and thence by No. 321 bus which runs between Watford Junction and St. Peter's Street, St. Albans.

Green Line coach No. 712 Luton—London (Victoria)—Dorking. No. 724 Romford— St. Albans—High Wycombe. Also routes 713 Dorking—London (Victoria)— Dunstable and 714 Dorking—London (Hyde Park Corner)—Luton to St. Albans centre and thence by bus No. 321 or 361.

The fare stage at which to alight from bus or coach is The Three Hammers Inn, Chiswell Green. The gardens are half a mile along Chiswell Green Lane which is adjacent to the Inn.

Visiting Arrangements for 1971

The Gardens will be open from Saturday, 12 June to Saturday, 2 October, at the following times:

Monday to Friday	9 a.m. to 5 p.m.
Saturday	9 a.m. to 6 p.m.
Sunday	2 p.m. to 6 p.m.

The Gardens will be closed on Monday, 30 August. Members wishing to see the Gardens before 12 June or after 2 October may do so from Monday to Friday only.

Terms of Admission

Membership certificates, which are to be shown at the turnstile, will admit the holder and one guest free of charge and four additional persons on payment.

Affiliated Society Certificate will admit two persons free of charge and four additional persons on payment.

Affiliated Societies may arrange for a party to visit the Gardens during the above hours. Applications must be made in writing to the Secretary at least fourteen days beforehand, stating the number in the party and the proposed date and time of the visit. Holders of Certificates and accompanying guests as specified above will be admitted free of charge. Members of the party not covered by such certificates will be admitted on payment.

Price of admission to persons accompanied by a member or in the party of an affiliated society, but not covered by certificate is 10p each.

Price of admission to public (Monday to Saturday only), 20p adults, 10p children under 14.

Refreshments

There is no restaurant within the Gardens. A Visitors' Lounge is provided where hot and cold refreshments are available.

Picnics are not allowed in any part of the Gardens.

Luncheon may be obtained at The Three Hammers Inn, Watford Road (half a mile from the Gardens) from Monday to Saturday.

Car Park

A car park is provided but the Council accepts no responsibility for loss or damage to property or vehicles.

It is regretted that coaches cannot be accommodated in the car park or Grounds.

Disabled or Invalid Members

Two wheel chairs (not self-propelled) are available for the convenience of disabled members. Visitors desirous of using these should apply in advance.

Guides

An alphabetical list of varieties, giving their location in the Display Garden, may be obtained at the turnstile.

Photography

Amateur photographers may use cameras in the Gardens but photographs or transparencies must not be used commercially. Professional photographers must obtain written authority from the Secretary.

General Regulations

Dogs must be kept on a leash at all times.

Entry and exit shall be through the respective turnstiles.

Rose blooms, buds, trees or parts of trees must not in any circumstances be cut, removed or taken from the Grounds.

'GOLDEN CHERSONESE' (shrub)
R. ecae × *'Canary Bird'*
Raised by E. F. Allen
CERTIFICATE OF MERIT 1970
See page 175

'CHORUS GIRL' (floribunda)
'Highlight' × *seedling*
Raised by Herbert Robinson
CERTIFICATE OF MERIT 1970
See page 175

Report of the Council

For the year ended 31st December 1970

Membership

The first year of the uniform subscription of £1 has ended. The result has been a response by members which exceeded the most optimistic expectations of Council.

The losses sustained through resignations and death were larger than the number cf new members enrolled, but in spite of this the total membership at the end of the year was the not unsatisfactory total of 99,330.

In an endeavour to increase membership several innovations are being tried, in particular, the production of a two-page leaflet, poster advertisements at Garden Centres, etc. Once again the Council is indebted to the members of the trade for their help by permitting the inclusion of leaflets in their catalogues.

Bureaux were established at the Chelsea and Southport Shows, in addition to those of the Society and of the Groups. An information Chalet is also provided in the Rose Garden at Syon Park Garden Centre.

Finance

As expected income shows a welcome increase but already much of this is required to meet the ever increasing costs. It should be noted that the cost of the new Bulletin does not appear in these accounts.

Postage is less this year, partly as a result of a somewhat smaller mailing list, but more especially because last year's charges were inflated abnormally by several additional mailings. The increased rates, due to take effect next year, will be a particularly heavy burden and Council appeals to all members to help to contain this by paying subscriptions promptly or by making use of Bankers or Giro Standing Orders for making annual payments.

Publications

The Rose Annual was despatched to all members in April and once again the Editor, Mr Leonard Hollis, is to be congratulated for the production of another fine volume. An outstanding event of the year was the issue of *The Rose Bulletin* in November. The need for such a publication, to bridge the gap between the yearly editions of *The Rose Annual*, has been apparent for some time. It is hoped that *The Rose Bulletin* will continue to be issued in the autumn each year.

Council records thanks to the small group, led by Mr Gordon Edwards, who pioneered the work entailed in producing the first edition.

Shows

Our Patron, Her Majesty Queen Elizabeth, The Queen Mother, graciously honoured the Society by attending the Summer Show at Alexandra Palace.

Although the weather during the early part of the season caused some concern, there was a considerable improvement in June which enabled trade members to stage the best exhibits for several years. The Championship Trophy was won by John Mattock Ltd. for an extensive and interesting wall group. The amateurs and the Floral Arrangement Section were also well up to their usual high standard, and the combination produced a memorable spectacle. Unfortunately, inclement weather and some counter attractions resulted in a disappointingly lower attendance on the second day.

The Northern Show held in conjunction with the Roundhay Show at Leeds again coincided with torrential rain. The Roundhay (Leeds) Horticultural Society has now suffered severe financial loss over the last three years through inclement weather.

Amongst many outstanding features of the Autumn Show were the magnificent display which gained the Autumn Roses Challenge Cup for Bees Ltd., and the excellent exhibits staged in the Floral Arrangement Section.

The thanks of the Council are recorded to all exhibitors, in particular to members of the trade who, in spite of ever increasing costs, continue to support the Society's Shows.

The Trial Ground and Display Garden

The trials of new varieties conducted by the Society continue to be well supported by raisers from many parts of the world. During the past year no fewer than 1,500 trees were planted, representing altogether 258 varieties, of which 82 were sent by hybridists from overseas. The President's International Trophy and a Gold Medal were awarded to 'Alec's Red', raised by James Cocker & Sons, the most outstanding variety on trial; 'News', raised by E. B. LeGrice (Roses) Ltd., a floribunda showing a distinctive new colour break, received a Gold Medal.

Development of the Display Garden, including the collections of historical varieties and species, continues and planting of a large number of trees this autumn will bring the scheme a stage nearer to completion. The Edland Pavilion – a central figure of the lay-out – was formally opened in June by Mr E. J. Baldwin, O.B.E., D.H.M., senior Past President of the Society, who invited Mrs B. B. Edland, widow of the late Secretary, to cut the tape across the door. Council records its appreciation to Mr H. G. Clacy who was responsible for the design, and its execution.

On the same occasion the new flag was broken and flies proudly over the grounds on appropriate occasions.

Examination for Rose Judges

The second examination for rose judges was held at St Albans and as a result a further fourteen candidates received certificates of proficiency. Unfortunately, the examination cannot be extended so as to accommodate all those members who wish to be considered, because it is necessary to spread the selection amongst candidates from varying localities.

Groups of Members

A North Western Group of the Society has been established since the conditions were amended, and now joins Bristol and District Group and Cardiff and District Group.

The first show of the new group was held at Southport in September and attracted an encouraging number of exhibitors and a good attendance.

Provincial Display Gardens

Interest in these displays of varieties that have received the Society's awards continues, and Council wishes to record its appreciation to the various authorities responsible for their maintenance. Arrangements are in hand to establish a display at Redcar, and the beds at Pollok House, Glasgow, will be ready during 1971.

Offices

During the year the membership records have been computerized which provides for greater speed and efficiency with a consequent reduction in staff. Modifications to the office accommodation have also been completed.

Plant Variety Rights Exhibition

The Society was invited by the Plant Varieties Rights Office to participate in an exhibition illustrating the progress made in research work in connection with the introduction of new varieties of flowers and crops. This was held in the historical and beautiful surroundings of the Banqueting Hall of Whitehall Palace. Mr and Mrs E. F. Allen and Mr. W. A. James staged a very fine exhibit on behalf of the Society depicting the genealogy of the Gold Medal rose 'Grandpa Dickson'. The centrepiece of the exhibition, an island stand displaying many rose novelties, made a wonderful contrast to the famous Rubens ceiling.

Research

Continuing financial grants have been made to support research at the Universities of Bangor, Bath and Manchester.

Hon. Vice-President

Mrs C. A. Wheatcroft has been elected an Hon. Vice-President of the Society in recognition of her long and active service on the Council and the loyal support given at the Society's shows as a trade exhibitor.

Conclusion

In conclusion the Council desires to express its thanks to all Committee members, the Hon. Scientific Adviser, Editor, Horticultural Adviser and especially the Secretary and staff at Bone Hill, for their work during the year.

By order of Council
JOHN CLARKE

DEAN HOLE MEDAL

The Council is very pleased to announce that the Dean Hole Medal, the highest award of the Society, has been bestowed on Mr John Clarke for the many years of devoted service that he has given to the Society and the Rose.

R.A.—2

BALANCE SHEET, 30th SEPTEMBER, 1970

1969 £		£	£	£
	SURPLUS			
	Balance 1st October 1969	77,522		
	Add Excess of Income over Expenditure for the year ended 30th September 1970	4,074		
77,522				81,596
	SPECIAL FUNDS			
	F. P. Gaskill Prize Fund	100		
	L. Hewlett Prize Fund	100		
	A. E. Griffith Memorial Fund	100		
	Gilbert Burch Memorial Fund	100		
400				400
	RESERVE FOR DEVELOPMENT—TRIAL GROUND, DISPLAY GARDEN AND PROPERTIES			
	Balance 1st October 1969	14,000		
	Add Charge against Revenue Account	5,780		
		19,780		
	Less Expenditure during year	5,780		
14,000				14,000
	RESERVE FOR NEW EDITIONS OF PUBLICATIONS, FILM AND CONFERENCE			
	Balance 1st October 1969	14,000		
	Add Charge against Revenue Account	6,000		
14,000				20,000
	RESERVE FOR PENSIONS			
12,000	Balance 1st October 1969	12,000		
				12,000
	CURRENT LIABILITIES			
12,294	Sundry Creditors	5,499		
24,247	Subscriptions received in advance and one quarter of 1970 subscriptions (excluding Life Members)	26,927		
				32,426
154,463				160,422

1969 £		£	£	£
	FIXED ASSETS			
37,000	Freehold Properties			37,000
	Office Equipment etc.			
	Balance 1st October 1969		2,000	
	Additions during year		417	
			2,417	
	Less Sales	457		
	Amount written off	460		
			917	1,500
	Motor Vehicles, Mowers and Equipment			
	Balance 1st October 1969		2,000	
	Additions during the year		462	
2,000			2,462	
	Less Amount written off		462	
				2,000
2,000	Library at Professional Valuation (1967)			1,650
1,650				
42,650	**INVESTMENTS AT COST**			42,150
86,426	(Market Value 30th September 1970 £82,421)			86,426
(82,840)				
	CURRENT ASSETS			
	Stock of Publications, Badges, etc. as valued by the Secretary		4,123	
5,125	Sundry Debtors for Advertisements, etc.		1,074	
2,189	Cash at Bankers on Deposit and Current Account and in Hand		23,009	
15,820	Income Tax recoverable		3,640	
2,253				31,846
154,463				160,422

AUDITORS' REPORT

To the Members, The Royal National Rose Society

We have audited the above Balance Sheet dated 30th September 1970 and Revenue Account for the year ended on that date and have obtained all the information and explanations we have required. In our opinion such Balance Sheet and Revenue Account are properly drawn up so as to exhibit a true and correct view of the state of the Society's affairs according to the best of our information and explanations given us and as shown by the books of the Society. We have verified the Securities representing the investments of your Society at 30th September 1970 and have found the same to be in order.

EVERS & CO., *Chartered Accountants, Auditors*
2 NORFOLK STREET, LONDON, W.C.2. 14th November 1970

REVENUE ACCOUNT FOR THE YEAR ENDED 30th SEPTEMBER, 1970

1968/69 £		£	£	£	£
	PUBLICATIONS				
28,860	Expenditure		26,979		
481	Less Sales	567			
3,405	Advertising Revenue	3,974	4,541		
24,974					22,438
	SHOWS				
2,368	Prize Monies, Medals and Trophies		3,237		
4,704	Expenses		4,566		
7,132			7,803		
585	Less Proceeds		343		
6,547					7,460
6,940	**TRIAL GROUND AND DISPLAY GARDEN**				8,075
	ADMINISTRATION				
15,221	Salaries and Assistance, Superannuation Contributions and Supplementary Pensions		16,248		
	Computer Charges		4,104		
1,151	Rates, Lighting, Heating, etc.		1,086		
5,463	Printing and Stationery		5,118		
12,831	Postages		9,824		
2,002	General Expenses, Telephone, Hire of Rooms, etc.		2,761		
1,010	Repairs and Renewals—office and premises		658		
300	Auditors' Fee		350		
790	Bank Charges		785		
38,768					40,934
4,228	ADVERTISING AND PUBLICITY				5,156
282	PROVINCIAL DISPLAY GARDENS				359
1,300	GRANTS TO UNIVERSITIES FOR RESEARCH				500
3,413	RESERVE FOR NEW EDITIONS OF PUBLICATIONS, FILM AND CONFERENCE				6,000
4,049	RESERVE FOR DEVELOPMENT—TRIAL GROUND, DISPLAY GARDEN AND PROPERTIES				5,780
546	MOTOR VEHICLES, MOWERS AND EQUIPMENT—Amount written off				462
525	OFFICE EQUIPMENT—Amount written off				460
					97,634
—	BALANCE—Excess of Revenue over Expenditure for the year				4,074
91,572					101,708

1968/69 £		£	£
	SUBSCRIPTIONS AND AFFILIATION FEES		
83,118	Subscriptions	93,324	
926	Affiliation Fees	1,393	
84,044			94,717
	INCOME FROM INVESTMENTS ETC.		
6,665	Gross		6,991
484	FILM—Proceeds of Sale		—
379	BALANCE—EXCESS OF Expenditure over Revenue for the year		—
91,572			101,708

The President's Page

The developments and the progress made in 1970 by our Society are faithfully recorded in the Report of the Council, but several things remain outstanding in my memory. In early July our Patron, Her Majesty Queen Elizabeth The Queen Mother, honoured us by an informal visit to the Summer Show and, in so doing, once again afforded great pleasure to everybody at Alexandra Palace; and to none more so than the eminent rosarians from Victoria and Queensland, South Africa and New Zealand, who happily were with us on this occasion.

Our first Autumn Bulletin was published in early November (somewhat later than planned due to uncontrollable last minute delays in printing) and this I regard as an outstanding innovation with considerable potential. The experience gained in the production of this first issue will be brought to bear on the 1971 Bulletin, as will all comments and suggestions which we hope members at large will offer. Council is very much alive to the vital role that its publications play in the life of the Society and arrangements for managing them in the future have already been reviewed and modernised.

Rising costs, especially of postal charges, continue to pose serious problems, but do, I feel, prove how wise it was to face the prospect and change the subscription scale last year. In 1971 every reminder on payment of subscription will lose us about 5p, so I make no apology for underlining Council's appeal to either pay by Banker's Order, etc. or otherwise to remit subscriptions early in the year. Such savings as these will be doubly valuable in this and next year, during which the Society will have to expend much effort on metrication.

With the first two main phases of development of the display gardens and trial grounds at Bone Hill largely completed as planned, 1971 will be devoted mainly to consolidation of the designs and establishment of certain improvements. All gardens take time to mature and ours will continue to improve for several years, thus making a visit ever more worth while, especially now that the extensions to the motorway system have rendered access to Bone Hill so much easier and quicker than it used to be.

We shall continue our efforts to strengthen the links between the Society and its Groups and Affiliated Societies; and I shall do my utmost to attend or be officially represented at as many of the latter's shows as possible during 1971 and 1972. In connection with shows, a special word of thanks to those

Frank M. Bowen, C.Eng.
President 1971–72

enthusiasts who so willingly came to Bone Hill at their own expense and took our judging tests in 1969 and 1970. These two years have provided valuable information and possible improvements in the arrangements will be instigated in 1971. The value of any qualification rests on the quality of the tests one must pass to attain it; our judging tests are not easy but I am sure all candidates will agree that they have felt a sense of real achievement in passing them. I hope and believe that these tests have come to stay and, in the long run, will be of great benefit to this important and enjoyable side of our hobby. I would like to encourage all members, old and new, who have not tried it before, to take the plunge and exhibit—in however modest a way— at their local shows and, in due course, our own, because in my experience by so doing one learns much about roses, obtains great relief from the pressures of working life today and, above all, gains tremendous pleasure through meeting kindred spirits and making innumerable lasting friendships.

Undoubtedly, the outstanding event of 1971 in the rose world at large will be the International Convention in New Zealand. The length of journey and the cost and time involved are, of course, major obstacles to a large attendance from Britain, but the R.N.R.S. party tours are planned to extract maximum enjoyment whilst avoiding the error of attempting too exhausting an itinerary; they incorporate several days in Melbourne en route to attend the special show and banquet of the National Rose Society of Victoria. If these events attain, in quality and hospitality, the standard of those I attended in 1967 (and I shall be very surprised if they do not!) they will constitute an unforgettable preamble to the activities in New Zealand. The wonderful spirit of international comradeship and goodwill that prevails on these occasions has to be experienced to be believed and all members who can join our party will be very welcome.

From our 1970 Trials, Scotland has emerged supreme but 'News' and 'Picasso' also have proved that there is no end to the fascinating development of this wonderful flower the rose. The R.N.R.S., the largest body of its kind in the world, has made extraordinary progress in the past twenty years and for this we all owe a debt of gratitude to our predecessors. It is up to us to ensure that the progress will be maintained by continuing to widen our activities, not only for our own benefit, but also in anticipation of future advancements and needs for leisure and enjoyment of the generation that will succeed us. When all is said, the Society and our hobby are inextricably linked together. I esteem it a great privilege to have been elected as President of the Society and extend best wishes to members and friends everywhere.

F. M. BOWEN

Gallica Roses

TESS ALLEN

(Amateur gardener in three continents and sculptress)

Approximately four dozen different Gallica roses are available from nursery-men in England; with few exceptions those offered for sale are hybrids. However, they are only listed as such when the Gallica influence is not dominant. Gallica roses are rooted in antiquity and although there has been considerable cross-pollination, the group retains identifiable characteristics. They have a creeping root stock and when grown on their own roots will sucker and develop into small, erect shrubs three to four feet high; budded plants grow taller and do not sucker. The foliage is usually dark-green, thick and rough to the touch; the stems have bristles, some with thorns, others thornless. The scented flowers, generally solitary, are held erect on stiff stems, a carriage approved of by admirers of modern roses. Under different conditions of soil and climate the colours of the petals vary in intensity and range.

The colours are some of the gayest found in old roses, in fact 'Super Star' and flowers of that ilk are the only roses of brighter hue than newly opened flowers of *Rosa gallica officinalis* and 'D'Aguesseau'. Furthermore, one of the best and most vigorous shrubs with single roses, 'Complicata', belongs to the Gallica group; it is considered to be a hybrid of *Rosa macrantha*. The large roses are almost five inches across, the bright pink colour of the petals shading into a white band round the golden stamens.

Gallica roses were probably the first roses to be cultivated in the Near East and European gardens, and thus they are the ancestors of most modern roses. In 1888, W. M. Flinders, the Egyptologist, while excavating a tomb near the Labyrinth Pyramid in Upper Egypt, found a dried garland containing roses which were identified for him by the Belgian taxonomist Crépin as a form of Gallica. Also the roses found by G. A. Schweinfurth, the German ethnologist and botanist, in Egyptian tombs dating from 100 A.D.–300 A.D. belonged to the Gallica tribe. Greek and Roman citizens cultivated the ancient Gallica roses, but during the tumultuous years of the Middle Ages these roses were restricted to the monasteries, where they were grown for their therapeutic qualities.

When conditions improved there was a revival of the arts, and the Renaissance artists with great fidelity depicted *R. gallica* and its varieties in their religious and pagan paintings, as can be seen in one of the famous pictures of

22

the German school 'Madonna of the Rose-Bower' by Martin Schongaeur and Botticelli's 'Birth of Venus'. The laity were again able to cultivate these roses for many different purposes. The petals boiled in white wine, together with a selection of herbs, were alleged to have been successfully used by the physician Paré in the treatment of gunshot wounds. Distilled rose water was a panacea for fainting, trembling and shaking; it was further asserted that roses strengthened the heart and refreshed the spirit. The petals were also used for confectionery and a French conserve made of rose petals was so delectable and the demand for it was so great that a jam industry grew up round the town of Provins, south-east of Paris.

As the centuries passed, Gallica roses remained in cultivation and the legends of the rose increased as freely as the flowers doubled. In the eighteenth century Gallica roses were at the height of their popularity, when great numbers were raised by the Dutch, and the French took up the good work of hybridisation. After the repeat flowering China roses were introduced into Europe the hybrids of these became the most sought after roses and the Gallicas fell from grace, as they only bloom in summer. Fortunately the agreeable qualities of the best have survived the attrition of fashions and of time.

I have seen Black Spot on Gallica rose bushes growing in walled and enclosed gardens in Kent but in our exposed garden in Suffolk I have planted twenty different types of Gallica roses and neither Black Spot nor Rust has disfigured their leaves; some bushes are susceptible to mildew if the diet is too rich for their needs. As I do not spray these roses I took care not to plant them with any roses which receive and need frequent spraying. This precaution ensures that the unpaid labour force of beneficial insects, lace-wing flies, labybirds, hoverflies and bird allies, such as song-thrushes, robins, wrens, tree-creepers, pheasants and partridges do not get killed, go on strike or move house. In a year when the enemies of the rose muster in great force it is necessary to remove aphids from the sticky, young rose shoots either by rubbing them off by hand or by aiming a strong jet of water from the hose at the pests. Like all garden roses Gallicas need good drainage. The pruning requirements are negligible; gather the flowers, spare the buds and after the flowering season is over, remove any old, unproductive wood, and do any light pruning to shape the bush or simply leave it as it is.

Rosa gallica officinalis, also known as: *R. gallica plena*, *R. gallica maxima*, 'Double French Rose', 'Rose of Provins', 'Apothecary Rose' and 'Red Rose of Lancaster', differs from the type plant *R. gallica* (*R. rubra*) by its semi-double flowers and larger leaves. The crimson buds open to fiery-crimson flowers and fade to purple-crimson, the strongly scented petals retaining their spicy fragrance when dried. Our plant, originally a sucker, was given to us by a neighbour who thirty years ago planted a blush-pink crimson striped rose in a bed of poor garden soil. She called this rose 'York and Lancaster' and, although I very much doubt if the plant received any fertiliser, it continued to thrive and produce suckers, some of which reverted to the original crimson rose of *R. gallica officinalis*. Her rose was, of course, 'Rosa Mundi' but I never had the temerity to correct the niece of one of Miss Jekyll's most intimate friends. However, this reticence did not prevent me from enjoying the ensuing scene when anyone else did, or argued about the correct pronunciation of a plant name. In the latter case the enemy was always defeated by the simple manoeuvre of bringing forward a little book *Plant Names Simplified* by A. T. Johnstone and H. A. South. Our neighbour's gay assemblage of *R. gallica officinalis* and 'Rosa Mundi' never suffered from mildew whereas, in a mixed border receiving an annual rich mulch, I planted a budded bush of 'Rosa Mundi' and this regularly gets mildew in late summer. From this I deduce that Gallica roses do not like being over-indulged.

'Rosa Mundi', also known as *R. gallica versicolor* and *R. gallica variegata*, has never been surpassed and although, like all old Gallicas, it has only one flowering season you will, in spite of this, find it adding distinction to nurserymen's show exhibits of modern Hybrid Tea and Floribunda roses. The semi-double, pale-blush roses are dappled and striped with carmine and crimson; the contrast between the glint of golden anthers and the gay colours of the petals never fails to attract attention. Legend relates that this rose was named after Rosamond Clifford, the mistress of Henry II. She was buried in 1176 at the Nunnery Church of Godstow, a fact recorded in the old ballad 'Fair Rosamond'.

> *'Her body then they did entomb,*
> *When life was fled away,*
> *At Godstowe, neare to Oxford towne,*
> *As may be seene this day,'*

In his book, *The World of Roses*, B. Park quotes the unpleasant Latin couplet inscribed on her brass tomb. Henry's Queen, Eleanor of Aquitane, may have been the author of Fair Rosamond's epitaph, as Eleanor was the grand-daughter of the most famous of all troubadours and she carried on this poetic tradition. Her chronicler wrote of her as a "woman beyond compare", gay, beautiful, poetical and powerful. She had ten children, one of whom was Richard Coeur de Lion, but a rose does not bear her name.

'Camaieux', one of the three striped gallica roses I grow is a dwarf bush not nearly as vigorous as 'Rosa Mundi', and thus it needs good soil. The double flowers have blush petals splashed and striped with carmine changing to lilac and in hot, sunny weather, the stripes fade to purple and grey as the petals turn white.

'Tricolore de Flandres' grows to a neat bush about three feet high. This striped rose has numbers of small, cream petals marked with fine crayonings of carmine, lilac and purple. When the flowers are fully open the petals recurve and form pompons. The stems of my young plant are free from thorns and at Bayfordbury there was an old bush without thorns.

'Belle Isis' is a spruce, neat bush and the dainty, scented, cup-shaped flowers are flesh-pink in colour. It flowers early and freely, the small blooms gradually become paler as they expand. While the plant has more thorns than I like, on the credit side it is one of the parents of the lovely modern, shrub rose 'Constance Spry', raised by D. C. H. Austin.

'Gloire de France', a low growing bush with a few thorns, bears large, double flowers on short stems. The globular, pink buds open to lilac-pink roses which fade to blush. G. S. Thomas records in his book *The Old Shrub Roses* that this rose is known in America by the name of 'Fanny Bias'. In the American Rose Society's 1967–68 Handbook for selecting roses, a Gallica rose 'Jeannette' is rated 8.8—no other Gallica rose receives such high marks and yet in England we do not know this rose. Possibly we grow it under another name.

'Jenny Duval' has exquisite buds and blooms to incite one to use extravagant prose. Therefore, in order to be factual I referred to the Royal Horticultural Society's new Colour chart. Unfortunately, even the facts make a severe demand on the credulity of the reader, as on matching the buds, newly opened and mature flowers with the colour chart, the range of colours was even greater than I expected as I found numbers 57, 58, 59, 65, 75, 76, 78 and, in addition, tones A.B.C. and D. The red, coiled buds expand to show these colours: ruby, old rose, five different purples, lilac, grey and brown. Furthermore, in the centre of the fully opened flowers the base of the petals is cream, flushed with yellow and crowned by a cluster of citron-yellow styles. Most of the anthers are modified to form petals but in some flowers a few anthers and petaloid stamens can be found. 'Jenny Duval' has a pronounced fragrance and the blooms last well owing to the firm texture of the petals. The bush appreciates good soil.

'Oeillet Flamand' is something of a mystery. W. Paul in the 1863 edition of his book *The Rose Garden* describes 'Oeillet Flamand' as a white Gallica rose striped with rose and lilac and it is illustrated in *Rosen-Zeitung* 1892 as a striped rose. In Hillier & Sons' catalogue of rose trees a pink damask is listed under this name. I bought my 'Oeillet Flamand' from Edwin Murrell of Shrewsbury and in the catalogue it is described as a "glowing pink, almost salmon Gallica rose"; the nursery has been uncertain about the name of this thorny bush for some time as, unfortunately, they have no record of its source. The cup-shaped flowers are scented, but the bright colour of the petals fades as the flower ages.

'Charles de Mills' is a strong grower and flowers well. The buds as they open are ugly; they look like small beetroot with the tops cut off, but the open roses are beautiful. The large flowers are packed with firm petals, deep crimson and purple with pink on the reverse side. As the blooms reach maturity the petals turn to plum-purple and wine, but they continue to hold their shape well.

'Du Maître d'Ecole' has a vigorous constitution and flowers of pronounced scent. The almost thornless plant carries a generous crop of large blooms, rose in colour shaded with purple, lilac and grey. The nostalgic scent and the colours of this rose cast a shadow across the present and recall the silk popular with my grandmother's generation.

'Président de Sèze' is a strong, thorny plant with good foliage. Long sepals extend beyond the rosy pink buds which open to two toned flowers; the outside petals are pale-lilac and the centre royal-purple; as the blooms expand the two colours merge into a luminous lilac. An established plant of 'Président de Sèze' can be expected to provide large, double flowers for a comparatively long period.

'Duchesse de Montebello' is an erect, trim bush and even in its middle-age spread, it retains a comely shape and will grow five feet tall. The newly-opened roses are like shallow goblets, filled with scented, curved, rosy-pink petals. As the flowers mature the petals recurve to form pale-pink rosettes, blending beautifully with the glaucous-green leaves of this excellent shrub.

'Duchesse de Buccleugh' in my experience promises unrealized potentials. I grew my plant from a thornless cutting and I hope that when it attains its full stature the roses will at last become symmetrical in shape. The large, full flowers have a great number of confused magenta-pink, scented petals. Inclement weather may be the cause of its present distorted blooms. The leaves are large and feel like sandpaper.

'Duchesse d'Angoulême' ranks as a hybrid Gallica; it is a delicate but wiry bush, a rose mobile forever swaying in the slightest breeze. The young leaves are lemon-green in colour and, in maturity, they turn light green, but remain soft and smooth. Long, narrow sepals protect blush-coloured buds splashed with crimson, and the flower stems droop under the weight of the globular, scented flowers. The blush petals have the quality of fine porcelain and are tinged with deeper pink as if an artist, passing by with a brush saturated in paint, had with delicacy and lightness of touch shaded the petals. There is an exquisite painting of this rose by Charles Raymond in 'Part Two' of *Old Garden Roses* by W. Blunt and J. Russell. This rose seems to me to be more like the small Centifolia roses than the typical Gallica.[1]

Rosa × *francofurtana* 'Agatha' is another Gallica rose catalogued as a hybrid; it is a Gallica × *R. cinnamomea* and from this species has inherited the large, spreading stipules. It appears to be able to tolerate shade, as my bush has grown with contentment for five years in an unused corner of the vegetable garden, between an old oak tree and a small pear tree, backed by a double hedge of three foot high box and seven foot high thorn. The scented, lilac roses have petals like crumpled organdie and a conspicuous brush of yellow stamens adds to the effect of the semi-double, loosely formed flowers. They are not as evanescent as one would expect from their appearance. The foliage is decorative and the large leaves, grey-green with a blue undertone, pay me an annual dividend in beauty I do not deserve. I bought this rose on the false assumption that it was thornless. When the bush arrived bristling with thorns I was indignant and carelessly planted it in its present, unsuitable site and forgot about it. Years later, when trimming the box hedge, the unexpected beauty of the rose foliage attracted my attention. The leaves of *R.* × *franco-furtana* 'Agatha', like those of all sun-loving foliage plants, would be even more colourful if the plant received additional light. The four foot high bush has very few thorns now on the young wood.

Rosa × *francofurtana* is a lower growing bush than *R.* × *francofurtana* 'Agatha' and although the leaves have the same wide stipules, the foliage is not as decorative. However, it is a better garden shrub than 'Agatha' and the roses are a finer shape. The petals have the same unusual texture, but they are a more popular, rich-pink colour veined and shaded with a deeper rosy-pink. They lack the fragrance of the variety 'Agatha'. The rose is better known as 'Empress Josephine'—her name and old roses have become synonymous as it was at the Château Malmaison that Napoleon's first Empress grew the roses which Redouté painted. When my daughter and I last visited Malmaison eight years ago the rose garden was a sad sight and did not reflect the past extravagance and glory of Josephine's time, when she grew all the two hundred and fifty roses, of which one hundred and seven were Gallicas,

[1] Modern Roses–7 states the parentage as possibly *R. centifolia* × *R. gallica*. Ed.

known in her day. However, the shady corner of the 'English Garden' and the rocks, on which Josephine languidly reclines in Prudhon's portrait of her now in the Louvre, were structurally unchanged.

'Cardinal de Richelieu' was originally named 'Rose Van Sian' but it is under the later name that it is one of the best-known, purple Gallica roses. The floppy stems bear a few thorns and bristles and numbers of small, mauve-pink buds open to murky-purple, ball-shaped roses. As the sombre flowers age the colour turns to a dusty-purple. The colour is not as I expected it to be, the glowing-red of the Cardinal's vestments in his triple portrait, painted by Philippe de Champaigne, in the National Gallery.

'Hippolyte's' light-green stems have the merit of being almost thornless. It bears quantities of double, violet-purple flowers, smaller and brighter in colour than those of 'Cardinal de Richelieu', on stiff stems. They open flat and later develop into a ball of violet-grey petals. It is susceptible to mildew in our garden.

'Belle de Crécy' has latent possibilities and although I do not want to denigrate its flowers they have never lived up to their reputation in our garden. The bush is a large, unwieldy plant with dull green leaves. The lilac-pink buds open to full, flat flowers with a lovely range of colours: rose, lilac, purple and slate grey. A late frost will distort the shape of the flowers but, even at their best, they never surpass the elegant refinement of 'Jenny Duval'.

'D'Aguesseau' is a vigorous bush with most arresting, bright-red, full flowers. As the scented roses age the outer petals become paler and suffused with purple, but they retain their pagan air. It is diverting to reflect that this rose was immortalised by the mid-Victorian Dean Hole on pages sixty and sixty one of his book *A Book About Roses* as the rose which first aroused his interest in the *genus Rosa*.

Gallica roses have a future; they do not survive on recollections of vanished popularity, but are currently being used by discriminating hybridists. *R. gallica officinalis* has played a part in a programme for breeding hardy roses in Canada carried out by F. L. Skinner of Manitoba. 'Belle Isis' was one of the parents of 'Constance Spry'; the floribunda 'Dainty Maid' was the other parent. E. B. Le Grice has used the deep maroon-violet Gallica 'Tuscany Superb' as one parent and crossed it with his own 'Lilac Charm' to breed a bright, cerise-purple, semi-double, repeat flowering floribunda called 'News'.[1]

W. Kordes recommends his modern Gallica hybrid 'Scharlachglut' ('Scarlet Fire') for groups and hedges, as it provides good cover and pear-

[1] Awarded the Gold Medal of the R.N.R.S. in 1970. Ed.

A typical stem as required for the Single Stem Class
(*see page* 30)

Key

Gallica roses

1. 'Duchesse d'Angoulême'
2. 'Charles de Mills'
3. 'Belle Isis'
4. 'Cardinal de Richelieu'
5. 'Rosa Mundi'
6. Buds of *Rosa* × *francofurtana*
7. 'Hippolyte'
8. 'Jenny Duval'
9. 'Tuscany Superb'
10. 'Camaieux'
11. 'Belle de Crécy'
12. Buds of *R. gallica officinalis*
13. 'Duchesse de Montebello'
14. 'Tricolore de Flandres'
15. 'Du Maître d'Ecole'
16. 'Gloire de France'
17. 'President de Sèze'
18. Murrell's 'Oeillet Flamand'

Gallica roses (for varieties see key)

shaped heps for birds. This vast shrub, bearing large, five-petalled, scarlet flowers, can also be grown as a climber. It was the result of a cross between 'Poinsettia' and the Gallica 'Alika'. The latter rose I have not seen, but it is recorded as having been brought from Russia in the first decade of this century by N. E. Hansen, and flowers are reputed to be large and brilliant red in colour, without any purple. In 1960 W. Kordes raised 'Waldfee' ('Woodfairy') which he classes as a repeat-flowering Gallica in his book *Roses*. Possibly owing to its desirable remontant habit, 'Waldfee' has been listed as a Hybrid-Perpetual in Macfarland's *Modern Roses*–7. However, it may have been the precursor of a new race of recurrent-flowering Gallica roses.

SONG OF THE ROSE

My sister is the wild rose, she roams the countryside,
Beneath her filmy petticoats the ruined quarries hide,
And all along the sandy shore she flaunts her petals white,
Or rosy in the country lanes she scents the summer night.

A richer perfume fills the air around my garden home,
Old-fashioned and yet well beloved, we never seek to roam.
The seasons find us well content to flower in the sun
And with frost-tinted leaves beguile the days when flowering's done.

My daughter in her modern dress is never very sure—
Will she be maxi?—mini?—She flaunts her bold allure
In fashionable colours that are very bright and gay.
But when her long days' flowering's done and winter winds hold sway,
She lifts up arms all bare and brown, her charm all fled away.

And yet men love our different ways—pay homage to us all
From the lowly little dog-rose to the rambler on the wall,
We blossom for him through the gold of lazy summer hours,
As down the years, for time untold, befits the Queen of flowers.

VERA MACPHERSON

The Class for a Stem

J. L. HARKNESS
(Rose nurseryman and breeder)

At the end of a day judging in the Trial Ground, a few of the judges were chatting together. Many of the new seedlings had large heads of bloom on them, very beautiful. Where, asked the judges, do you draw the line now between hybrid tea and floribunda? Look at the truss of flowers on this alleged hybrid tea—could you disbud it to get a specimen bloom?

From there arose the idea—why not exhibit these beautiful heads of flower? How much more natural the Society's Shows would look, if instead of specimen blooms we had specimen inflorescences, or trusses, of all kinds of roses. The idea went to the Exhibitions Committee, and a class was put into the schedule.

Unfortunately, the exhibits up to now have not succeeded in fulfilling the ideas behind this class. So now I am detailed to try and explain what is wanted. It is really very simple:

"One stem bearing a number of blooms, the exhibit to consist entirely of young growth."

It is the proviso about young growth which causes difficulty, both to exhibitors and judges. It means just this: the stem ought to have grown into a flowering head by breaking into side shoots *before the centre (or terminal) flower bud came into bloom.* The class is *not meant* for stems which had a centre (or terminal) flower and then some weeks later put out side shoots. To express it another way, the difference in age between the stem and its subsidiary flower-bearing stems ought to be as little as possible. The whole lot should be from one non-stop impulse to grow.

In judging this class last year, we looked for this quality of youth. We did not find it helpful to see the main stem cut, or stopped, though it was understandable that the centre flower had to be removed, having passed its best. Where the main stem was noticeably older than the flower stems, we did not consider the exhibit to comply with the schedule.

Most exhibits were too tall. The ideal is to enable the flower stems to stand clear of the vase, the whole at a height which the spectator can look down upon. Bare stem is no attraction.

Exhibitors, just think how pretty this class could be. I hope that these notes as to its origin, intention and execution will help to make it a success.

The Famous Fragrant Reds

DERRICK EVERITT

(*Amateur rose grower and hybridist*)

> "*Ere twice the shades o' dawn are fled*
> *In a' its crimson glory spread,*
> *And drooping rich the dewy head,*
> *It scents the early morning*".
>
> Burns

The red damask-scented rose is perhaps symbolic of all that is desirable in our National Flower. In fact, one wonders whether the rose would to-day be held in such esteem were this colour absent. It gives one food for thought.

If we go back but a mere century we find the hybrid perpetuals at the zenith of their popularity. Many of these were of red or crimson colouring, most were blessed with fine fragrance and among their ranks are several worthy contenders for entry to our Hall of Fame. One stood out above all others; the great 'Général Jacqueminot', raised in 1853 by Roussel of France and named in tribute to an officer of Napoleon's army.

That illustrious rose grower of the period, William Paul, author of *The Rose Garden*, one of the great rose books, considered the "General" one of the best. In fact it was probably the very best. Popularly known as "General Jack", this rose of bright scarlet colouring and intense fragrance, with its gently nodding camellia-shaped blooms, set a standard by which others were judged. Most of the subsequent important reds up to the present day can trace their ancestry back to this refulgent beauty.

Although countless fine red roses were introduced in the intervening years we have to wait for more than half a century before the next aspirants to greatness came along and then, in the same year, 1905, two of considerable merit put in a belated appearance.

The first, which also claimed a lofty military status, was 'General Mac-Arthur', of unestablished parentage, but its habit allocated it to the hybrid tea class. Rose-red and very fragrant, this can still be found in many a proud owner's garden. Of lesser petallage than most and less rich colouring, it nevertheless held a high position for many years in the merit tables as published in *The Rose Annual*. The American, McFarland, no mean authority on the subject, once wrote that were but a single red rose admitted into the garden, it might easily be this one.

Its contemporary was 'Hugh Dickson', named after the head of the cele-
brated Irish firm that raised it. Genetically it would seem to be a hybrid tea,
but the hybrid perpetuals usually claim it. High centred, amply perfumed,
richly crimson shaded scarlet and of rampant growth, "Hugh" needs to be
pegged down to be grown successfully. A fine bed so fashioned can to-day
be seen at Kew and should be sought out by all rose-loving visitors. One of
the foremost exhibition and garden roses of its time and still available, it has
surprisingly been most unnoteworthy as a parent and its progeny can be
counted on the fingers of one hand.

Just a few years later, in 1912 to be exact, and thanks to the same family,
Alex Dickson presented 'George Dickson', the recipient of an N.R.S. Gold
Medal the previous year. Despite its pendulous habit and too often poor form
it was widely acclaimed and won much fame on the show bench. Undoubtedly it graced the gardens of all self-respecting exhibitors. Well endowed with
perfume and of fine colouring, crimson deepening to maroon, the huge
blooms as if chastened hang their furiously-blushing heads.

The first world war over, Verschuren's 'Etoile De Hollande' was hastily
introduced in 1919, a rose of great decorative value but, alas, not always
impeccably formed. Of Continental origin, it can boast no gold medals as
apparently it was not sponsored by a British firm, but for many years it was
unquestionably one of the most highly esteemed red hybrid teas. Like many
roses of this colouring it often failed to hold its blooms erect and probably
for this reason its climbing sport eventually superseded the bush form in
popularity. Widely grown even now, its prodigious first flush of bloom in
early summer makes a spectacular display when seen embellishing a house wall.
Here its nodding blooms can be seen to their best advantage.

We are indebted to Wilhelm Kordes for our next representative, the
appropriately christened 'Crimson Glory', the finest red of its day. For many
years Kordes had been striving for the perfect red and the story leading up to
the introduction in 1935 of 'Crimson Glory' makes interesting reading. This
was narrated by Kordes himself in an address to the 1938 International Rose
Conference held in London and which can be found faithfully transcribed in
The Rose Annual of the following year. Its fragrance is a by-word and this
attribute, coupled with fine velvety-textured crimson colouring, ensured it
an unassailable position at the top of the N.R.S. merit tables for most of the
war and early post-war years. Naturally a Gold Medal winner, it eventually
relinquished the throne in 1950 to one of its own offspring, the equally
famous 'Ena Harkness'. 'Crimson Glory', like its forebear 'Général Jacqueminot', has proved to be a prolific parent of fine calibre red roses.

'CITY OF GLOUCESTER' (H.T.)
'Gavotte' × *'Buccaneer'*
Raised by John Sanday (Roses) Ltd.
TRIAL GROUND CERTIFICATE 1970
See page 176

'CHARLES DICKENS' (floribunda-H.T. type)
'Paddy McGredy' × *'Elizabeth of Glamis'*
Raised by S. McGredy IV, N. Ireland
TRIAL GROUND CERTIFICATE 1970
See page 176

An amateur, the late Albert Norman, a retired diamond setter, gave the world 'Ena Harkness'. Still a current favourite, few gardens are without her; "Ena" accomplished the dual feat of gaining both the N.R.S. and Portland Gold Medals. Of impeccable form and colouring, with fragrance to match, this doyen of red roses has the unforgivable fault, shared with many of her predecessors, a tendency to droop her elegant head. For this reason the standard form is a better proposition.

My first acquaintance with 'Ernest H. Morse' engendered admiration mixed with pessimism as the brilliant turkey red colour is not held too well, but the more I see of this comparative stripling convinces me that here is the best red rose in commerce today. A little above average height with an exemplary habit, it really fills a bed; no red hybrid tea I know is so generous of flower. Rarely a prey to mildew, "Ernest" has few apparent faults and I've never heard an unkind word said of it. Some roses have greatness thrust upon them; this one will surely earn it on merit alone.

'Fragrant Cloud' is not a true red, being neither crimson nor scarlet, and when the weather is uncompromising a rather wishy-washy shade of coral, but I feel it is close enough. Prone to Black Spot and unhappy in the rain, the fantastic scent and beautiful form must ensure it a prominent place in rose history.

No apologies are made for the omission of the other fine red roses of which a few perhaps are superior to some of those selected, as it is doubtful if they have achieved equal greatness. 'Josephine Bruce' was left out after much heart searching and another may have included her. 'Christian Dior' was never in the race, having too many faults and no fragrance, whilst Kordes 'Independence', famous progenitor of so many similar red cultivars fails to qualify for similar reasons. 'Charles Mallerin', 'Chrysler Imperial' and 'Papa Meilland' have given joy but more often than not despair. On the other hand that admirable bedder, 'Mme Louis Laperrière', deserved distinction but somehow never made it; an inexplicably underrated rose.

Of the newcomers, 'Red Devil' is just not for our climate. Tantau's 'Eroica' is well spoken of by the Editor, but I don't know it well enough to recommend it. 'Alec's Red' and 'Red Planet' are still on probation, but both having pocketed the President's International Trophy has given them a good start in life. Only time will tell, but inevitably many more fragrant reds will achieve the accolade of high office and rosarians everywhere wait impatiently for their introduction.

The Enthusiast

W. R. JOHNSON

(Amateur rose grower)

It all started with the beetroot—when we were first married I had a sudden rush of blood to the head and planted rows and rows of beetroot seed. I watered them and exercised the necessary vigilance but when the great day came, I dug them up and found to my horror that without exception they were all tall and thin and just like the ladies in that form—very uninteresting.

My wife, who has no sense of humour whatsoever, surveyed the sorry scene and said—though of course she is very ignorant when it comes to gardening—"You realise what you've done wrong, of course!" "No", I said, mystified as ever. "Beetroot should always fatten out, and they can't if you let them grow downwards. Put a flat piece of wood underneath each seed when you plant them and this forces them to grow horizontally".

This sounded logical to me and anything having this as a basis appeals to me, although I found it hard to understand how she had acquired this rather technical knowledge. Well naturally I believed this story, and it was not until after she had recovered from a violent attack of hysterics that I discovered her story was a complete fabrication.

From that day on my reputation as a gardener was established and we turned to other things. It either rained and wasn't fit to do any gardening or the sun shone and it was too nice to stay in and we pushed off to the coast. So apart from turning it over in my mind, I let the garden have its head.

I was once looking for a football we had lost at the bottom of the garden and the chap opposite greeted me as "Dr. Livingstone I presume!" I had always disliked the fellow—his garden was always immaculate. He never went off to football matches on a Saturday afternoon, but spent the time digging or something utterly futile—to cap it all, he even seemed to enjoy it! When we removed, gleefully leaving the jungle to our successors, we bought a house on a corner site and the garden had a hedge of roses on two sides. The vendor dug most of them up when he left so I hurriedly replaced them in April with 'Queen Elizabeth' on one side and another kind on the other. These turned out to be 'Orange Sensation' and I was the first in the area with them and secretly rather proud of the fact, although I didn't know what colour they were when I bought them.

Gradually we bought more and more roses—I even began to like gardening

—I can manage half an hour's pruning as well as the next man.

I let my wife help as well—it's good for married people to have joint activities—she does the digging mainly and wheels the stones and refuse down to the tip. She's not very good at the pruning and spraying and besides, it keeps her slim as well as giving her an interest.

Sometimes she tries to help with the planning and to humour her I listen. "Try turning the bed on the South Wall over to roses" she said one Sunday morning after bringing my breakfast to bed. This, of course, was absolute nonsense. I knew at once that the lack of air would cause them to suffer from mildew. Kindly, but firmly, I told her that the idea was ridiculous.

In that perverse way women have, she persisted with the idea. In the end, I gave way and knowing full well it was stupid said I would give it a try.

Even now she wasn't satisfied and wanted to discuss the roses I intended buying. This was too much, although I was prepared to tell her the variety and colour.

"Why don't you try shading them"? said the little woman—"start with white at one end and go through the pinks and reds, finishing with a deep red—say—'Ernest H. Morse' at the other end?"

I don't know where she had dreamed up an idea like this. It was as if she wanted to ruin the bed completely. Knowing that events would prove me right I decided to humour her. Benevolence pays on these occasions.

They arrived one Friday evening and it rained all day Saturday; no football either that day, so we decided to tackle the planting. We work quite well as a team—I act as general supremo and take the vital decisions—should 'Piccadilly' go to the left or right of 'Bettina' or whether to put 'Fragrant Cloud' in place of 'Super Star'. My wife does the things which require no thought or planning—she digs the holes whilst I decide upon the order of the roses and prune the roots.

By some strange stroke of luck, this particular rose bed is far and away the best we have—I think it must be the way I organised the planting and the post-natal care. The neighbours are very impressed with the shading, but when my wife explains to them the knowledge I have accumulated over the years, they begin to realise that those of us who take the trouble to learn about our hobbies will always get better results than those who just jog along.

The vicar called round last July and admired the bed on the South Wall. "God and Man make a fine team, Mr Johnson" he said. "They do indeed vicar" said my wife, "but you should have seen it when God had it on his own!"

William Paul - Victorian Rosarian, (1823-1905)

BETTY MASSINGHAM
(Amateur rose grower)

The name 'Paul' in connection with roses still means something to the gardener today thumbing through a catalogue or making a selection from a nursery garden. One of the most prolific and reliable of all red roses is, of course, 'Paul's Scarlet Climber'. 'Paul's Lemon Pillar', profuse in flowering in June and of superb colouring—white with a touch of ivory or palest lemon—is also vigorous in growth, sometimes achieving a height of ten to twelve feet. 'Paul's Himalayan Musk Rambler', blush to rose in colour and having a rich scent, will attain a height of about 40 ft and is grown to some effect through a yew at Hidcote.

William Paul's life must provide one of the best examples of time well spent. He died in his eighty-third year having devoted his energies not only to roses but to the profitable culture of fruit trees, how best to grow camellias, the cultivation of pelargoniums, ivies, hollies, the planting of ornamental trees and ideas on landscape gardening. A lecture read in 1869 at a Manchester show on *The Improvement of Plants* remains as one of the most important horticultural contributions on this subject. It was illustrated by personal experience of improvements carried out on subjects as diverse as brussels sprouts, common parsley and hollyhocks, involving scientific principles such as the Mendelian hypothesis and De Vries' theory of mutation.

But it should be acknowledged that these were interesting sidelines compared with the major part of his work which was undoubtedly concerned with roses. He must have been surrounded by roses, by talk about roses, and his earliest recollections must have been connected with them. His father's nurseries at Cheshunt, Hertfordshire, were founded in 1806 and Adam Paul was one of the four big names in rose-growing in the early nineteenth century in England.

Dean Hole, reminiscing about the early days of rose-growing, writes: "I like to think of Lee of Hammersmith complacently surveying those standard rose-trees which he introduced from France in the year 1818, which were the first ever seen in England ... I like to imagine the elder Rivers looking on a few years later, half pleased and half perplexed, as Rivers the younger budded his first batch of briars ... Then I wonder what those other heroes of the past, Wood of Maresfield, Paul of Cheshunt, and Lane of

Berkhampstead, would say to their sons and grandsons, could they see the development of the work which they began ..."

Certainly the opportunities were there at such a time of pioneering and development, and Adam Paul's son made the most of them. He made such good use of the chances surrounding him, of the knowledge to be accumulated and stored away in his mind, of his father's experience and reputation that, at the early age of twenty-five, he was in a position to have published one of the most important manuals on the rose ever written in this country— *The Rose Garden*. But even before this he was a contributor to the *Gardeners' Chronicle* in its early days and had already published *Observations on the Culture of Roses in Pots*. In their review of the second edition of this booklet the *Gardeners' Chronicle* remark: "Beginners, in this kind of cultivation, will find this a most useful pamphlet, and it may doubtless be read with advantage by persons even experienced in the art. The excellence of Mr Paul's roses, in pots, at our great metropolitan exhibitions, forms perhaps the best guarantee that could be offered of his ability to teach; and those who would wish to obtain similar results cannot do better than follow his instructions implicitly ..."

And so, as a young man, he was already an authority on the culture of roses in pots which was a relatively new idea at that time. Advocating this method of growing for exhibition he wrote: "Roses in pots during this season form highly interesting objects among the French; and why should they not do the same here, since it is allowed that our general cultivation of roses in the open ground is quite equal to theirs?"

As a young man, too, he came into contact with J. C. Loudon. As Loudon was taken seriously ill in October, 1843, dying two months later on the 14th December when he was struggling to finish his *Self-Instruction for Young Gardeners*, it may, perhaps, be surmised that William Paul, being at that time about twenty years of age, was one of the "Young Gardeners" Loudon might have had in mind as he dictated far into the night to try to get the book finished before he became too ill. (The work included instruction in:— arithmetic and book-keeping, geometry, mensuration, practical trigonometry, mechanics, hydrostatics and hydraulics, land-surveying, levelling, planning and mapping, architectural drawing and isometrical projection and perspective.) It is interesting to think that Loudon's teaching might have been responsible for William Paul's later ideas on landscape gardening or the planting of ornamental trees.

At about the same time the young man also came under the influence of John Lindley, Professor of Botany at University College, London, and

Assistant Secretary of the Horticultural Society. Professor Lindley had also worked with Sir Joseph Banks as an assistant in his library, and it seems likely that the literary influence of both Loudon and Lindley would be invaluable to William Paul as a training and of lasting importance in his later work. ·

The publication in 1848 of *The Rose Garden* was a landmark in both the rose world and in William Paul's own career. Its well-deserved success was soon established—it eventually went into ten editions—and anyone reading through it might well be astonished at the vast store of personal experience which lies behind the knowledge expounded in its pages, especially taking into account the youth of the author.

In 1849 a much smaller publication entitled *Morning Rambles in the Rose Gardens of Hertfordshire* made its appearance and was reviewed in January, 1850: "The object of these descriptions is to give 'rose fanciers' who live at a distance, and who might therefore be prevented from seeing these gardens, an opportunity of knowing what they contain and the modes of growth under which different varieties of roses flourish at their best." This little book proved to be a useful guide, giving a brief outline of the type of garden, how to get there and some of the most important roses to be found in it — a fore-runner of the present-day booklet brought out annually under the National Gardens Scheme. For example, Mr Warner's garden at Hoddesdon ". . . about a mile from the Broxbourn Station on the Eastern Counties Railway . . . is remarkable for the diversified surface it presents . . ." and includes amongst a long list of roses a "splendid Felicité et Perpétue".

But in spite of all this literary activity combined with practical fulltime work at the Cheshunt Nurseries, William Paul was one of the three chicf rosarians (the others being Mr Charles Turner and Mr Rivers) who promised to work with Dean Hole when he invited them, in 1857, to help him to organise the first National Rose Show.

In 1860, the now well-known and respected author of *The Rose Garden* parted from the Cheshunt Nurseries and started out on his own under the new name of "William Paul and Son, of Paul's Nursery," at Waltham Cross. The rose catalogue for this year comes under the new heading with a reproduction from a wood engraving of a standard rose on the cover, taken from chapter X of *The Rose Garden*.

Perhaps some of the most important tributes to his practical knowledge of roses came some thirty years after his death in the various mentions made by Mr Edward Bunyard in his rose classic *Old Garden Roses*. Messrs. Lee, Rivers and Wood all have single references made to their opinions but it is William Paul's advice that is most frequently quoted.

Discussing the Boursault, for example, Bunyard writes: "Mr William Paul points out that the shoots are very long and flexible, often nearly thornless, the leaves far apart, and the flowers in large clusters. He also says they do well in cold northerly exposures where other varieties would not thrive." The author also attributes to William Paul the interesting fact concerning the change of colour in most of the China roses owing to dull weather or bright sunlight, especially mentioning the now well-known case of 'Madame Pierre Oger.' He writes: "William Paul was the first, I think, to point out that these roses deepen in colour as they grow older, and as the sun strengthens, unlike the Damasks and Albas, which grow paler." Of these rare Damask roses it was William Paul who included twenty-three varieties in his list and perhaps the most outstanding tribute of all comes in connection with the Double Sulphur Rose (*R. hemispherica*): "W. Paul, from his great experience, advises the production of a moderate growth, overgrowing being fatal to flower production . . ."

"From his great experience" is the phrase which indicates clearly the scope of his life's work. He had the Victorian capacity for conscientious application to a task to be done with all the integrity and energy of which he was capable. Like Loudon he must have worked through all the hours that came. He also had the Victorian love of collecting, not only roses in his garden but a vast number of gardening and botanical books in his library. Another Victorian trait—that of an upright character, with a streak almost amounting to severity—is illustrated in his remark when it was suggested that a good name for one of his new roses might be 'Queen Mab', the queen of the fairies. He is reputed to have queried: "Was she a good woman?"

When I am dead, my dearest,
Sing no sad songs for me;
Plant thou no roses at my head,
Nor shady cypress tree:
Be the green grass above me
With showers and dewdrops wet;
And if thou wilt, remember,
And if thou wilt, forget.

CHRISTINA ROSSETTI

Symposium on Roses for Rainy Districts

LEONARD HOLLIS
(Editor and amateur rose grower)

The variable weather in different parts of Great Britain and Northern Ireland is always a lively topic of conversation among rose growers. It was felt that a Symposium contributed to by rosarians living in notoriously rainy districts might produce information of value to other members also resident in areas of high rainfall.

Our contributors are: Dr A. Dick, Glasgow; Mr L. Poole, Cardiff; Mr J. Craig Wallace, Newtownards, Northern Ireland; Dr J. T. Watts, Cheshire; Col. W. B. Wright, Bideford, N. Devon. All are experienced growers and Mr Poole and Col. Wright are former amateur champions of the Society. Each was invited to deal with the following matters, *inter alia*, in his reply:

1. Approximate average annual rainfall in his area, sub-divided into monthly averages, if possible.

2. A general indication of the petallage of roses which open well in the rain. It was expected that very full-petalled varieties would tend to "ball" under such conditions.

3. An indication of the contributor's experience of varieties with spreading growth or sprawling habit, the blooms of which would tend to become splashed with soil in heavy downpours.

4. Particular defects in varieties making them unsuitable for rainy districts, e.g. brittle footstalks or delicate colouring which is highly subject to staining in the rain. A short list of varieties found to be intolerant of rain.

5. Varieties recommended as particularly suitable for growing in rainy districts (a) hybrid teas (b) floribundas.

6. Any special treatment recommended for ripening the lush, soft growth produced in areas of high rainfall, or special points on feeding.

7. Any other observations considered to be relevant to the subject under discussion.

Not all of our contributors followed this outline, but a considerable amount of useful information was supplied, and it is convenient to follow the outline in commenting on the various points.

1. *Approximate annual average rainfall:* The following statistics of rainfall have been provided by the Meteorological Office:

Month	ENGLAND AND WALES			SCOTLAND			NORTHERN IRELAND		
	Average 1916/1950	1969	1970	Average 1916/1950	1969	1970	Average 1916/1950	1969	1970
	All figures expressed in millimetres								
January	92	97	106	154	146	118	109	131	109
February	66	73	82	106	82	139	76	79	126
March	57	77	64	89	43	91	66	48	84
April	60	59	85	88	73	95	67	69	85
May	63	115	26	87	116	75	72	107	35
June	55	57	46	87	86	75	71	79	56
July	79	71	70	114	78	144	96	51	94
August	81	76	80	122	87	116	102	55	109
September	76	39	65	128	125	144	96	39	122
October	92	18	56	158	118	184	111	59	117
November	95	142		143	170		104	132	
December	88	89		143	111		111	113	
Annual Total	904	913		1,419	1,235		1,081	962	

Note: 1 inch = 25·400 millimetres.

These statistics covering each of the three countries will clearly differ from those given by each contributor for his own particular district. The difference between the Scottish average for 1969 (1235 mm.) and that for Dr Dick's district in the West of Scotland (915 mm.) is illuminating, as one might have expected an average for the whole of Scotland to show a lower figure than for a district in the West of Scotland.

The monthly figures are useful as an indication of the extent to which rainfall during the flowering period, from June to October inclusive, contributes to the annual total, as it is the rainfall during these five months which can adversely affect the opening of the flowers or otherwise damage the open blooms.

2. *Petallage:* While our contributors agree that the very full-petalled varieties are most likely to "ball" in wet weather, this is not the only factor. Some with fewer, but soft-textured petals ball readily, as do some others with a high-centred bloom and therefore long petals. Col. Wright is more specific than his fellow-contributors and finds that hybrid teas with from 27 to 35 petals open well in the rain in the Bideford area. Dr Dick, Dr Watts and Col. Wright refer to high relative humidity rather than high rainfall as such at the time when the flowers are opening, as possibly having some bearing on "balling".

3. *Spreading growth and sprawling habit:* Dr Dick feels that the problem of varieties with a spreading type of growth can be overcome after the first year by judicious pruning and good cultivation. He mentions the floribunda 'Europeana', which bears particularly heavy trusses, as being unsuitable for rainy districts. Col. Wright also finds varieties with spreading growth no

great problem if they are pruned to inward-facing buds and the same rule is followed when cutting and dead-heading.

4. *Particular defects in varieties making them unsuitable:* Some varieties with brittle footstalks are mentioned, including 'Perfecta', 'Liberty Bell', 'Liebestraum' ('Red Queen'), 'Lucy Cramphorn', 'Super Star' and 'President Eisenhower' among the hybrid teas. Floribundas mentioned as having brittle footstalks include 'Queen Elizabeth', 'Celebration', 'Tombola' (particularly vulnerable in my garden), while 'Dearest' and 'Europeana' are considered unsuitable, the former because of balling and the latter because of the heavy trusses, as already mentioned. Hybrid teas referred to by our contributors as balling badly in wet weather include 'Montezuma' (black-listed by all of them) 'Red Devil', 'Karl Herbst', 'Memoriam', 'Royal Highness', 'Anne Letts', 'Brilliant', 'Margaret', 'Perfecta' and 'Liberty Bell'. It will be observed that all of these are of specimen bloom type and favoured by the exhibitor.

5. *Varieties recommended as particularly suitable:*

Hybrid teas:	Votes	Floribundas:	Votes
1. 'Peace'	5	1. 'Allgold'	4
2. 'Ernest H. Morse'	4	'Iceberg'	4
'Grandpa Dickson'	4	'Orange Sensation'	4
'Wendy Cussons'	4	'Queen Elizabeth'	4
5. 'Ballet'	3	5. 'City of Leeds'	3
'Mischief'	3	'Evelyn Fison'	3
'Piccadilly'	3	'Lilli Marlene'	3
'Stella'	3	'Orangeade'	3
9. 'Brasilia'	2	9. 'Anna Wheatcroft'	2
'Diorama'	2	'Arthur Bell'	2
'Fragrant Cloud'	2	'City of Belfast'	2
'Garvey'	2	'Escapade'	2
'Ginger Rogers'	2	'Europeana'	2
'Mme L. Laperrière'	2	'Flamenco'	2
'Peer Gynt'	2	'Frensham'	2
'Pink Favourite'	2	'Ice White'	2
'Prima Ballerina'	2	'Irish Mist'	2
'Red Lion'	2	'Manx Queen'	2
'Rose Gaujard'	2	'Marlena'	2
'Super Star'	2	'Paddy McGredy'	2
'Uncle Walter'	2	'Paprika'	2
		'Pink Parfait'	2
		'Tombola'	2

(a) *Hybrid teas:* Only 'Peace' was recommended by all five of our contributors, but 'Ernest H. Morse', 'Grandpa Dickson' and 'Wendy Cussons' each received the blessing of four of them.

(b) *Floribundas:* No variety was recommended unanimously, but 'Allgold', 'Iceberg', 'Orange Sensation' and 'Queen Elizabeth' found favour with four of our contributors.

6. *Any special cultural treatment recommended:* Most of our contributors recommend a dressing of sulphate of potash before the end of August at from 1-2 oz per sq yd to help with the ripening of the growth. Dr Watts finds this of value in ripening only the early growth, and considers that late growths might as well be cut out, as they will become frost-damaged in the winter. Our contributors are agreed that bloom protectors are essential to the exhibitor in a rainy district, coupled with the tying of the individual stems to canes to prevent movement as far as possible.

Mr Craig Wallace suggests that general purpose and proprietary rose fertilisers should not be applied after early to mid-July. Col. Wright has found that foliar feeding has helped to counteract the leaching of fertilisers applied to the soil.

7. *Other relevant observations:* Col. Wright mentions the combination of rain with strong to gale force winds in North Devon, and this is, of course, a particularly damaging combination. Some of our contributors feel that the advantages outweigh the disadvantages in rainy districts. Mr Craig Wallace refers to the extended blooming period in a moist, cool climate, coupled with the production of a big, leafy plant. Dr Watts, too, brings out some interesting observations on the influence of the weather on the colour intensity of the blooms; he also comments on the reduction in pests and diseases compared with drier parts of the country. Certainly when I grew roses in Lancashire diseases, other than Mildew, were conspicuous by their absence, but I attributed this to the fungicidal effects of smoke pollution rather than to the heavy rainfall. I would agree with him that there are fewer problems associated with rainy districts than with trying to grow roses in a dry part of the country, especially on a shallow soil, with a ban on watering in most seasons, and *always* when watering would be beneficial.

DR A. DICK, GLASGOW

Rainfall

My garden is situated on the outskirts of Glasgow seven miles to the south west, and just over 400 feet above sea level. It is exposed but the area is by no means the wettest in the West of Scotland; there are few high hills in the immediate vicinity.

It has proved an interesting exercise to obtain accurate rainfall statistics for the past two years, the monthly figures of which are shown in the table below.

RAINFALL STATISTICS FOR 1969-70

Month	1969 Rainfall		1970 Rainfall	
	inches	mm.	inches	mm.
January	4·26	108·2	3·60	91·4
February	1·07	27·2	4·75	120·7
March	0·90	22·9	2·20	55·9
April	1·67	42·4	3·22	81·8
May	4·00	101·6	1·80	45·7
June	2·75	69·8	2·70	68·6
July	2·49	63·2	2·69	68·3
August	3·14	79·8	3·54	89·9
September	3·23	82·0	5·10	129·5
October	2·47	62·7	6·94	176·3
November	6·44	163·6	6·61	167·9
December	3·61	91·7	2·52	64·0
Total	36·03	915·1	45·67	1160·0

In 1969 it was generally accepted that the West of Scotland enjoyed an excellent summer and roses were exceptionally good. In fact, reservoirs were at their lowest level for many years; in some areas even water rationing was enforced and I was not permitted to hose my garden or wash my car from August onwards. I would therefore have expected the rainfall for 1969 to be well below the annual average of 40 inches but it was only slightly lower, largely the result of 10 inches of rain which fell between November and December. The monthly figures, however, reveal a moderate fall each month from June until October. I think the rain must have fallen at night because quite frankly it did not seem to affect the roses adversely and I have not seen 'Red Devil' and 'Bonsoir' look better.

Turning to 1970 we, in Scotland, have universally lamented a sunless, wet summer with only three weeks of excellent weather at the beginning of June and one week at the beginning of August. This year the hybrid tea roses have never been comfortable in the damp, sunless weather and I have rarely seen more "balling" and have had to cut off thousands of abortive blooms which failed to open. I have often wondered why I grow so many roses!

Reference to the rainfall statistics shows that the total for 1970 of 45·67 in. is considerably in excess of the annual average of 40 in. and represents an increase of 26% over 1969.

We are mainly concerned with the adverse effect of rain during the flowering season, which may be said to extend for six months from May until October. I include May because shrub roses such as 'Canary Bird' and climbers such as 'Gloire de Dijon' grown on south-facing walls are often in full bloom by the middle of this month. If we compare the rainfalls during this period (May–Oct.) we find, as might be expected, 18·08 in. fell in 1969 and 22·77 in. fell in 1970, an increase of 26 per cent. On the other hand, during the earlier part of the flowering season (May–Aug) the respective rainfalls were 12·38 in. and 10·73 in. Although the amount of rain was actually lower in 1970 roses "balled" badly in the early summer and I can only suggest this might in part have been due to the high relative humidity which was experienced from July onwards.

Could it be that the total rainfall in itself is not so important as other weather factors such as sunshine, wind and temperature, which might assist in the rain drying off the petals quickly? At any rate with roses looking so terribly miserable at the end of September as I write this article, I think it is an excellent time in which to select varieties which have stood up best to the wet; unfortunately, few varieties have escaped completely without some weather damage. It is interesting to note that this season has resulted in a high incidence of rose disease, both Black Spot and Rust, in several areas in the West of Scotland. It seems obvious that in selecting suitable varieties for rainy districts it is desirable, if not essential, that such varieties should be as disease resistant as possible.

Petallages

It is generally agreed that very full-petalled varieties, which on account of their numerous petals tend to open slowly, are the most likely to "ball" in wet weather. Varieties which I would include in this category are 'Perfecta'. 'Montezuma', 'Margaret', 'Gavotte', 'Bonsoir', 'Red Devil' and 'Liberty Bell'. But these are by no means the only varieties that "ball" and in July varieties like 'Royal Highness', 'Memoriam', 'Fred Gibson' and 'Elizabeth Harkness' were badly affected by rain; these pale varieties have fewer petals, but the texture is exceedingly soft and if the outer petals are affected in the early stages of opening then they become stuck together and the bloom fails entirely to open.

Other varieties with few petals which "ball" are 'Brilliant' and 'Show Girl' and I suggest the cause for such varieties failing to open is more the formation of the high centred bloom, which tends to open exceedingly slowly, rather than the texture of the petals.

Apart from complete "balling" certain varieties are marked more readily by rain

than others and, while the blooms will open, they are considerably blemished because
of the soft texture of the petals. In this category I would include varieties such as
'King's Ransom', 'Alec's Red', 'Fragrant Cloud', 'Mullard Jubilee', 'Prima Ballerina'
and 'Silver Lining', to mention a few.

It seems, therefore, that to open in wet weather a variety should not have too many
petals, the texture must not be too soft and the formation of the bloom must not be
too tight.

Spreading Growth

A few hybrid teas tend to have a spreading type of growth which means that some
blooms may be near ground level. Thin outer stems bearing heavy blooms might
therefore touch the surface or be splashed by rain. I refer to varieties such as 'Josephine
Bruce', 'Gavotte', 'Rex Anderson' and 'Percy Thrower'. After the first year I consider that with good cultivation and judicious pruning a sufficiently large plant will
be produced whose outer blooms will not be damaged by rain. Personally, I much
prefer a variety with upright growth and I have now discarded these varieties except
'Percy Thrower'.

One floribunda which bears very heavy trusses which become badly marked by soil
in wet weather is 'Europeana' and this variety cannot be recommended for rainy
districts.

Climbers, including ramblers, bearing heavy trusses must be adequately supported
against a wall, fence or pillar to prevent their blooms being marked by touching the
ground.

Brittle foot-stalks

After severe, heavy rain, rain with wind or even wind alone I can count on many
blooms with their foot-stalks lying on the ground and the roses involved can be
accurately restricted to less than a dozen varieties. Amongst hybrid teas the worst
offender is 'Perfecta', followed by 'Liberty Bell' and 'Liebestraum', all full-petalled
varieties. 'Lucy Cramphorn' may also be affected and to a lesser degree 'Super Star'.
Amongst floribundas 'Queen Elizabeth' is easily the worst offender, with 'Celebration'
and 'Tombola' involved to a lesser degree; the latter variety carries fairly heavy, multi-
petalled blooms, which snap off easily.

Varieties suitable for rainy districts

In selecting suitable roses to grow where the summer rainfall is considerable one must
exclude the exhibitor, who is prepared to give certain roses some protection in really
wet weather, and cater for the average gardener, who will expect his roses to flourish
and give reasonable quality blooms in all weathers. Floribundas and climbing roses are
less likely to suffer than hybrid teas. Some varieties of hybrid teas have only the outer
petals spotted by rain and may be recommended, but varieties which "ball" completely
must be excluded in wet districts. During exceptionally wet weather in September

(5·10 in. rain) a variety which has been outstanding in my garden on account of its tough petals which have borne few blemishes is 'Uncle Walter'.

My selection of diseases resistant varieties for growing in wet areas would include the following—

Hybrid teas

'Ballet'	'Grandpa Dickson'	'Pink Favourite'
'Brasilia'	'Milord'	'Red Lion'
'Duke of Windsor'	'Mischief'	'Rose Gaujard'
'Ena Harkness'	'Pania'	'Stella'
'Ernest H. Morse'	'Pascali'	'Super Star'
'Gail Borden'	'Peace'	'Sutter's Gold'
'Garvey'	'Peer Gynt'	'Uncle Walter'
'Gold Crown'	'Piccadilly'	'Wendy Cussons'

Floribundas

'Allgold'	'Iceberg'	'Orangeade'
'Apricot Nectar'	'Ice White'	'Orange Sensation'
'Arthur Bell'	'Irish Mist'	'Paddy McGredy'
'City of Belfast'	'Jan Spek'	'Paprika'
'City of Leeds'	'Lilli Marlene'	'Pink Parfait'
'Evelyn Fison'	'Manx Queen'	'Queen Elizabeth'
'Golden Treasure'	'Marlena'	'Sweet Repose'
'Heaven Scent'	'Molly McGredy'	'Tombola'

Climbers

'Bantry Bay'	'Etude'	'Parkdirektor Riggers'
'Casino'	'Golden Showers'	'Pink Perpetue'
'Danse du Feu'	'Morning Jewel'	

Special Cultural treatment

I do not consider my locality with an annual rainfall of just over 40 inches is excessively wet; In many coastal districts in the West of Scotland the rainfall exceeds 60 inches and such areas can legitimately be designated wet.

I am sure it is quite wrong to apply a nitrogenous feed too late in the season, especially when there is much rain. I maintain the last general feed should be applied by the end of July. Sulphate of potash takes several weeks to be effective after application to the soil, so this likewise is less efficaceous if applied too late in the season. I suggest that potash should be given before the end of August. Luscious basal growth is more likely to be found in a wet, sunless season and this may be the result of excessive nitrogen release caused by bacterial action owing to the prevailing weather conditions. In a wet season I would favour the use of more potash and less nitrogen. Potash undoubtedly aids the ripening of wood but after a severe winter much frost damage is usually encountered following an exceptionally wet summer.

I have had no personal experience of deficiency disease arising as the result of essential elements being leached out of the soil by excessive rain.

Those of us who wish to grow the multi-petalled or soft petalled varieties must be prepared to give some protection in a wet, sunless season if we wish to obtain top quality blooms. At the Scottish National Rose Society's Summer Show (1970) the three most frequently exhibited varieties were 'Royal Highness', 'Gavotte' and 'Red Devil' in that order; all these varieties had obviously been protected. However, bloom protectors definitely affect the colour of some varieties, especially reds. Where protection is necessary I consider it is desirable to use transparent plastic bloom covers. Some exhibitors use frame sashes to cover their roses, as do chrysanthemum growers, but this seems to me to be carrying things too far! The challenge to the hybridiser is to produce more weather resistant hybrid teas.

LIONEL POOLE, CARDIFF

Perhaps one of the country's most ideal testing grounds for roses is at Cardiff's Roath Park. I am in the fortunate position of being able to pay frequent visits to these grounds as well as to be able to observe the performance of roses in my own garden.

It is well known that most western areas of the British Isles, including Wales, get more than the country's average rainfall, and as a result of this, most rosarians residing in these areas tend to choose roses that will tolerate frequent wet conditions. Taking for example 1969, the year's total rainfall for the Cardiff area was 32·45 inches, and sub-divided into monthly totals was as follows:

	inches		mm.
January	4·9	(wetter than average)	124·5
February	1·9	(average)	48·3
March	3·0	(wetter than average)	76·2
April	1·9	(average)	48·3
May	4·28	(wetter than average)	108·7
June	1·82	(drier than average)	46·2
July	3·26	(wetter than average)	82·8
August	2·6	(average)	66·0
September	1·78	(drier than average)	45·2
October	0·54	(drier than average)	13·7
November	3·82	(average)	97·0
December	2·65	(drier than average)	67·3
	32·45		824·2

'PICASSO' (floribunda)
'Marlena' × ['Evelyn Fison' × ('Orange Sweetheart' × 'Frühlingsmorgen')]
Raised by S. McGredy IV, N. Ireland
CERTIFICATE OF MERIT 1970
See page 175

'GRACE ABOUNDING' (floribunda)
'Pink Parfait' × *'Circus'*
Raised by R. Harkness & Co. Ltd
TRIAL GROUND CERTIFICATE 1970
See page 176

It will be noted that there were four *wetter* than average months, four *average* months and four *drier* than average months throughout the year. Even so, the final total is somewhat lower than the average for the Southern Wales area.

In such a year as 1969 a true test of rain-prone varieties may not have been evident, but over the period of the past three or four years, during which 1967 and 1968 were abundantly wet, 1969 slightly drier and 1970 probably average, certain factors leading to weather damage became evident. In almost all cases of hybrid tea roses damaged by rain, the varieties were either full or long-petalled, and being thus formed, are rather slow to open. The very formation of the flower makes it easy prey, for a short spell of even the lightest of drizzle followed by sunshine will do damage at any time after the sepals have dropped and the bud is fully formed. Sunshine on rain droplets still lodged on the fully-formed bud will burn or bleach through many of our most popular varieties. Heavy downpours of rain during the formative period of the flower will do even more damage—and once again the full, long-petalled varieties suffer the most. Many flowers become sealed in a soggy mess of rotting petals.

I cannot mention one white or blush hybrid tea variety that is able to withstand even moderate rain, without some petal damage being caused. Pale pinks fare a little better, but those who grow 'Anne Letts' will no doubt agree that she gives of her best only in dry, sunny weather. Deep pinks are, on average, much more rain resistant than most other colours—perhaps because there are so many to choose from. Salmon and bright orange varieties are a mixed bag, but one only has to think of 'Montezuma' at the end of a day's rain to seek a divorce from this variety. Reds and crimsons can be quite devilish—some are brave and resist all but the heaviest of downpours; there are, however, certain rogues that will always succumb, namely, 'Karl Herbst' and 'Red Devil'. The final colour, yellow, contains many good rain-resistant varieties, perhaps because most are short-petalled and not overfull. Even so, exhibitors will bear out that 'Ethel Sanday' is not for cutting when rain is about.

The most obvious solution in choosing rain-resistant varieties is to visit the nearest rose gardens after a period of heavy rain, and it will soon become evident that those blooms remaining undamaged would be one's choice. Those varieties with weak footstalks would also be evident, as the weight of rainwater held within the petals of the full blooms soon causes the whole flower to keel over, and in many cases completely to snap off in any accompanying wind. This is typical of the hybrid tea roses 'Perfecta' and 'Liberty Bell'.

Where hybrid tea roses are grown expressly for garden decoration or cutting, no amount of good cultivation will help to protect the blooms against rain damage if the varieties grown are known to be intolerant. One would be more inclined to grow for effective colour and perhaps length of stems, rather than classic form and size which is sought by the exhibitor, who should be prepared with shades and stakes to protect his blooms from rain, drizzle and strong winds.

The use of sulphate of potash, applied at a rate of 1 oz. per square yard during August, is advised if the summer has been excessively wet. This would help to ripen new basal shoots which otherwise may become victims of severe frost during the ensuing winter. I would hesitate to advise the August application of sulphate of potash every year, especially when roses are grown in heavy soil. Regular applications of most modern rose fertilisers provide ample potash in sufficient quantities for the bushes' requirements throughout the year.

I have made no mention of floribunda roses. In the majority of cases the flower heads are much more rain resistant than hybrid teas, simply because the flowers, which are either single or semi-double in petallage, are more easily able to shed rainwater.

The lists now given, showing the most rain-resistant hybrid teas and floribundas in the South Wales area, compare most favourably with the tables in *The Rose Annual*, although perhaps not in the same order.

MOST RAIN-RESISTANT VARIETIES IN SOUTH WALES

Hybrid Teas	*Floribundas*
'Charlie's Aunt'	'Allgold'
'Chicago Peace'	'City of Leeds'
'Diorama'	'Escapade'
'Ernest H. Morse'	'Evelyn Fison'
'Ginger Rogers'	'Frensham'
'Grandpa Dickson'	'Iceberg'
'Mischief'	'Orangeade'
'My Choice'	'Paprika'
'Peace'	'Princess Michiko'
'Piccadilly'	'Queen Elizabeth'
'Prima Ballerina'	'Stephen Langdon'
'Stella'	'Sundance'
'Wendy Cussons'	

J. CRAIG WALLACE, NEWTOWNARDS
(Secretary/Organiser, Rose Society of Northern Ireland and City of Belfast International Rose Trials)

Climate

Average annual rainfall in Northern Ireland 42·55 in. (1080·8 mm.)
Average monthly figures during flowering season:

	inches	mm.
June	2·80	(71·1)
July	3·79	(96·3)
August	4·00	(101·6)
September	3·78	(96·0)

Roses grow well in Northern Ireland, exceedingly well. Visitors from drier, sunnier areas in the British Isles and from overseas invariably pass comment on the strong, leafy growth of our hybrid teas and floribundas. Because of later springs and cooler weather in May and early summer compared to the south-east of England for instance, flowering commences later with us. Generally early July sees the peak of the first flush in gardens. In later more exposed aspects, for example, the Belfast Rose Trials at Dixon Park, often this peak is not reached until the third and fourth week of the month. This also applies to "maidens" in the nursery fields. Again because of cooler conditions in mid-summer, it is not a question of a wild riot of colour one day and gone tomorrow. This first flush lingers on over several weeks; at the same time, seldom lacking moisture at the roots, the bushes build up plentiful growth for later in the season. I think perhaps it is this flowering on the strong growths of spring and early summer coinciding with the lushness of the basal shoots for the second flush, together making for big leafy plants, which so impresses those used to something smaller and "harder".

What we lose in the early part of the season is compensated to some extent by a long mild "back-end" (an Ulsterism referring to the end of the season, in this case the autumn!). This means roses through the autumn, even to Christmas. A dry settled spell in October or November will bring out the blooms on late growths as fine as any in July. The Rose Society of Northern Ireland has held a members' show as late as the third week in November—and no question either of "tatty", bedraggled, "good in the circumstances" type of exhibits.

It should be apparent from all this, however, that roses which don't stand up to the rain and moisture are out, with a big OUT. I don't want to give the impression that we live under a continual summer deluge and have developed webbed feet; on the other hand the freshness of the Ulster countryside—and it is beautifully fresh and ever changing—and our green grass don't come as the result of weeks of summer drought and hot sunshine. Our garden roses must be those which can shake off the raindrops and come up smiling for the sunbeams to follow.

With this prologue, Mr Editor, to put readers in the picture regarding the climate which conditions rose growing in Northern Ireland, herewith are my lists of varieties for your symposium. I am going to take perhaps the more positive attitude and name in the first instance those found most suitable:

Hybrid Teas

'Alec's Red' (after a season's experience, I believe this to be a top rater), 'Bond Street', 'Colour Wonder' (can be quite marvellous in autumn), 'Diorama', 'Ernest H. Morse', 'Fragrant Cloud', 'Garvey', 'Grandpa Dickson' (a good wet weather rose for a yellow), 'Lady Seton', 'Lady Sylvia', 'Madame Butterfly', 'Madame Louis Lapperrière', 'Mischief' (quite outstanding in my opinion), 'Paris Match', 'Peace', 'Peer Gynt', 'Peter Frankenfeld' (in my own garden this makes a big, husky plant—it hasn't been given the attention it merits), 'Piccadilly' (the colour of this variety is rather insipid with me in dull, wet weather, but the blooms do stand up to the rain), 'Picture', 'Pink Favourite', 'Pink Supreme' (very good in the Belfast Trials, always in flower), 'Rose Gaujard', 'Shannon', 'Shot Silk', 'Spek's Yellow', 'Super Star', 'Timothy Eaton',

'Violinista Costa' (very good, always reliable), 'Wendy Cussons', 'Western Sun' (a yellow rose which seems to get better and better—it should be more widely known).

Floribundas

'Alamein', 'Allgold', 'Ama', 'Arthur Bell', 'City of Belfast', 'City of Leeds', 'Elizabeth of Glamis', 'Escapade', 'Europeana', 'Evelyn Fison', 'Firecracker' (always bright and cheerful), 'Flamenco', 'Fred Loads', 'Frensham', 'Goldgleam', 'Iceberg', 'Ice White', 'Irish Mist', 'Jane Lazenby', 'John Church' (very reliable), 'Kerry Gold', 'Korona' (still going strong in many gardens—hard to beat), 'Lavendula', 'Lilli Marlene', 'Manx Queen', 'Marlena' (an outstanding little rose), 'Meteor', 'Orangeade', 'Orange Sensation' (both these orange floribundas are very happy with us), 'Paint Box', 'Queen Elizabeth', 'Red Favourite', 'Rodeo', 'Rose of Tralee', 'Scarlet Queen Elizabeth', 'Tip Top', 'Tombola'.

Varieties which Dislike the Rain

Hybrid Teas
'Anne Letts', 'Baccara', 'Bridal Robe', 'Brilliant', 'Frau Karl Druschki', 'Isabel de Ortiz' (this variety seems to need more sunshine than it gets with us), 'Karl Herbst', 'Konrad Adenauer', 'Liberty Bell', 'Margaret', 'Memoriam', 'Mojave' (although a small-flowered variety it has a crumpled look in the rain), 'Montezuma', 'Mister Lincoln', 'Peaceful', 'Percy Thrower' (the flowers suffer because of sprawling growth), 'Perfecta', 'Red Lion', 'Red Devil', 'Royal Highness', 'Vienna Charm'.

Floribundas
The floribundas are generally excellent with us. There are comparatively few which could be called really unsuitable, although 'Dearest' is definitely unhappy with too much rain and 'Rumba', with its habit of holding on to its petals and brown stamens, can become very shabby. The ones which I have mentioned are, in my experience, outstanding in the way of shrugging off the worst which our summers can offer.

Special cultural treatment

In some years we get autumn and winter dieback associated with stem botrytis. I feel that this is connected with too generous applications of high nitrogen fertilisers late in the summer which encourage the lush, rank growth which is particularly susceptible to this type of trouble. This means, I think, avoiding general purpose and proprietary rose fertilisers after early to mid-July. An August dressing of sulphate of potash at 2 oz per sq yd is a usual recommendation to help ripen growth.

DR JOHN WATTS, CHESHIRE

Location and climate

My garden is in north-east Cheshire, roughly half-way between Manchester and Macclesfield.

In writing this note, I have tried to follow a pattern set out by the Editor and to comment on any queries he raised. All roses do well in this area of the north-west, but some do better than others. Years ago I was interested in the "Three R's"; to-day I live in an area of the "Four R's"—Roses, Rhododendrons, Rain and Rheumatism! The amount of annual rainfall is only slightly above the national average, but of course the clay soil, on which so many of us grow our roses, does retain the moisture, and my own view has been for a long time now that we have an area of high humidity, not necessarily of high rainfall. When I arrived in Manchester some thirty years ago and complained about the humidity, my listener replied that it was good for cotton. Now I know that it is good for roses.

Manchester Weather Centre has kindly provided the data which is quoted later. Looking at the annual rainfall over twenty-five years the figure of 32·04 inches compares very favourably with the average figure for England and Wales quoted by Leonard Hollis (*The Rose Annual 1967*, page 46)—35·6 in. (1916–1950). Also the rainfall in July, August and September at a figure of 9·7 inches is not greatly in excess of the England and Wales average, 9·3 inches.

Rainfall—1942–1966 (25 years)	June	July	August	September	Year
Average Falls (inches)	2·5	3·18	3·50	3·02	32·04
Average Falls (mm.)	63·5	80·8	88·9	76·7	813·8
Average number of wet days	11	12	12	13	139
Most in 24 hours ⎫ (inches)	1·11	1·75	2·73	1·55	2·73 (Aug.)
Year ⎭	1958	1946	1942	1965	1942

Since we are considering "Rainy Districts" the monthly average rainfall throughout the year must also be included and, as in the previous table, the average is based on data collected over 25 years (1942–1966).

	Average monthly fall		Average No. of
	inches	mm.	wet days
January	2·82	71·6	13
February	1·94	49·3	9
March	1·85	47·0	9
April	2·08	52·8	10
May	2·35	59·7	11
June	2·50	63·5	11
July	3·17	80·5	12
August	3·50	88·9	12
September	3·02	76·7	13
October	2·69	68·3	11
November	2·91	73·9	13
December	3·21	81·6	15
	32·04	813·8	139

Petallage

The defect of some roses in a rainy district is that the blooms fail to open, balling instead, thereby leaving the decaying remains of petals where the bloom should have been. At first sight, the number and texture of petals may be thought to account for this behaviour, but with this note in mind I kept a careful, though amateur, record of rainfall and temperature in my own garden during the first and second flush of blooms this year. The first flush began on June 22 following a few days of fine weather. Between June 22 and June 29 three days were fine, the temperature ranged from 42–70° F. and 0·79 in. of rain fell. By June 29 many of the hybrid teas and some floribundas e.g. 'Fashion', 'Spartan' amd 'Ivory Fashion' had balled. 'Winston Churchill', 'Montezuma' and 'Queen Elizabeth' were amongst the first to ball. Every bloom of 'Winston Churchill' was spoiled independent of the state of opening.

By a strange coincidence the second flush of blooms, starting on Sept. 27, had a very similar sequence of weather i.e. three dry days, a range of temperature 38–75° F. and 0·94 inches of rainfall. Today, October 4, very few of the roses show signs of bruising, let alone balling and even one bloom of 'Winston Churchill' (the only flower) is unaffected.

There would appear to be, therefore, other factors involved in the balling up of roses, besides rainfall and number and texture of the petals. Whatever these factors are, there is no doubt that floribundas give a better show of colour through the flowering season than hybrid teas. Perhaps the large number of buds and sequential opening, in part, accounts for this.

The question is, why did the sequence of weather conditions detailed have such a devastating effect on the June flush of blooms? Spring and early summer feeding? There were no signs of mildew at either time, but petals from floribundas and hybrid teas in June immersed in sterile sugar solution for a few days did produce fermentation. Perhaps this may be the case with the autumn roses, but there has been no time to check. If 'Winston Churchill' can be persuaded to bloom without balling, under slightly adverse conditions, by some modification in the growing technique, then I think that balling in other varieties can be almost eliminated.

Spreading Growth

One hybrid tea regarded as typical of spreading or sprawling growth i.e. 'Josephine Bruce', has this year decided to be upright and has borne its blooms two to three feet from the ground. Black Spot infection has been very slight; usually this attacks leaves near the ground, but Black Spot has been almost completely absent this year.

Particular Defects in Varieties, Making Them Unsuitable for Rainy Districts

Brittle footstalks occur in only one variety known to me i.e. 'President Eisenhower'. This rose is liable to break off even when picked dry. Others, such as 'Perfecta' and 'Lucy Cramphorn', have never presented any difficulty. Before this year, I would have included 'Gavotte', 'Margaret', 'Tiffany' and 'McGredy's Ivory' amongst roses intolerant of rain. But 'Gavotte' flowered beautifully in June, 'Margaret' and 'McGredy's Ivory' in September, whilst in June two bushes of 'Tiffany', one on Multiflora, the other on unknown rootstock, flowered differently. The one on Multiflora, on a lower and wetter rose-bed, bloomed whilst the flowers on the other one balled. No serious conclusion can be drawn from this, as it is only one observation on two rose bushes.

Varieties

As I mentioned at the beginning, all roses do well in this area, but the following varieties have given a good show this year:

Floribunda Roses
'Dearest', 'Iceberg', 'Anna Wheatcroft', 'Flamenco', 'Paddy McGredy', 'Europeana', 'Copper Delight', 'Pink Parfait', 'Queen Elizabeth', 'Orange Sensation'.

Hybrid tea type roses
'Frau Karl Druschki', 'Fragrant Cloud', 'Prima Ballerina', 'Wendy Cussons', 'Helen Traubel', 'Mme. Louis Laperrière', 'Peace', 'Eden Rose', and 'Ballet'.

Special Cultural Treatment Required in Rainy Districts

My own experience with the sulphate of potash treatment to ripen growth before the winter, is that it helps with the early growth, but late growth might as well be cut out when cleaning up the rose beds during the winter. It will die back anyway after the frosts, and potassium sulphate treatment will not prevent it.

Growing roses for exhibition in a rainy district presents difficulties. It is hopeless for hybrid teas without bloom protectors, and as there is usually a good blow before a show, it is a wise precaution to tie the rose stem to a cane as near the bloom as possible, so that it has no movement whatever. The use of three or four canes holding the bloom protector ensures that this does not sway in the wind across the tip of the bloom. Tilting the protector slightly into the wind helps to prevent drips being blown from the rim across the bloom. Even with such precautions, I have in the past collected quite a number of shades from the adjacent cornfield at harvest time.

The heavy feeding and watering programme (half a gallon per bush per day, when there was no rain) which I used to carry out in order to grow large blooms of hybrid teas for exhibition, did contribute to a tendency to ball, even with 'Peace', and a considerable amount of time and skill had to be devoted towards keeping moisture off the blooms.

As regards feeding, I always added magnesium sulphate and Plaster of Paris to every fertiliser mix or slurry I used, arguing that the magnesium sulphate would soon leach out and fertilise the woodland below, whilst the Plaster of Paris or Gypsum helped to break down the clay through the drainage channels.

Special Comments

Since I have been studying the colour of roses according to the hues given in the

R.H.S. Colour Chart, I have been surprised by the wide variation in hue which occurs throughout the season according to weather, one of the factors being sunshine.

In the case of many of the reds, sunshine seems to emphasise the yellow undertone and change the colour from something which can be described as deep velvety crimson to something like bright currant red. For example, 'Josephine Bruce' well grown and flowered in soft weather has a sheen and hue similar to black velvet with a crimson undertone, but flowered in dry sunny conditions—yes, we did have a few summer days this year—it lacks the sheen and in colour is approximately currant red.

Similar remarks apply to 'Ena Harkness', 'Mardi Gras', 'President Eisenhower', 'President Adenauer', 'Brilliant' and many others.

Some of the yellows appear bleached by a dry spell, e.g. 'Dorothy Peach' and sometimes 'Peace'. The latter also has the pink edging of its "ballet skirt" influenced by the weather.

One advantage of growing roses in a rainy district, besides the beauty of the flowers, is the reduction in pests and diseases; no Rust, very little Black Spot or Mildew this year and no aphids. The only serious pest we had at the beginning of the season was leaf-rolling sawfly.

I hope that my comments have shown that I enjoy growing roses in a "Rainy District" and regard the advantages as offsetting any disadvantage such as "balling".

COL. W. B. WRIGHT, BIDEFORD, N. DEVON

Rainfall Source: (Chivenor Met. Office, N. Devon).

Average Monthly
(based on 16 year-period)

	mm.	inches	1970	
			mm.	inches
January	80·3	3·16		
February	61·8	2·43		
March	51·0	2·01		
April	59·5	2·35		
May	55·7	2·19		
June	47·7	1·88	35·3	1·39
July	74·1	2·92	72·5	2·85
August	87·2	3·43	75·2	2·96
September	85·2	3·35	72·0	2·83
October	86·6	3·41	68·9	2·71
November	107·4	4·23		
December	92·3	3·64		
Annual	888·8	35·00		

Petallage

Most thin hybrid tea roses with 27 to 35 petals open well in the rain, although there are some full petalled roses too which open well, such as 'Princess', 'City of Bath', 'Ballet' and 'Grandpa Dickson'.

Spreading Growth

I have only a few varieties with low, spreading growth (e.g. 'Gavotte' and 'Josephine Bruce'). These I always prune to an inside bud, not forgetting to do the same when cutting blooms or dead-heading. The result is the blooms are rarely spoilt by rain splashing up from the soil.

Particular Defects in Varieties

Weak footstalks: 'Perfecta' and 'Liebestraum' with the weight of water held in the bloom.

Tendency to ball badly: 'Red Devil', 'Karl Herbst', 'Memoriam', 'Royal Highness', 'Montezuma'.

List of Varieties Recommended as Particularly Suitable (Alphabetical order).

Hybrid Teas		*Floribundas*
'Ballet'	'Grandpa Dickson'	'Allgold'
'Brasilia'	'Peace'	'Anna Wheatcroft'
'Bristol'	'Red Lion'	'Anne Cocker'
'City of Bath'	'Stella'	'Lilli Marlene'
'Embassy'	'Uncle Walter'	'Orange Sensation'
'Ernest H. Morse'		'Vesper'
'Fred Gibson'		(*Note:* I grow only very few varieties of
'Ginger Rogers'		floribundas)

Special Cultural Treatment

Foliar feeding has helped to counteract the leaching of fertilisers applied to the soil.

Otherwise normal feeding, i.e. a general Rose fertiliser after pruning and again in July, with a good mulch of farmyard manure after pruning.

For exhibition work bloom protectors are essential for protecting blooms from the rain, but they must be used with discretion. If gales occur more damage may be caused by the blooms striking the protector or the stakes supporting the protector.

A common occurrence in this district is the combination of rain and strong to gale force winds. In these circumstances nearly every variety suffers, many buds and blooms snapping off and other blooms being badly marked and torn.

Humid weather with periods of hot sun seems to increase the balling and to cause many buds to rot. The most outstandingly good hybrid tea in wet weather in my garden is 'Stella'.

Steve's Maggot

W. D. ROBERTS

(Amateur rose grower)

Anybody who is at all familiar with botanical or zoological nomenclature will know that it is common practice to name biological species after the people who discover them. Thomson's gazelle hoofs around Africa shamelessly unaware that a distinguished gentleman dignified it with his own name; *Betula pendula youngii* throws its shade indiscriminately on man and beast, greenly indifferent to what any of them are called—including itself. This is all so self-evident that it is difficult for anyone to believe that a maggot—of all things—could concern itself with human activities and become involved with a particular field of human endeavour. However, evidence has gradually accumulated during the past few years, and matters have now reached a stage where Steve's Maggot is positively recognised by exhibitors, although he has yet to be sighted. Let's go right back to the beginning.

It was at the RNRS Summer Show at Alexandra Palace in 1967. The staging of the exhibits was finished, and the judging of the amateurs was going on in the Palm Court; time was creeping on and exhibitors were beginning to gather around the entrance, waiting to be admitted into the hall to see the results. One group of about six of us included Steve. To set the record straight at the outset, let it be understood that Steve's surname is Stevens; he has a Christian name as well, but it has so atrophied through disuse that he has probably forgotten it himself.

We were all whiling away the time, as usual, with rose-talk, and Steve's contribution was characteristically vivid and hilariously descriptive of the occasion a year or two previously, when he was putting the final touches to an exhibit which he was staging at one of the major shows. There was one bloom in particular of which he expected great things; it was a good one even to Steve's critical eye, and there it was, securely ensconced in the back row of a box of six. It was nearly time for exhibitors to leave the Hall for the judging to commence, and Steve decided that THE bloom would be even better if one petal were opened out just a little. One deft tweak with finger and thumb, and the job was done—really done. The movement of the petal was like turning aside a curtain in the Chamber of Horrors, and Steve suddenly felt as if his boots had exploded, such was the enormity of the revelation. The cause of it all was a small hole, $1\frac{1}{2}$ mm in diameter, a perfect circle forming the entrance to a tunnel as straight as a laser beam. Once revealed it could never again be concealed; it was no use even trying to turn the bloom to face the other way; the North face was identical to the South. Good as it was, the bloom had to come out, and was replaced, in traumatic haste, by something of baser degree but of unpunctured integrity.

As the tale unfolded, our little knot of enthusiasts was joined by others who became engrossed, amused and very nearly (but not quite, of course) hysterical at Steve's rendering of a seemingly ordinary incident of no great entomological rarity. The end of the story was more or less coincident with the end of the judging, and we passed into the Hall to see the results.

In one class, I had a rather nice specimen of 'Royal Highness'—not good enough to save the other five from anonymity, but a very fine bloom, nevertheless. Knowing that one bloom in the show must win the silver-gilt medal, I paid my first visit to it. With the increasing warmth of the day, it had opened a little in the past hour. . . . Steve's maggot had another scalp on his belt, and, moreover, he had so timed it that the cynics could see for themselves that a truly worthy adversary had really arrived.

A number of shows have come and gone since that day, and the reports of S.M.'s activities have been steady and well authenticated. S.M. has outlived the scepticism.

Although nobody has yet seen S.M., it is possible to give an accurate character study, based on examination of evidence, and on *modus operandi*. Firstly, S.M. is the super-perfectionist, drilling a shaft of ram-rod straightness from pole to pole, passing through the exact centre of gravity of the bloom. Unlike a gunshot, the exit wound is as neat as the entry and both are perfectly circular with precision-finished, punched-out edges. Nor does he make the mistake of over-playing his hand; one good hole is always enough, and if you see a rose looking like a mass-produced colander, you may depend upon it, Steve's Maggot would shudder at the sight as much as you do yourself.

Secondly, S.M. is selective. He will under no circumstances operate on rubbish, and his work is to be seen exclusively at the better shows. S.M., you see, is a bon-viveur, a gourmet, having an educated palate which he indulges with an incomparable sense of occasion. Only Henry Moore can possible vie with S.M. when it comes to positioning a hole to obtain maximum artistic and dynamic fulfilment.

Thirdly, he is a master tactician who has studied guerilla operations in all their aspects, including the secrets of immunisation against all known insecticides. He strikes quickly and decisively, covers up all tracks, and vanishes under cover of the resulting consternation, as one would expect of the Pimpernel of Maggotry.

As plain exhibitors, we cannot do more than set out this report of the events as we have observed them. We confess that we have been unable to find any remedy, and are reduced to consoling ourselves with the thought that even S.M. is not immortal; but we also suspect that shortly after one writer has completed his obituary, another will be writing an article called "Son of Steve's Maggot". It is therefore clear that if a solution is to be found, superior brains must be brought into play, and the Society's Scientific Adviser might do worse than drop everything else and espouse this very pressing cause.

Over to you, Mr Allen—but just catch him, eh?—don't kill him!...

The Rose and William Cowper

DR MICHAEL BALL
(Minister of Religion)

Although many poets make use of the rose, as a symbol of beauty, transience or corruption lurking under a lovely exterior, few can have known as much about the practical aspects of gardening as William Cowper, who lived from 1731 to 1800. He is famous for his hymns, as well as his other verse. Being a gentleman, he did not undertake the hard work involved. He was content to supervise those with "robust tough sinews, bred to toil" since "lubbard labour needs his watchful eye, oft loitering lazily if not o'erseen, or misapplying his unskilful strength". Cowper would have been mystified by the theories of Ruskin and Morris or by the poem of Wordsworth "To the Spade of a Friend" with its line "Spade! with which Wilkinson hath tilled his lands."

However, Cowper assumed personal responsibility for tasks "such as may amuse, not tire, demanding rather skill than force", and this included pruning. Although there is surprisingly little difference in content between his pruning advice, and that still given, Cowper's lovely blank verse makes it far more pleasant to read:

> "*No meaner hand may discipline the shoots,*
> *None but his steel approach them. What is weak,*
> *Distempered, or has lost prolific powers,*
> *Impaired by age, his unrelenting hand*
> *Dooms to the knife; nor does he spare the soft*
> *And succulent, that feeds its giant growth,*
> *But barren, at the expense of neighbouring twigs*
> *Less ostentatious, and yet studded thick*
> *With hopeful gems. The rest, no portion left*
> *That may disgrace his art, or disappoint*
> *Large expectation, he disposes neat*
> *At measured distances, that air and sun*
> *Admitted freely may afford their aid,*
> *And ventilate and warm the swelling buds.*"

During winter, like many another gardener, he looked on his garden and clothed it with spring and summer glory, in impatient imagination:

> "*These naked shoots,*
> *Barren as lances, among which the wind*
> *Makes wintry music, sighing as it goes,*
> *Shall put their graceful foliage on again,*
> *And more aspiring, and with ampler spread,*
> *Shall boast new charms, and more than they have lost.*"

After mentioning the laburnum and syringa, he continues:

> "*The scentless and the scented rose: this red,*
> *And of an humbler growth, the other tall,*
> *And throwing up into the darkest gloom*
> *Of neighbouring cypresses, or more sable yew,*
> *Her silver globes, light as foamy surf,*
> *That the wind severs from the broken wave.*"

According to a footnote in my 1806 copy of the poems, the latter rose is not a true rose at all, but the so-called guelder rose, more properly known as *Viburnum opulus*.

The imagery in Cowper's poem *The Rose* is both original and moving. He describes a rose picked for indoor decoration, following a shower, its flower bowed down with water. He picked it up, and clumsily swung it around too violently in an attempt to shake off the rain, unfortunately snapping its stem. The poem surely relates a genuine incident—many of us have experienced similar mishaps! But Cowper goes on to treat the story as an auto-biographical parable of the damage suffered by sensitive people from well-meaning, but rough, friends and relations. Cowper was himself morbidly sensitive to the extent that he suffered devastating mental breakdowns, and the poem could refer to his friendship with the Rev. John Newton, a cheerful extrovert who was psychologically incapable of understanding Cowper.

Although Cowper's garden at Olney was only small, his taste was catholic, and he grew such rarities as citrus trees, pineapples, geraniums and cucumbers. He delighted to sit in his greenhouse. "Is not our greenhouse a cabinet of perfumes? It is at this moment fronted with carnations and balsams, mignonette and roses, jessamine and woodbine" he wrote to a friend.

In another poem, *The Rose and the Lily*, these two flowers argue as to which should be queen. Cowper diplomatically suggests they should reign jointly, but I am sure his verdict is a symbolic plea for peace between Britain and France, political rivals and enemies in his time, not a horticultural preference. My guess is that he would have given the crown to the rose, if he had lived nearer our own day. Indeed, I have a double regret that he never saw more of the potential of the rose family, since developed. He himself would have taken great pleasure in the multitude of beauties produced since his time. And we should probably be enjoying some wonderful prose or poetry from him about our favourite flower, and how to grow it.

Rose Foliage

F. FAIRBROTHER
(Amateur rose grower and successful exhibitor)

One of my great delights in late spring is to stand on the N.E. side of my rose garden in the afternoon or early evening and look across the rose beds with the sunlight glinting on the rose foliage. The colours are enchanting—starting with crimson, ruby-red or bronze-red and passing through plum-purple and chocolate-bronze to the varying shades of green from the palest, delicate tints to a dark olive shade. I find great satisfaction in looking at the foliage even when there are no blooms. The genus *Rosa* is unique in the great variety of colour of the foliage, particularly in the early stages of growth. Then again, what other genus gives us such a variety of shapes of foliage in the odd number (3, 5, 7 etc.) of leaflets which share a common stem?

As one approaches to make a closer study of the leaves one notices variations which often lead to identification of the variety.

The common stem which is shared by the leaflets is called the *rachis*. The part of the leaf stem between the lowest pair of leaflets and the main shoot of the rose tree to which the leaf stem is attached is called the *petiole*. Near the base of the petiole and decorating each side is an interesting bit of variously shaped greenery called the *stipule*. One notices the shape of the stipule when budding. It is the part of the leaf stem which one holds when inserting the bud into the bark of the stock, and what fascinating shapes there are on the different varieties. In fact the differing shapes of the stipules may be a useful guide in determining varieties. Sometimes the breadth of the stipule is almost leafy as in *R. alba* or it may be much more reduced as in the China Roses and even more reduced, almost to a mere hair, in the Banksian Roses.

The rachis of some varieties is well provided with vicious, hook-shaped thorns—a well-known hazard to the exhibitor and flower-arranger as they are apt to tear other foliage in the vicinity or get hooked up with it, even with the slightest movement.

Sometimes the main stems of a variety have few or no thorns but the rachis has a plentiful supply e.g. 'Pink Favourite'. Other varieties have thorny stems but no thorns, or very few, on the rachis e.g. 'Maigold', 'Gipsy Boy', 'Mme Isaac Pereire'. The most common amongst the hybrid

teas and floribundas are those with thorny stems and many thorns on the
rachis; also in this class one must place 'Schneezwerg', and *R. sinowilsonii*.
'Zéphirine Drouhin', the Bourbon climbing rose, has practically no thorns
on the main stem or under the leaves and that delightful shrub, 'Canary
Bird', is also practically thornless. Some varieties have tiny thorns on the
main stem and also on the rachis e.g. 'Baron Girod de l' Ain', that charming
hybrid perpetual with Burgundy red blooms edged with white. Some
thorns are distinctly decorative in themselves e.g. those on the young wood of
R. sericea pteracantha (R. omeiensis pteracantha).

Another interesting variation in the foliage is the shape of the leaflets.
While these are, in general, of some type of oval, the detailed shape of the
oval varies. Some leaflets have the broadest part of the oval at the base or
lower half; such a shape is called *ovate*. Others have the widest part in the
half nearest the tip; these are said to be *obovate*. In order to be able to identify
the class to which some of our old garden roses belong it is most important
to know what the species look like, for they are the parents of our garden
roses. The serrated edges of the leaves give some clue to the ancestry of a
given variety e.g. *R. centifolia* has large teeth which are very prominent, but
on closer examination these are seen to be composed of two or three small
ones. In *R. rugosa* the smooth, small rounded teeth hardly show for they are
rolled under. *R. damascena bifera* also has small rounded teeth but these stand
out clearly.

The surface of the leaves of different species varies widely. Some have
smooth, shiny surfaces e.g. the tea roses, a character inherited from the
China roses. This is seen in such varieties as 'Maréchal Niel' and all the
Polyantha or Rambler roses. In *R. alba* the leaves are not shiny, and are a
blue green colour; the varieties 'Celestial' ('Celeste') and 'Maidens Blush'
are good examples. The leaves of the Gallicas are different again as may be
observed by a few minutes study of the rose 'Rosa Mundi'. A comparison
of this with the Centifolias e.g. the old cabbage rose, will be rewarding. The
Rugosas are outstanding and easily recognized by their thick, dark green,
heavily veined leaves, the underside of which is a lighter green. In the
autumn these leaves are a vivid pale gold and set off the tomato-coloured
fruits to great advantage. *R. hugonis* and its descendant 'Canary Bird' have
fern-like leaves, the leaflets of which are elliptical shaped. 'Canary Bird' is
very attractive, especially when the fifteen small leaflets of the leaves are the
background of the single yellow flowers which are produced in abundance.

Another interesting species is *R. rubrifolia*. The foliage is the chief feature
of this species and it has a unique combination of colours with grey, green

'Canary Bird'
(*see page* 64)

ROSE FOLIAGE

R. rugosa 'Scabrosa'
(*see page* 64)

R. sericea pteracantha
(see page 64)

ROSE FOLIAGE

R. multiflora watsoniana
(see page 65)

and bronze shades predominating. Species with grey foliage are *R. fedtschen-koana* and *R. beggeriana*, both belonging to the CINNAMOMEAE group.

Several rose species have foliage which assumes brilliant tints in the autumn. *R. virginiana* is an outstanding example. Not only is the young foliage glossy and richly coloured in spring, but shades of beetroot purple, followed by bright orange-red and yellow are revealed with the colder autumn weather. Other species noteworthy for their vivid-tinted foliage in the autumn are *RR foliolosa* and *nitida*.

A particularly curious variant is *R. multiflora watsoniana*. This has willow-like foliage, very narrow and linear and not resembling a rose leaf at all. It appears to be a sport, as seedlings develop as normal foliaged *R. multiflora*.

No other genus provides such a variety in shape, colour and texture of foliage, as the genus *Rosa*. In view of this I wonder why flower arrangers need to add such things as bull-rushes to their arrangements, particularly at a Rose Show? It should be their pride and joy to show what can be done with rose foliage alone as a background to well grown roses.

The rose is fairest when 'tis budding new,
And hope is brightest when it dawns from fears;
The rose is sweetest washed with morning dew,
And love is loveliest when embalmed in tears.
                                    SCOTT—*The Lady of the Lake*

Roses from Kitchen Window Cuttings

F. C. H. WITCHELL

(Amateur rose grower)

The types of roses with which this article is concerned are the hybrid teas and floribundas, which are rather more difficult to propagate successfully from cuttings than are the ramblers.

The first consideration is whether the effort is worthwhile; whether the resultant plants will ever become comparable in vigour and longevity with budded trees. My own experience, so far, suggests that, on average, bushes on their own roots are manifestly inferior for the first two or three years but, in time, most of them will develop into equally vigorous trees. In some varieties, they may even outgrow budded plants. However, it must also be admitted that a few will prove to be miserable failures.

On the question of longevity, I have not yet had to discard any "own roots" bushes because they showed signs of senility but, as some indication of their life potential, I can point to the fact that the most massive of the bushes of 'Rose Gaujard' in my present garden is a four foot thick, twelve year old specimen grown from a cutting. I believe that there are some even older examples of other varieties still thriving in my previous garden, which I left more than ten years ago.

The second consideration is whether a solution can be found to the principal problem one faces in growing roses from cuttings, that of obtaining plants of an acceptable flowering size in a reasonable time with minimal resources—in particular without the facility of a heated greenhouse.

Cuttings taken in November and rooted in the open ground seldom produce good-sized flowering plants in less than three and a half years. Cuttings taken in July, from shoots which have borne the first flush of bloom and similarly rooted, will normally produce good plants in just over three years. In both cases, it is desirable to use cloches for twelve months or more to assist in rooting and initial plant development.

If one possesses a heated greenhouse, the process can be accelerated considerably. I used to root hormone treated cuttings, taken in July and planted individually in five-inch pots, each pot being sealed for the first few weeks in a polythene bag. When a cutting appeared to have rooted, the bag was loosened a little and left for twenty-four hours, then loosened a little more and, after repeating this process for four days, the bag was finally removed.

The important point here is that it is essential to change only very gradually the degree of humidity in which the cutting has been living for all these weeks. If the plant is suddenly subjected to the drastic change from being totally enclosed to being totally exposed, it will usually collapse and may not recover. After removal of the bags, my plants remained in their five-inch pots through the winter, being potted on the following spring into eight-inch pots. They were slowly hardened off during the latter part of May and were put in their flowering positions in the open ground in June. Maintaining a minimum greenhouse temperature of 45° F during the winter, the resultant plants were of acceptable size and grew on to make very satisfactory bushes. If one propagates and plants out roses from pots in this way, it is very necessary to treat them in the same fashion as container grown bushes. They need well prepared, friable soil to encourage rapid root extension and they must never be allowed to become dry at the roots during their first summer in the garden. Varieties which I propagated in my greenhouse, using the above method, included 'Masquerade', 'June Park', 'Rose Gaujard', 'Karl Herbst' and 'Ethel Sanday'.

But, many people do not possess a heated greenhouse and, for them, the problem is how to obtain good plants in something like twelve months without that facility.

The solution was found, as solutions so often are, by accident. Blundering clumsily around amongst my roses in late June 1968 I succeeded in breaking off two strong shoots, both of which bore promising buds showing colour. Feeling annoyed with myself for my clumsiness and not wishing to waste what appeared to be good material, I wondered whether I might be able to root cuttings from the broken shoots. Now I do not possess a greenhouse in my present abode, but I do have an indulgent and green-fingered wife and we do have a large, north-facing kitchen window. So we decided to experiment with these unflowered shoots and, to make the experiment worth while, we also decided to try more than one variety. In the event, we prepared four cuttings, all from shoots which had buds showing colour, by reducing them to about eight inches in length, cutting them cleanly immediately above an eye at the top and below an eye at the bottom. All but the top set of leaves were removed. We then dipped the bottoms of the cuttings in Murphy hormone rooting compound and set them, one to a five-inch pot, in the kitchen window.

The four varieties were 'Elizabeth of Glamis', 'Princess', 'Ena Harkness' and 'Red Devil'. It is interesting to note that, for these cuttings, polythene bags were not used. Although they were not thus protected from moisture loss, it appeared that the atmosphere of a sunless north-facing kitchen was sufficiently humid for their needs, because they all prospered and produced acceptable sized plants which were planted out in June 1969 and which produced several blooms during that summer. At the time of writing, in autumn 1970, they have wintered perfectly, flowered reasonably well, and promise to make useful trees. Compared to nursery stock of the same varieties and of the same true age—that is to say, stock which was budded in June 1968—the plants of 'Elizabeth of Glamis', 'Princess' and 'Ena Harkness' are still noticeably smaller. The plant of 'Red Devil', however, has grown magnificently, and has produced blooms of such quality that I was able to include one in an award winning specimen bloom class exhibit at the 1970 Autumn Show.

Too few to prove anything conclusively, these results at least demonstrate that much knowledge and some success can come from bold experimentation and should give you, dear reader, considerable encouragement to risk a few experiments of your own. Apart from the suitability of a north-facing kitchen window for rooting cuttings, the most useful discovery made through this experiment was that rose shoots may be ripe enough to use as cuttings even before the flowers open. Thus, cuttings can be taken two or three weeks earlier than was previously considered wise and the resultant plants given that precious additional time to develop before the winter sets in.

A Tale of Five Cuttings

PATRICIA HONNOR
(Amateur rose grower)

When we moved, in September 1967, from an acre in Surrey to half an acre in Hampshire we had no intention of taking any of our plants with us. But we had a ten year old 'Cécile Brunner' which, for sentimental reasons, we wanted to keep. The thought of transplanting an ageing rose in full flower in the midst of all the preoccupations of a move did not appeal to me, so I decided to attempt to take a cutting from our bush; at least we could have the offspring of our loved rose.

Accordingly, some time in July, I cut five mature stems from the bush and pressed them firmly into the soil around it; no hormone powders or other mumbo jumbo for me; with luck from five I might get one substitute for our "Cécile". A week before the move I lifted the cuttings and put them all into one small pot. So far, no sign of root formation, but the shoots were obviously still alive.

I can't remember how they travelled to our new home, but probably it was in the boot of our car. Eventually they were found and put onto the kitchen window sill to await a site in the garden. Here they remained for about three weeks, being watered when I thought of it and twice being rescued when the cat knocked the pot over. The second time this happened I found, to my great surprise and delight, that the spilt soil was full of long, soft roots. I quickly found an unused corner of the vegetable garden and heeled them in, thinking that I could now leave them in peace at least until the spring. It was at this point that the master of the house decided that the vegetable garden was to be turfed over. Oh well, just one more move and one more temporary home!

At last, in March, we found the perfect spot, two small beds let into the terrace, where Bindweed and Snow-in-Summer were having a life and death struggle in soil consisting of builder's rubble and gravel. The beds were cleared, the soil enriched with compost, and the cuttings, all five of them apparently still alive, were installed in their final home.

That summer, to my joy, they all produced a few blooms, and by the next summer each had put out several shoots and gave us blooms from June to September. This year, 1970, after fairly hard pruning, we have five sturdy bushes, 2 ft. across and 3 ft. tall, bearing great trusses of exquisite inch long blooms, like tiny replicas of 'Madame Butterfly'.

I don't know what the moral of this story is, but perhaps it is that the best results in gardening are sometimes achieved by not trying too hard. I did not deserve to succeed with even one of my cuttings, but, bless her heart, 'Cécile Brunner' gave me five lovely daughters to remember her by.

Roses from Cuttings

LEONARD HOLLIS
(Editor and amateur rose grower)

Probably most amateurs confine the raising of roses from cuttings to those groups for which this is a recognised and simple method of propagation. On the one hand there are the rampant ramblers, usually of the Wichuraiana group, which are strong enough to show the necessary vigour to succeed on their own roots. In this category one could also include some of the Old Shrub Roses and the very vigorous floribunda shrub roses, such as 'Queen Elizabeth'.

On the other hand there are the miniature roses, where the aim is to perpetuate the dwarf character of this group, which is one of their most appealing traits. When budded onto rootstocks the resultant growth may be too vigorous and therefore out of character. This acknowledges the fact that roses are normally not as vigorous when grown on their own roots as when budded onto a strong-growing rootstock, although this fact may not be apparent when the variety concerned is so rampant that it will still give every satisfaction when grown from cuttings.

The budding of roses is simple with a little practice, and yields a high percentage of strong maiden plants at the end of the second season after planting the rootstock, i.e. from rootstocks planted in January or February, 1970 and budded in the early summer of that year, maiden plants will flower in July, 1971. By this time very few, if any plants raised from cuttings will have attained the size of a budded plant. The root system, such as it is, will tend to be shallow and more susceptible to frost damage in the winter.

Apart from the interest of raising the bedding roses from cuttings and the desirability of curbing the vigour of the miniatures, as already mentioned, it would appear that the main advantage lies in the absence of suckers from plants raised in this way. If one could rely on the vigour of the resulting plants and their ability to survive transplanting this would be a cogent point, as one tends to spend a lot of time going round removing suckers when the garden contains a fairly large collection. Subsidiary advantages are that cuttings can be prepared from prunings which, otherwise, would be consigned to the bonfire.

Several years ago my sister-in-law took an armful of prunings from my floribunda roses in the spring. These were inserted without fuss in a border in her garden which was shaded to some extent by large shrubs in her neighbour's garden. I have been surprised at the high percentage of these that struck and eventually made satisfactory plants. I am satisfied that this was largely because of the sandy nature of the soil. The varieties were mainly 'Iceberg', 'Queen Elizabeth' and 'Shepherd's Delight'. Cuttings of 'Queen Elizabeth' were also inserted against a chain link fence on the opposite side of the same garden. These have never been transplanted and now form a six ft hedge with no noticeable gaps where cuttings have failed to root.

About seven years ago, when our Shetland sheepdog was a puppy, I pushed some prunings of the floribunda rose 'Mandy' into the soil around some miniature roses planted in a border near the house, to discourage his attentions. Although these prunings were not prepared in any way, as they were merely needed to form a barrier, several of them rooted and were transplanted the following year to the floribunda border. One of them died following transplanting, but the others flowered in due course. What I did notice, though, was that they never had the vigour of the budded plants and had a short life, succumbing to severe frosts which nearly all the budded plants survived.

The main argument against cuttings is that it seems to be problematical as a method of propagation for hybrid tea type roses, and rarely succeeds with yellow, orange and flame-coloured hybrid teas.

Writing in the 1961 spring number of *The Rose*, Dr R. Selby sets out the results of his fairly extensive experiments in rooting rose cuttings and, more important, indicates how the rooted cuttings fared in the ensuing five years. He lists by groups a total of 207 which were rooted out of some 1,600 cuttings inserted (approximately 13 per cent "take"). Of the 207, 118 either died or made poor plants and were discarded, leaving only 89 which were successful, or not much more than 5 per cent of the original cuttings inserted. Results by groups indicated that 16 floribundas out of the 62 rooted eventually made good plants. All the Poly. poms. that were rooted (25) proved satisfactory, as did 41 out of 102 hybrid teas (40 per cent). Of these, 20 were in shades of pink and carmine and this may help to explain the relatively high percentage of successes.

Among Dr Selby's conclusions the following are particularly interesting:

"(ii) Rooting does not seem to mean that survival necessarily follows.

(iii) The roses nearest to their original species seem to survive. A deal of inbreeding does not produce sturdy stock—any more with roses than with humans.

(iv) The ramblers and the climbers do well."

It seems significant that Dr Selby adds that he now depends for propagation on budding on Canina seedlings, with an 80 per cent take compared with only 5 per cent from cuttings, and good plants in one year from budding compared with good plants in three years from cuttings.

Back to 1913

ARBEL M. ALDOUS
(Amateur rose grower and successful exhibitor in the Artistic Classes)

I see from my National Rose Society Note Book (not then 'Royal') for 1947 that a press representative, Miss Picton-Jones, asked to be introduced to "an old rose-grower with a past". There is a reference to this fact in the 1948 *Rose Annual* and, though I cannot recall the conversation, I distinctly remember the very beginning of the "Past".

It was June 23rd 1913, the first Queen Alexandra Rose Day. Walking across Trafalgar Square I saw the gaily decorated booth and stopped to buy a rose, and one of the four ladies asked if I would stay for a little time while two of them went for a cup of tea. That is how I first met Mrs Courtney Page.

When they returned they were accompanied by a gentleman who gave me a ticket for a forthcoming Rose Show in Regent's Park. That is how I first met Courtney Page and that is how I went to my first Rose Show—over fifty-seven years ago!

I can't claim to remember details of that show, but the table decorations impressed me, as lovely "tables" were also a feature of the then-flourishing Colchester Rose Show.

But I can remember many things about 1925. For the Spring Show, the R.H.S. Hall seemed quite full and there were actually seven table decorations; and from that day I came to expect that Mrs Courtney Page would be first. And from that day I got to know that Mr Goodwin would show twelve perfect blooms of 'Maréchal Niel' every year—and would until his death in 1936, after winning First Prize for 23 years in succession.

That Show was then a revelation to me. All those roses and all those people on April 24th! I thought of it on April 28th 1970, for the once-great Spring Show is now being painfully resuscitated. It is to be hoped that the valiant efforts of the faithful few will be increasingly supported, especially by those members of the Council who opposed the motion.

But it was the Summer Show of that year, 1925, under canvas in Regent's Park, that laid the foundation of my life-long interest. From that day, Saturday July 4th, I belonged! I had started the nucleus of a rose garden at my week-end cottage and I knew all the Colchester rose people—well, nearly all! I was very fond of Mrs Cecil Cant of the original Benjamin R.

Cant firm and it was Captain Frank Cant of the breakaway branch who later came to verify my boast that I had no greenfly one year when it was very prevalent.

I knew the Warner family of the Boxted Rose Garden and the Priors at their prime. On one occasion when I had done a basket of the dark, velvety red single, 'Donald Prior', Courtney Page said: "That's the best thing the Priors ever put out."

I like to remember that I saw the début of 'Dainty Bess' and I knew her raisers, Mr and Miss Archer. They gave me 'Bonnie Jean'.

I remember the first occasion when I watched Mr and Miss Hart put up their exhibit—not, of course, the great displays of the professional, but big enough to make me wonder if I could ever do that! Why not? But I never did.

In the amateur section Dr Turnbull had prizes and I knew his garden. Nice Mr Fieldgate, of my Oliver & Parker Grocers, took me to lunch. Mrs Harry Barton did a table with 'Betty Uprichard' and gave me the roses to take back to my Hendon flat. (All Colchester people).

Those tables. Twenty-nine of them! It was a sunny day and the golden light from clean canvas flooded the white expanse of snowy damask, each with one large and four small splashes of colour, for it was then *de rigeur* to have a central glass bowl and four corner pieces. The criticism of monotony was not really justified as there was plenty of diversity and, with a set standard, judging was fair and equal, depending on the rose itself and the decorative skill, uninfluenced by extraneous matter and material.

At that time there were decorative exhibits in the Nurserymen's Section and here, and for many years, I can recall the names of Mrs. Bide, Mrs Chaplin, Mrs May, Miss Archer and Mrs Tisdall who outstayed them all.

In the "Ladies Artistic Classes" there was a class for single roses and I can still see the lovely 'Irish Fireflame', 'Irish Elegance', 'Mrs Oakley Fisher' and 'Isobel'. The last was often used by Miss Newsham whose single plant[1] rambled completely over her tool-shed. There was a class for roses that could be bought, but the most exciting was for ladies who grew and staged their own roses unassisted. Here Mrs Courtney Page led the way year after year, followed by Mrs Charlton, Miss Griffith, Mrs Cowan, Mrs Chalmers-Hunt, Miss Newsham and Mrs Oakley Fisher herself, among others.

At this point in my reminiscences it came as a shock to realise that Miss Hart and I seemed to be the sole survivors of 1913. So I wrote to ask her if she knew of others; she could not give me any living names but mentioned Miss

[1] This was a tall-growing bush variety. It still survives in my father's garden. Ed.

Willmott and Mrs Darlington. Both, of course, I had known "by sight". By the 1925 Show I think Mrs Toogood (surely "Miss X" at that early date) must have started showing "singles" to which she is still devoted, as witness her lovely bowl at the Alexandra Palace in 1970. She too will remember the arrival of 'Dainty Bess'.

Of the names that appear in the lists of Council members today there was none in the 1926 Annual and Mr Anstiss (1932), Mr Bertram Park (1933), Mr Hollis (1934), Mr Baldwin and Mr Fairbrother (1936), were the earliest; but I am here concerned with the "Ladies Artistic Classes", especially with Table Decorations.

Her Majesty Queen Alexandra died during the autumn of that year (1925) and there is no doubt that it was with those spectacular tables in mind that Eric Holroyd gave the much-coveted Queen Alexandra Rose Bowl as a Memorial Trophy. Queen Mary, the new Patron, approved the design and herself gave the heavy jade base on which it stands and as the years passed Mrs Courtney Page headed the list of the "ladies who grow and stage their own roses unassisted."

I think Mr Hollis will remember the year 1933, for I believe it was the first time one of his articles appeared in the Annual[1] and it was also the last time that Eric Holroyd's name appeared in the list of the Council Members, for he died in the autumn.

Miss Woollard ("Gwen" affectionately to us all) will also remember 1933. She took first prize in the class "for those who had not previously won a first prize in the decorative section"—the Novices' Class in fact! It was amusing to think of Gwen as a novice when her exquisite table arrangements had been an outstanding feature at Shows at Colchester, Ipswich, Saffron Walden, Bishops Stortford and everywhere in that district. For perhaps thirty more years she did at least one lovely table at R.N.R.S. exhibitions. She still visits us—generally as a judge.

Mrs Thorn also is with us still, though she appears to have given up staging exhibits. I think both she and Mr Thorn appeared first at the Spring Show in 1934 before moving from Wooburn Green to Colchester.

1935 was the year of the disastrous May frost and the cancellation of the Summer Show. I have many notes of 1936. The Summer Show was held at Chelsea. My friend Mrs Grech and I camped out in my car parked in Lime Tree Avenue and we were wakened (by request) at 5 a.m. by the Police with a cup of tea. Those were the days! I had bought a new piece of ground from a young man who kept pigs and I never had such roses before or since.

[1] Sorry, Miss Aldous—the first time was 1931! Ed.

In 1937 I went to Southport for the first time, having been invited to stay with a rose-growing friend at Bolton. I went again in 1939 against the advice of wiser people. It was not actually a Rose Society Show but there were N.R.S. classes. Both coming and going were memorable. Going, I dropped off to sleep when held up by traffic at Ormskirk—it was a long drive from Colchester to Southport!

Then after a three-day show we were called back by wireless for emergency duties. I had my special permit but could not get off until 9 p.m. on Friday and I drove blind through fog and mist and a tremendous thunderstorm. At Stony Stratford I found an off-the-road place outside a garage and fortunately waited until a glimmering of light appeared, because there was an axle-deep flood outside Bedford. But from Cambridge onward it was dry and I was opening corned-beef tins by 9 a.m. ready for our evacuees.

Soon the lights were to go out over Europe and the N.R.S. had to make concessions, but the slim little Annual for the 'forties testifies to its courage; for after the first year of the War the Society managed to produce the bi-annual Show which I always managed to visit. I picked and packed at dawn, did my day's work, and set off for London by 6 p.m. When I had done some unofficial police work I was allowed a little official police petrol and, by walking miles, I used to hoard my own ration and could drive up, do the staging during the night and back again in the early hours. More than once, especially for the Autumn Show, it was the train for me. That meant being at Liverpool Street by 4.10 a.m. I enjoyed the walk from West to East and was glad of coffee and a sandwich at the stall of the Silver Lady on the Embankment. On the first occasion she said tactfully: "You needn't pay if you can't afford it."

We were all saddened in 1942. Some weeks after the shock of a car accident Mrs Courtney Page died "suddenly and peacefully at the home she loved so well". This was all the more poignant because it happened only a few days after Mr and Mrs Courtney Page had received many congratulations on the occasion of their Golden Wedding, having been married on September 3rd, 1892. When talking to Courtney Page when next we met he told me that they had decided to join the Society on their wedding day.

For a year or two Miss Courtney Page (Cherry) carried on her mother's tradition and we were all sorry when she gave up.

Then in 1947 Courtney Page himself died, after some months of failing health. He had been the autocrat of the Society, almost a dictator for the last years; but everyone respected him and many—myself included—liked him very much. Mr Harry Edland ("Harry" to those who knew him well) had

had a good training and was thoroughly competent to carry on and extend the work.

Bertram Park, with his wide knowledge of rose matters and rose people all over Europe and North America and an experienced photographer and a linguist, became the Editor of the Rose Annual until he resigned in 1963 and Mr Hollis took over.

But the biggest undertaking of the Council at that time was the transference of the Trial Ground from Haywards Heath to Oaklands, two acres of land loaned by the Hertfordshire Institute of Agriculture. I was not invited to the Official Luncheon on June 26th 1950, but I waited outside and "gate-crashed" when Mr Farr opened the memorial gates "IN MEMORY OF COURTNEY PAGE, HON. SEC. 1915–1947". However, the Society rapidly outgrew the ground and now it has a permanent home at Bone Hill, St. Albans.

It really was a tragedy that Harry Edland, who had steered the ship through many storms and finally brought it to harbour at Bone Hill, did not live long afterwards. He died suddenly on December 15th 1964 and I write this only a few days after witnessing the dedication of the pavilion erected in his honour and to be known by his name in the Royal National Rose Society Gardens at St. Albans.

But the wind of change had set in. The Age of the Flower Arranging Societies had begun, inaugurated by Mrs Pope of Dorchester and closely followed by Mrs Desmond Underwood of Colchester, with whom I went to start off the branch at Leicester.

It was Mrs Barker (of Colchester) who broke away from the conventional centre bowl and four smalls for the Table Decoration Class. She placed a boat-shaped glass "container" with 'Picture' obliquely across one corner. She was "wizard" with flowers and once she had a well-deserved First Prize with 'Lydia' in the elbow of a jaggedly broken drain pipe.

But supreme among the artists of the unconventional was Miss Hambley-Parker. She, once and for all, launched the "theme" idea, making still-life modern pictures with her rose arrangements. Some of us remember the eye-catching Chinese shawl cast nonchalantly over her sideboard.

The passing of the white damask napery was marked in 1951. I noticed a crowd round a table and went to investigate. A group of W.I. members were all making ejaculations of admiration at Mrs Clacy's lovely cloth used with her winning entry for the Queen Alexandra Memorial Trophy for Table Decoration.

By that time the Schedule "Ladies Artistic Classes" had become "Artistic

Classes" because Mr V. R. Vyner Brooks, a specialist in "drapes", had entered the lists, and in due course clever Brian Green, the son of a clever mother, joined him. (I can't call him "Mr" for I knew his father when he was a boy.)

By 1962 the Summer Show had outgrown the R.H.S. Halls and had been transferred to the Alexandra Palace. There, the "tables" as such were crowded out and instead there was Class 92, "a table decoration of roses suitable for a buffet for a special occasion to be stated by exhibitor, any rose foliage and accessories allowed".

Oh, those accessories! The revised rules certainly printed in heavy type "Roses must predominate" but it was *not* the roses that caught the judges' eye! What would Eric Holroyd have thought? *Verbum sap!*

This year of grace 1970 our own Royal National Rose Society Flag, the gift of our President, Mr Clarke, was displayed outside for the first time. Inside, for the first time also, a big board on the wall boldly proclaimed "Floral Arrangement Section" for the decorative classes.

"What a lovely thing a rose is!" He walked past the couch to the open window and held up the drooping stalk of a moss rose, looking down at the dainty blend of crimson and green. It was a new phase of his character to me, for I had never before seen him show any keen interest in natural objects.

"There is nothing in which deduction is so necessary as in religion," said he, leaning with his back against the shutters. "It can be built up as an exact science by the reasoner. Our highest assurance of the goodness of Providence seems to me to rest in the flowers. All other things, our desires, our food, are really necessary for our existence in the first instance. But this rose is an extra. Its smell and its colour are an embellishment of life, not a condition of it. It is only goodness which gives extras, and so I say again that we have much to hope for from the flowers."

SIR ARTHUR CONAN DOYLE, *The Naval Treaty*,
in *The Memoirs of Sherlock Holmes*, 1893.

On Safari through Senghenydd

ANON THROUGH BRYNDORION (SWANSEA) & DISTRICT ROSE SOCIETY

You may well ask, "Where's Senghenydd?" Actually it has nothing to do with this account—merely a place one nearly misses when travelling through the Rhondda Valley.

All agog and armed with pen, paper and the Rose Society's advice to "beginning" judges, we set off to sit in judgment, without fear, favour or malice, on the Rhondda Society's Annual Rose Show. Not forgetting a buttonhole. It's the hallmark of having "arrived" on the rose scene. When shaking hands and meeting the welcoming committee, one feels ten feet tall under the green-eyed gaze of men who quite obviously have never seen a dead 'Circus' before.

The first problem was in actually finding the show. One naturally assumes that one's fellow judge knows where the venue is. Such is human frailty. Neither of us had a clue. We passed through four seasons climbing to the head of the Rhondda Valley. The Gods, frowning in anticipation of such inept students of the rose, sent down a blanket of mist which engulfed everything including the dead 'Circus'—we'd have to ask.

"Rose Show?" The first six laughed. The next three wore expressions of gentle compassion whilst the last lady, shepherding her two young daughters to her ample waist, muttered something about having read about "the likes of us", before. As the car number was not "local", we were obviously a duo of Saxon sex maniacs let loose on an unsuspecting Welsh valley.

How we found it I'll never know. Perhaps if one drives long enough up and down valleys one is bound to find one's goal. Even in a North Sea mist.

Anyway there we were. Minus all rank, medals, whiskers, or shooting sticks. But wouldn't we show them how to judge roses!

The first thing we noticed was the calm of the place. Nothing seemed to be moving. The occasional lady carrying driftwood, Grecian urn and purple drape sneaked self-consciously along past the unknowing Non-conformist chapel. An old gent with a Vase of Three smiled—but we stared stonily back. Maybe we'd unbend a little after judging, but rules are rules. Fraternisation was out, right out.

Well, we judged the Show, retired for lunch, returning later to sit back

78

and listen to the praises of the winners. As far as we could, we'd given everybody a prize.

The congregation (it was in a Church Hall) was 100 per cent female. There wasn't a man to be seen anywhere. I'd read about this in African villages. Some inexplicable mist madness drove the ladies to consume their partners in a fit of gastronomic delight. Surely not here? We made for the door. We were willing to forego our travelling expenses to see Swansea City in the Third Division next season.

We discovered the reason for the lack of males. Apparently every club in the area had gone to Porthcawl for the day. Twenty-two buses had taken hundreds of fully paid-up members to the sea-side. We were glad we didn't have to judge the trippers.

In actual terms we got on fine with the remainder of the community and indeed we are looking forward to this year's outing—which doesn't coincide with the Rose Show. But that's another story. Any interested female reader requiring the date of this exodus should write to us (including a stamped addressed envelope—under plain cover, of course).

We returned to Swansea under a welter of good wishes and praises. "Could you judge a Baby Show in August?" "We'll be a second-row forward short this season, what about it?" "Plaid Cymru want to raise a Welsh rose, can you suggest a name?"

Homewards, we travelled under a warring thunderstorm and arrived home to witness the complete destruction of the following week's winners in our local Rose Show.

C'est la vie. You can't win them all.

The Men behind the New Roses

NIGEL RABAN

(Amateur rose grower and art dealer)

As you walk round your rose beds on a summer evening, delighting in the form, colour and fragrance of the blooms, do you ever stop to think of the men who have spent years raising the new varieties that now grace your garden? For every new rose which is brought into commerce thousands of seedlings have failed the test and been destroyed. It was the thought of such an immense labour that prompted this series of thumbnail sketches of some of today's leading hybridists.

From the correspondence and tape recordings certain common denominators have emerged. Nearly all the breeders with whom there has been contact are agreed that hardiness and disease resistance are vital pre-requisites. Without these qualities, a rose is not worth putting out and one hybridist went so far as to say that his great fear for the future was that too many breeders would send too many geese to market, believing them to be swans, and that a rose should only go out after the most stringent tests.

It is noteworthy that Monsieur Gaujard refers specifically to colour. Since the war the French hybridists have paid particular attention to this problem and under their conditions of brilliant light and sunshine it is understandable how they strive to give us rich, even startling colours. One is tempted to compare this approach with the work of the painters of the Impressionist school, who taught the world to see pure colour for the first time for centuries.

Although the raisers are agreed on the importance of fragrance, none has so far placed it in the front rank of vital qualities. Nevertheless, few good roses of hybrid tea type are without scent today and the cliché which is still at times trotted out by the ignorant, that the modern rose has lost its scent, should be recognized for the nonsense that it is.

In trying to link the men with the roses, personal experience often has the greatest impact. For some ten years I was an ardent exhibitor and during that time I hardly put up an exhibit that did not contain one or more blooms of 'Karl Herbst'. To Wilhelm Kordes, therefore, I feel I owe the prizes that I managed to win. Last year a friend came to me in some concern as her florist had let her down and she needed white roses for two pedestals at a church

Edward Le Grice
(*see page* 85)

Wilhelm Kordes
(*see page* 83)

Top Left:
Jean Gaujard
(*see page* 81)
Top Right:
Louis Lens
(*see page* 87)
Left:
Samuel McGredy
(*see page* 88)

festival. She went away with an armful of 'Pascali'. To Louis Lens we gave our grateful thanks. In June 1969 some friends came to see the roses, but as it was a very late season, not many varieties were in bloom. However, they were able to enjoy a good show of 'Irish Mist' and 'Elizabeth of Glamis'. How thankful I was to Sam McGredy, whose work had enabled me to have some colour in the garden at the right moment. A keen flower arranger came asking for "something different" to use at the local rose show. She was able to cut good sprays of 'Vesper', thanks to Edward Le Grice and his work in producing these new colours so suitable for flower arrangement.

In the words of Ecclesiasticus, 'Let us now praise famous men . . . '

JEAN GAUJARD

About the year 1820, a number of rosarians at Lyon in France began the selection of roses in an attempt to obtain new varieties. This method had been started by Descemet who had been a gardener at Malmaison when the Empress Joséphine was forming her comprehensive collection of the then known roses. Descemet had simply taken the ripe seeds from the plants after the flowers had been pollinated by the bees.

In Lyon, Claude Ducher took the matter a stage further by selecting the parents and controlling the pollination himself. Matters advanced so well that, in 1845, the Horticultural Society of Lyon organized an exhibition cf new roses. This had a considerable success and Ducher decided to specialize in the production of new varieties. In 1879 another rosarian in Lyon, Joseph Pernet, married Marie Ducher and so was founded the firm of Pernet-Ducher. The new firm continued its emphasis on hybridization and in 1890 introduced one of the great classic roses, 'Mme Caroline Testout', following this with 'Mme Abel Chatenay' in 1895.

As he was walking one day in the new Parc de la Tête d'Or in Lyon Pernet-Ducher was struck by the sight of two rose species in full bloom—the 'Persian Yellow' (R. foetida persiana) and R. foetida bicolor, and determined to produce roses in these colours with the added quality of remontancy. Crossing the species with his own hybrid, 'Antoine Ducher', he obtained the first seedlings of a strain which was to become known as the Pernetiana, but it was not until 1900 that he was able to produce 'Soleil d'Or', the first satisfactory hybrid having both the required colour, orange yellow shaded nasturtium-red, and the freedom of flowering. From 'Soleil d'Or' × 'Mme Mélanie Soupert' came 'Rayon d'Or', the first rich yellow, in 1910.

Pernet-Ducher's two sons had to leave the nursery at the outbreak of war in 1914 and tragically both were killed that autumn, fighting to stem the German advance. Their father was thus left alone to carry on the work of hybridizing. In 1924 he asked the young Jean Gaujard to join him in his work. M. Gaujard comes from a family with a long tradition as nurserymen. One of his ancestors worked at Versailles with LeNotre as far back as 1648 and the family had remained in the Versailles area until the Revolution and had then gone for safety to Chateauroux in central France where Jean was born in 1903.

Very shortly after joining Pernet-Ducher, the young man knew this was to be his vocation and he wrote to his father, telling him that this was to be his life's work and that he would abandon the profession of general nursery-man.

Pernet-Ducher died in 1928, but by that time he had handed over the day-to-day control of his establishment to M. Gaujard and the mantle of the 'Magician of Lyon' fell on this young man of 25. Soon the nursery became too small for his needs, and a move was made to Feyzin in 1930, where he created a great modern installation for the culture of the rose.

Over the past 40 years, Gaujard's work has been crowned with many great successes. Five times he has won the Gold Medal at the Bagatelle and seven times the award of 'La Plus Belle Rose de France' and other international successes have been a frequent occurrence. His work has been officially recognized by the State which created him Chevalier de la Légion d'Honneur and Commandeur du Mérite Agricole.

Amongst the famous varieties raised by him during this period are 'Julien Potin' (1928), 'Quebec' syn. 'Mme Marie Curie' (1943), 'Opera' (1949), and 'Rose Gaujard' (1957) to name but a very few.

Since 1950, M. Gaujard has made many crossings with a view to obtaining good varieties for the cut flower market. For some years now the glasshouse trade has been demanding stock which will give a greatly increased number of flowers to the plant, thus making the project more attractive commercially, and it is to this end that the Gaujard nurseries have been working at their new research station at St Remy in Provence, which was started in 1957. Altogether the nurseries produce 25 to 30,000 seedlings annually and from these no more than 3 or 4 ultimately find their way into commerce. The actual selection of the chosen varieties presents enormous problems and, if the task of choosing the parents for the crossings is hard, the final selection of 3 or 4 from tens of thousands is the most arduous of all.

Two sons, Jean Jacques and Patrice, have joined their father and this team ensures the continuity of the breeding programme of the Gaujard roses.

In speaking of their aims M. Gaujard still places great emphasis on the search for new and brilliant colour which led Pernet-Ducher to 'Soleil d'Or' and it is still the main objective of his successor to seek for reds which do not 'blue' and to find true orange varieties which do not fade in the sun. He believes that 'Guitare', coming from 'Golden Slippers' crossed with unnamed seedlings, is a new step along this road. In addition, like other hybridists, he aims for disease resistance and freedom of flowering. As he himself says. "Rosarians nowadays want their roses to bloom until the frosts come."

WILHELM KORDES

Charles de Gaulle once maintained that 1891 was the year of the finest vintage. That same year, Wilhelm Kordes was born in Holstein four years after his father had set up a general nursery on abandoning a career at sea for which he had been intended.

Young Wilhelm served his apprenticeship in a large German nursery, moved to Switzerland and then on to Orléans where he spent a year with the Chenault establishment, at that time the most famous propagating and hybridizing firm in Europe. In 1912, he went to England, working at Bide's nursery in Farnham and the following year started on his own with Max Krause at Witley. This project was one of the casualties of the war, as Kordes was interned in September 1914 and spent the next four and a half years in the Isle of Man.

On his return home Kordes, like so many of his countrymen, had to start from scratch and the first step was to move from his father's old land at Elmshorn to Sparrieshoop where, after 50 years, the nurseries have grown in size to 200 acres, producing some 4 million rose plants annually.

When he first started hybridizing after the first world war, he used 'Mme Caroline Testout', then the most popular rose in Germany for cutting, as the seed parent. By using 'Général Jacqueminot' as the pollen parent, he was hoping to produce a red "Testout", but the first crosses were valueless and it was not until 1930 that he launched 'Cathrine Kordes' ('Mme Caroline Testout' × 'Willowmere') × 'Sensation', bright red in colour and similar to "Testout" in form. Crossing a seedling from this rose with 'W. E. Chaplin' gave 'Crimson Glory' (1935), one of the great classic roses and parents of modern times.

In Holstein the climate is very difficult. The winters give extremes of temperature ranging from mild to a blistering cold, with dry winds from the East, which make the over-wintering plants appear as if a blow-lamp had gone over them. In addition, less hardy varieties are very subject to the fungus diseases. Reviewing this situation, Kordes realized that his aim had to be hardiness combined with disease resistance, in addition to the standard quest for colour and freedom of flowering. It was *R. spinosissima* and *R. rubiginosa* which were to give the necessary hardiness and now after 20 or 30 generations, we have the results in roses such as 'Perfecta', 'Colour Wonder' and 'Peer Gynt'. Freedom of flower was realized by using the China hybrids and the habit of forming trusses came from the poly. poms.

By chance, a crossing of 'Robin Hood' with 'J. C. Thornton' gave a batch of disease resistant seedlings. Both parents have Noisette hybrids in their strain so it is in part from *R. moschata* that have come the strong, healthy shrub roses of to-day.

One of Herr Kordes' greatest successes in his long experience of hybridizing must be the introduction of the hardy, perpetual flowering climbers, now known as Kordesii. He was always much attracted to 'Max Graf' (1919), a cross between *R. rugosa* and *R. wichuraiana*, which was often planted for ground cover and has fine disease resistant foliage and large, single flowers. For many years it refused to set heps, until one autumn when it gave two seed pods from which came three seedlings. Two were killed off by the winter cold but the third survived and produced light red, double flowers and plenty of pollen. This seedling gave big heps full of seed, but freedom of flowering was lacking. However, after a few more generations, 'Hamburger Phoenix' (1950) appeared—the first of an important new group which has been still further improved by the introduction into the strain of *R. rubiginosa* hybrids. These Kordesii varieties, which include 'Dortmund', 'Leverkusen', 'Parkdirektor Riggers' and 'Ritter von Barmstede', are admirable pillar roses reaching 7 to 9 feet with recurrent blooms, unlike the old climbing roses which flowered once profusely and were then finished for the year.

Another aspect of Herr Kordes' hybridizing activities has been the production of a group of floribundas. After the arrival of 'Else Poulsen' in 1924, nurserymen and amateurs began to demand new varieties of this type, and Kordes started a programme on these lines, producing seedlings with more petals and a greater range of colours than the prototype. 'Rosenelfe' (1939), was the first to achieve a big success but 'Rudolf Timm' proved of greater importance, as this had *R. rubiginosa* in its parentage and, being tetraploid, was of great value to the breeding programme. In this rose, the raiser brought together the qualities of hardiness, disease resistance and remontancy. Another special virtue of this strain is its capability of producing a large quantity of cut flower bloom under glasshouse conditions. Finally, the introduction of 'Independence' ('Kordes Sondermeldung') (1950), into the line has given stronger growth and longer-lasting flowers.

In looking into the future, Herr Kordes feels that an attempt should be made to reduce the number of thorns apparent on some of the newer varieties, probably due to *R. spinosissima* in their parentage. He emphasizes that the problem lies in the correct choice of parents. Unless they have the qualities for which he is seeking their offspring will lack them also. In the words of the old German saying, "The soup ladle will only bring out what is already in the tureen".

E. B. LE GRICE

Born in 1902, Edward Le Grice comes of a family which has lived in East Norfolk for hundreds of years. He was educated at Paston Grammar School in North Walsham—a happy chance as the school ran special classes in Agricultural Science from which he was able to benefit. He decided not to enter his father's shop but to take up a horticultural career and shortly after the end of the First World War obtained a position with Henry Morse & Sons with whom he spent two busy and happy years.

It was quite by chance that he became a specialist rose-grower. As a beginning, the Morses encouraged him to plant a few stocks and in 1920 he started on his own. Despite the demands of a growing business, he has always taken a keen interest in social work and local affairs; lay preacher and scoutmaster for more than 20 years, local councillor, and, during the Second World War, a member of a busy Rescue Squad which, being on the flight path of allied squadrons on their way to the Third Reich, meant not infrequent attendance on aircraft, which having staggered back across the channel, crashed or had to force-land in this country.

Married in 1944, he has two sons who have joined him in the business, the younger having had a spell of training in the United States. His activities have been somewhat curtailed recently by ill-health but as he now spends more time in writing and lecturing in addition to watching over his seedlings, one is forced to wonder whether he pays much attention to the doctors. His two books, *Rose Growing Complete* and *Rose Growing for Everyone*, are standard works for all rosarians.

Mr Le Grice's first attempts at hybridizing were modest, being carried out in his father's vinery and the crosses were all experimental. It was not until 1938 that he really made a mark with his famous floribunda 'Dainty Maid', which received a Certificate of Merit in that year. Then came the war and with it disappeared the greater part of the experimental work that had been going on, particularly some crossings of a remontant form of R. moschata with 'Kirsten Poulsen' in an attempt to achieve repeat flowering. But three important seedlings survived those years. Two were hybrid teas, 'Wellworth' and 'Ellinor Le Grice', which have proved themselves as parents, the former producing 'My Choice' (1958) and the latter, the famous 'Allgold' (1956). The floribunda seedling saved from the wreck of war was 'Dusky Maiden'. This was introduced in 1948 and won him his first Gold Medal from the R.N.R.S.

During these years the Le Grice nurseries were famous for their strain of 'Maid' roses which dominated the breeding programme and brought Gold Medals for 'Charming Maid' (1953) and 'Bonnie Maid' (1955) and culminated with 'Lilac Charm' which won its Gold Medal in 1961.

With 'Allgold' came an abiding interest in the production of new colours, particularly with a view to the needs of the rapidly growing and popular Flower Arrangement Societies. 'Lavender Pinocchio' had always fascinated him with its unusual colouring and his seedlings, 'Lavender Lady' and 'Overture' showed the possibilities lying hidden beneath the surface. Other seedlings from R. californica had exciting new characteristics; one was a single, brown in colour; another led to 'Lilac Charm'. The brown caught his attention, in particular, and after many experiments and crossings with old garden roses came 'Amberlight', with its unique scent and 'Vesper', so good in growth and habit and an interesting light golden-brown in colour. From exploiting all these crossings came, at last, the 1970 Gold Medal rose, 'News', which has combined the vinous colour, so much loved in many of the old fashioned varieties, with the health and freedom of flowering of the modern floribunda.

After forty years of trial and error, Mr Le Grice still prefers an experimental programme to one run on strictly planned lines of routine crossing. He quotes the figures of last year's work as being 34 named varieties as seed-parents, with 78 pollen parents and about another 25 unnamed seedlings to make separate crosses. As soon as something promising appears from a cross he aims to raise a thousand seedlings in a further year. He allows himself a maximum of three such extended crosses each year and if after that period no further progress has been made, the cross is discarded.

All along he holds to definite aims for his new varieties. In hybrid teas he looks for self colours and perfume—this latter an unpredictable quality—and 'City of Hereford', 'Incense' and 'Ellen Mary' are examples of a successful outcome. In the floribundas he wants freedom of flower and a clean shattering, regarding both as essential and more important than size. Of the future, he hopes for a tall, full, unfading golden variety, either hybrid tea or floribunda, but despite hundreds of crosses and thousands of seedlings, the goal seems as elusive as ever; but as he says, his work is only part of the structure of the building—the coping stone of perfection will be placed there by future generations.

LOUIS LENS

One hundred years ago, Louis Lens Senior dreamed of founding a nursery and in 1873 he was able to make this dream come true with the purchase of 25 acres of land at Wavre Notre Dame in the vicinity of Malines. This land still forms, today, the nucleus of the Lens nurseries.

From the beginning, Louis Lens was interested in the cultivation of the rose. It was an important period in the history of rose breeding. In 1867, the variety 'La France', fore-runner of the hybrid teas, had been introduced and 1875 saw the birth of the first of the polyantha pompon roses, 'Paquerette'. Shortly afterwards Joseph Pernet-Ducher began his experiments, carried on over twenty years, which were to introduce exciting new colours.

Louis Lens Senior had three sons, Emile, Henri and Victor who took over the running of the firm from their father. Unfortunately Emile died in 1933 and Henri went off on his own to become a successful orchid grower. Victor was, therefore, left alone to carry on the rose nursery and, as he had never been blessed with robust health, he devoted much of his personal time and effort to the production of new varieties and became one of the most prominent raisers in Belgium. The rose 'Ville de Malines' (parentage un-known) a salmon pink variety with orange tones, was brought out in 1929 and this was followed in 1932 by 'Madame Louis Lens' syn. 'White Briarcliff', ('Briarcliff' × 'Kaiserin Auguste Viktoria') × ('Briarcliff' × 'Mrs H. Stevens'). This was a white rose, much used in the cut flower trade and was named in honour of his mother.

The years of the second World War naturally put a stop to all hybridizing activities, but the work was restarted in 1949 by Louis Lens Junior and in 1956 he took over the personal direction of the firm from his father, who died in 1969.

Undoubtedly, the firm's most important introduction in the last few years has been 'Pascali' ('Queen Elizabeth' × 'White Butterfly') which won the 'All America' award in 1969, having already achieved a Trial Ground Certificate and Certificate of Merit from the RNRS. It is certainly one of the most popular white hybrid tea varieties, both for cutting and bedding purposes today. Amongst other distinctions which this rose has achieved, is the honour of being used by the Belgian Government for an issue of postage stamps on a horticultural theme in September 1969.

Of the large number of roses introduced by Monsieur Lens, British rosarians will know best 'Dame de Coeur' ('Peace' × 'Independence') TGC 1958, 'Bel Ange' ('Independence' × 'Papillon Rose') × ('Charlotte Armstrong' × 'Floradora') TGC 1962, 'Percy Thrower' ('La Jolla' × 'Queen Elizabeth)' TGC 1962 and 'Blue Diamond' ('Purpurine' × ('Purpurine' × 'Royal Tan')) TGC 1964.

There is no evidence to show that Victor and Louis Lens have followed a specific breeding line, though some of their most successful parents have been 'Independence' and 'Queen Elizabeth'. Rather, by making various crossings they sought to produce roses of attractive form with particular emphasis on cut flower work. It is clear from their group of introductions that elegance, in blooms of moderate size, has taken pride of place in contrast to the style further south where, in the French nurseries, it is colour which is the predominant theme.

SAM McGREDY

Having been born in 1932, Samuel Darragh McGredy is very much a man of the post-war era, with no pre-conceived notions of the style of rose-breeding of earlier years.

His father died in 1934 leaving a flourishing rose nursery and breeding establishment in trust for his son. Sam went off to boarding school in Enniskillen in 1939 when the war started, and stayed there until he won a scholarship under the English Speaking Union exchange scheme, which gave him a year at Mercersburg Academy, Pennsylvania, and he speaks of this episode as one of the happiest years in his life.

Back in Northern Ireland in 1949 he went, somewhat reluctantly, to Greenmount Agricultural College, where he studied under Crosbie Cochrane whom he regards as the best teacher he ever had and who gave him an enthusiasm for practical horticulture. From Greenmount he went on to

Reading University, where the pleasures of playing Rugby outweighed his academic interest. For the rose world, this was probably a lucky chance, for had he passed his finals he might well have gone into journalism as a career. Instead, after a year at Walter C. Slocock's nursery in Woking, he came back to Portadown at a time when the business was beginning to be rebuilt after the war. The plant breeding activities had almost folded up, and the records of his father's work in the years between the wars had been misguidedly pulped to help the war effort. Typical McGredy productions at that time were roses like 'Armagh', 'Pink Spiral' and 'Misty Morn', which were not equal to the new roses coming from Europe.

Diving in at the deep end is often a salutary experience and, without much genetic knowledge to help him, he started off by reading *Modern Roses* several times from cover to cover and all the old National Rose Society *Annuals* on which he could lay his hands. Then he went into his greenhouses, discarded all the old strains, took the best of the new roses from Europe and America, put them all in one house and threw pollen about to see what would come out.

Three parents gave notable results—'Spartan', which became the background of his whole strain of floribundas from 'Flamenco' to 'City of Leeds', 'Irish Mist' (via 'Mischief'), and 'Molly McGredy'; 'Cläre Grammerstorff' which gave 'Arthur Bell', now in its turn in the background of many of the new varieties which will be appearing in the next few years, and lastly 'Karl Herbst', affectionately known to all hybridists as "the old bull". From this came 'Piccadilly' and further along the line 'John Waterer' and 'National Trust'.

Like so many hybridists, he realized at once how important hardiness and disease resistance were to his strain and to this end he introduced Spinosissima blood by the use of 'Frühlingsmorgen'. At first the seedlings were of no commercial value, but after several generations came a red variety with a white edge which was named 'José'. This was very free-flowering and hardy but was marred by ugly blotches on the foliage; this defect proved difficult to eradicate in later generations, but after many crossings, including some with *R. microphylla,* success is at last in sight, and he has a new strain which will soon be available and to which he refers as his "handpainted" series. The first of these is 'Picasso'.

Asked about his policy for new varieties, he replies that he is not now interested in producing hybrid teas or floribundas as such, except for sale in America where there is still a call for the traditional hybrid tea type. He believes that health and vigour are all-important and that, without these qualities, a new variety is useless. He thinks in terms of plants being required to fulfil certain definite roles. At the present time there is the need for low-growing roses, very free-flowering, which will act as good ground cover and smother weeds. Secondly, he believes in the future of the Floribunda/H.T. type, and is constantly working to produce seedlings which will give clusters of good-sized blooms, each with the perfection of form of the old hybrid teas.

A further development at Portadown in the last few years has been a remarkable series of remontant climbers. This started quite by chance. He thought that Kordes' shrub, 'Heidelberg', offered great possibilities and he undertook an extensive programme, crossing it with almost everything on which he could lay his hands. The results were spectacular with 'Handel', 'Galway Bay', 'Swan Lake' and 'Santa Catalina'. These new, repeat-flowering climbers are a great advance and can serve a dual role, in that they may also be grown very successfully as shrubs. Of all his introductions, Mr McGredy gives pride of place to 'Handel' with its refreshing colour and vigorous habit.

Another field in which he has been at work is that of the miniatures. His crosses started with *R. roulettii* and 'New Penny', and he is now far along the line. The problem has been the tendency of many miniatures to flower once and then to go to sleep. He does not mind if the resulting varieties are not tiny; he looks for good shape, low and bushy, and lots of bloom. In this way he links his twin aims of low-growing floribundas giving ground cover, and the production of new miniatures. He thinks that in the next few years results along these lines will be startling, as many of the hybridists are already working with this goal in view.

Of all the satisfactions that his work has brought him, none has been greater than his friendships with his European colleagues. Both Reimer Kordes and Niels Poulsen were groomsmen at his wedding and he is god-father to Poulsen's daughter, Lisa. It is for him an enduring delight to walk through the seedling houses in their company and to know that all of them express their thoughts absolutely freely and that, without commercial enmity, they can discuss roses and enjoy one another's company.

There is no space here to record his triumphs and awards, which started with his Gold Medal for 'Orangeade' in 1959, but it should be noted that his standing amongst his fellow hybridists is such that, for six years, he was President of CIOPORA, the powerful international organization of orna-mental plant breeders, succeeding Wilhelm Kordes and being followed in turn by Kordes' son, Reimer.

It is hoped to continue this series in future editions.—Ed.

Seasonal Notes in 1970

VERA F. P. DAY, N.D.H., FOLKESTONE

(Professional gardener and Botanist)

Looking back on some random notes made at the beginning of the year, I found this:

"Trees and shrubs retained their full green leaves almost to the end of November. Wet weather in December prevented plants of all kinds from dying down. By mid-December buds on roses were swelling, in some cases producing green shoots—the state usually reached by mid-January in this area—so I pruned earlier than usual. . . .

"The old rhyme runs:

> *"If Candlemas Day be foul with rain,*
> *Winter has gone and won't come again.*
> *If Candlemas Day be clear and fair,*
> *The half of the winter's to come—and more!"*

"I have found this to be remarkably consistent, so was prepared for the worst when February 2nd dawned gloriously bright and cloudless, and the sun sank in a clear sky, followed by a brilliant full moon with not a cloud in sight—but did not expect to wake next morning to find a white countryside after a heavy snowfall in the small hours. . . . Snow and hard frost and high bitter winds throughout the month even discouraged small boys from tobogganing!"

I was not troubled about my winter pruned roses, for modern roses are as hardy as the wild ones, and will stand up to anything except fire, flood or landslides, and I reckoned they could look after themselves as usual. They did.

There was no spring worth mentioning in 1970, but when what passed for spring eased out into early summer, and growth was making definite progress, I only had to remove a few damaged tips (it is unwise to be too precipitate in removing frosted stems), and found, as I have found before with early and light pruning, that most of the frosted buds threw off small, damaged outside leaves, and the shoots emerged unhurt. In fact, there were fewer blind shoots than last year, when this form of damage was exceptionally high generally.

Flowers were late in appearing: in this area I can usually cut the first in mid-May, sometimes earlier; but this year there were no blooms until May

28th, when I cut four perfect, delightfully scented blooms of 'Etoile de Hollande', a variety by no means usually the first to flower. 'Shot Silk' is usually the first—this year when it did bloom the first flowers showed the strange malformation that appeared after the severe winter of 1962-3, a hard central growth, pale green and divided into four stiff thick horns. None of the double varieties threw single petalled blooms, as I have known to happen on two occasions after very severe frost.

By mid-June roses were resplendent all over the town—then on July 6th at the height of their beauty came a severe storm at sea, with a whirlwind on Romney Marsh, leaving gardens littered with full blown roses and half-opened buds. Luckily secondary growth had hardly started, so subsequent blooming was not affected. But for some reason, I suspected the prolonged severe drought, my second crop was a long time in maturing, few of the buds opening until September. (My rain-water tanks never ran dry but could not be spared for the roses.)

I have never known a year so free from pests of all kinds. Being close to the sea, we are rarely troubled with greenfly and I never spray for it. An old fashioned remedy, recommended when I was at College, namely, finger and thumb, if applied early in May when the "mother aphid" appears on young shoots, not only gets rid of viviparous females but the subsequent broods as well. Of course, this is only practicable with small gardens and few plants. Black fly is always a major pest and almost impossible to control because of the many elder trees in the chalk country; but this year it more or less confined itself to the dahlias. Leaf rolling sawfly caterpillars, usually a serious pest locally, only made a very brief appearance, as did gooseberry sawfly. Late caterpillars, like those of vaporer moths, were entirely absent.

I only saw one bedraggled specimen of the large cabbage white butterfly, and no caterpillars, and there were very few small whites or cabbage moths; cuckoo spit, another serious pest, was negligible this year. Asparagus beetles, usually a serious nuisance, succumbed to one application of derris dust; white fly and flea beetles were absent, leather jackets were in short supply and consequently there were no daddy-long-legs. Major nuisances were ants and wasps.

What caused this blissful time and money saving, not to mention plant saving, absence of pests this year, I do not know, unless the long drawn out cold spring, with plant and animal growth at a low ebb, induced birds to hunt more diligently for insect eggs and immature larvae.

Mildew on roses in this area was not troublesome. I have no ramblers so do not expect it, but it did not occur in the neighbours' gardens. Rust is uncommon in the neighbourhood and I have not seen it in local gardens.

I have long since given up trying to cope with Black Spot, other than to rake up fallen leaves in autumn and water beds and plants with a weak solution of Jeyes. There has been very little of it so far. (I had better not speak too soon, it is only mid-September!) I have been told "we sprayed our roses and had no Black Spot until the autumn" but this is less likely to be due to spraying than to the fact that it rarely appears before late summer. When it does appear early, I have not found it on young vigorous shoots at this time, but always on leaves arising from old and rather worn out wood. These growths are nearly always blind, and the affected leaves are usually small and have a look of maturity from the start, always green and never showing the juvenile colouring of young shoots, which varies considerably with the variety. Later in the year, all stages of growth are attacked.

Hard pruning was thought to prevent disease by removing material likely to harbour infection, but in fact hard pruning was chiefly concerned in cutting back year old growth and often a ring of old stumps was left around the plant. Further, the fashion coincided with the production of varieties not susceptible to the disease. In fact Black Spot only became a menace in the early '20's, when the yellow and orange shades began to predominate in the rose garden; the first Black Spot I saw was in our own garden on a pretty salmon pink variety called 'Los Angeles'[1] (no longer in commerce) which was promptly destroyed. It is not always possible to remove all the old wood from plants that are slow to make growth, but as soon as new growth is made the old should be removed wherever practicable to avoid disease.

It was about this time that advice was given to mulch rose beds as a possible preventative, it being suggested that perhaps lack of moisture aggravated the trouble. This has not proved to be the case; but in fact roses do benefit from mulching. Grass mowings were—and are—advised; and this would seem to point to the best time of application, starting in early summer, when bulbs and early perennials like doronicums that make their principal growth in spring, are dying down, and winter killed grass is already disintegrating. This year my neighbour invited me to remove her compost heap—I spread this on top of the remains of the hyacinths growing under the roses, and whether this kept Black Spot in check I do not know, but perhaps our grandfathers' advice does check spores arising from fallen

[1] This variety had very poor foliage when I grew it in Lancashire and it was a martyr to disease. Ed.

leaves that have been overlooked—I wouldn't know. The next natural mulch occurs in late autumn.

Why is it that stocks growing up in the form of suckers are so prevalent these days? Are they extra strong? It is to be expected that when roses are old and worn out, sickly, or weak growers that fail to "get away" satisfactorily after planting they will degenerate, and the stocks take over; but why should a lusty, strong growing bush of 'Eden Rose', with blooms like cabbages, throw suckers right, left and centre? Its vigour seems unimpaired; could it be that it has imparted its strength to the stock? This has been known in the case of fruit trees. Incidentally, 'Eden Rose' is one of the first to be affected by Black Spot in my garden, and 'Super Star', which Dr P. J. W. Saunders lists as resistant[1] is another sufferer, and on our soil, not a strong grower. There is something in our peculiar soil that makes quite a number of varieties take on the colour of 'Super Star'. 'Vilia' is one of them.

[1] See page 119 of *The Rose Annual 1970*. Ed.

ROSEBUDS

Sweet rosebud on thy slender stem
The glistening dew thy diadem,
Caressed within thy cradled coomb
The promise of a perfect bloom.

Thy petalled folds in flaming flush
By youth's first fervent virgin blush,
Untarnished yet by rigours rude
That rock thee in thy maidenhood.

So soon thy lovely petals part
To bare thy vulnerable heart,
And swift the passage of thy prime
On wingèd transience of time.

The cycle of our lives engage
Through seed, maturity and age,
As all is drawn to deep decay
So waste and wither thou away.

Yet from thy source there soon will be
Another bud as chaste as thee,
As nature ever circling flows
To thus perpetuate the rose.

                                             IRIS WHITTAKER

The Rosarian's Year Book, 1890

J. L. HARKNESS
(Rose Nurseryman and Breeder)

Do you know that feeling of wanting something to read? And as you look at your bookshelves, you realise you know your favourites all too well?

It was in such a mood one evening that my fingers hooked out an old Rosarian's Year Book. I could feel the scorn of my distinguished entertainers left on the shelf. Dickens and Browning, long neglected, seemed to be appealing to Lord Peter Wimsey and Philip Marlowe to do something about it. Nevil Shute and Dornford Yates were complacently sure of my speedy return. They were wrong.

I opened the 1890 Year Book to find Keynes Williams & Co. of Salisbury advertising "Climbing Niphetos Rose, Price 7/6 each, the most valuable introduction since Maréchal Niel was sent out. Distributed in May 1889". Lower down on the page are the words: "TEAS IN POTS". I suppose pots are what you expect to find Tea in, but to avoid confusion they add "Strong Plants in April and May". So—container-grown roses were going strong in 1890.

George Prince, of Oxford, has a "NEW TEA ROSE, Souvenir de S.A. Prince, a pure white sport from Souvenir d'un Ami". It won the Gold Medal at the Crystal Palace on 6 July 1889.

G. Bunyard & Co. tempt their customers to Maidstone with: "Frequent Trains on the South Eastern and Chatham and Dover Railway".

Alex Dickson & Sons give their address as "The Royal Nurseries, Newtownards, Ireland"; a reminder that Ireland was one country then.

What happened to Ewing & Co., Seaview Nurseries, Havant, Hampshire? They bought a page to commend themselves in the third person and elegant phrases: "Their terms as to *carriage* and *package*, in the case of *prepaid* orders, are extremely liberal". Their catalogue "is not compiled only with a view to selling their trees, but also for the purpose of imparting to their customers valuable information . . . Price *post free 4d*. Gratis to customers."

While this Ewing of Hampshire was busy proving that his roses ripened wonderfully well in consequence of exposure to south coast sea breezes, the page facing him had unfortunately been sold to Dicksons Ltd of Chester. They made the point, unkindly enough, of their roses "eventually succeeding in positions where roses from southern and more favoured situations have failed". But they rather spoilt this good impression with their next sentence: "*Roses* in pots are largely grown for Greenhouse culture, and for forcing." Roses are not the only plants advertised. We have Ant. Roozen & Son (Successors to the late Baron van Pallandt), of Haarlem, Holland, offering Dutch and Cape Bulbs, Direct from the Growers, Delivered entirely free to any Railway Station in London, Edinburgh, Leith, etc., etc., etc. Philanthropists, obviously.

Frank Cant, Benjamin R. Cant and James Cocker & Sons are well-known names advertising in 1890. But we can assume that Thomas S. Ware, Hale Farm Nurseries, Tottenham, London, was built upon long ago, and can no more shout "Roses! Roses!! Roses!!!"

In the advertisement section, and strangely enough headed "Advertisements", we come to the "Report of the Committee for the Year 1889". It does not mince matters, but in its second line introduces the following bitter disaster:

"The circumstances under which the Metropolitan Exhibition was held at the Crystal Palace were particularly unfortunate. Her Royal Highness the Princess of Wales had signified to the Secretaries her intention of visiting the show early in the day. The Shah,[1] however, having afterwards expressed a wish to be also present, and not being able to attend until the evening, this idea had to be abandoned;[2] while the necessity of keeping the building clear for the Royal party compelled the Directors of the Crystal Palace to hold the Exhibition in a tent, to the great detriment of the Roses, and the great inconvenience of both exhibitors and visitors."

As if that was not enough trouble for one season, the Committee are next obliged to report: "The Provincial Show, at Sheffield, proved less extensive than any held by the Society in recent years." I love the moderation of the words "less extensive". How much more diplomatic than saying "this was the lousiest turn out we had seen for ages".

One wonders what went right in 1889 when we read about the National Conference, held in Chiswick in conjunction with the R.H.S.: "It is only to be regretted that the attendance of visitors was not larger."

The Committee turned from their troubles to warn exhibitors against "dressing" rose blooms at exhibitions. This, they "cannot but regard as prejudicial to the best interests of the Rose, and as likely, if generally adopted, to bring discredit on Rose showing".

On the facing page, back in the advertisements proper again, and apparently unconcerned about the ethics of artificial aid, Messrs Harkness & Sons of

---

[1] of Persia.   [2] He means the Princess had to come later too.

'GOLDEN TIMES' (H.T.)
'Fragrant Cloud' × *'Golden Splendour'*
Raised by J. Cocker & Sons Ltd
TRIAL GROUND CERTIFICATE 1970
See page 176

'STEPHEN LANGDON' (floribunda – H.T. type)
'Karl Herbst' × *'Sarabande'*
Raised by John Sanday (Roses) Ltd
TRIAL GROUND CERTIFICATE 1970
See page 177

Bedale were offering not only their Roses (70,000 Plants Propagated Annually) but "Exhibition Boxes, Tubes, Supports and all Accessories for Exhibiting Supplied". And eventually we reach a delightful

PREFACE

Kind friends, some well-known to readers of the Year-Book and some new ones, have contributed to make up the Cargo of my little craft, which although not so bulky as some of its predecessors, may yet prove that, like the old Spanish Galleons of former days, she carries a valuable freight in a small space.

VIVAT REGINA

It was for some years the custom to begin the subject matter with a photograph and article depicting a well known rose grower. The subject in 1890 was Mr R. N. G. Baker, of Exeter, a successful exhibitor of Hybrid Perpetuals grown on Manetti stocks. Some of these plants being 15 years old, the writer gleefully seized upon the chance of a little pro-Manetti propaganda, by citing his own two splendid plants of 'Souvenir de la Malmaison', 38 years old, and hard pruned every year.

The second article is "Rose Growing in Mauritius", which probably appealed to a somewhat small minority of members. In fact the author, Mr Edward C. Fraser, begins by saying as there is "a good deal of doubt in many quarters as to the whereabouts of Mauritius, so I will begin by stating that it is a small island in the Indian Ocean, in latitude 20 degrees S. and longitude 57 E." Thus at least all seafaring rosarians were put clearly in the picture. He goes on to say that Mauritius has six months of hot weather, and six months of cool, and distinguishes them by a mean variation of 5° F.

Standards were not in vogue in Mauritius, owing to hurricanes; and the best stocks were *R. robusta* and *R. multiflora*. The former was imported from India, and "grows like a willow from cuttings". Briar and Manetti were of no use in the Mauritius climate, but *R. rubiginosa* "grows admirably". His most successful consignments (imported in April) were packed in "an ordinary case in charcoal (dust and pieces the size of a nut) the roots being wrapped in a ball of earth covered with moss". Another, which did admirably, was "packed in a Wardian case".

It is extremely interesting to note these words when Mr Fraser is commenting on the performance of varieties; "on the debit side were Gloire de Dijon, which deteriorated so much as to go almost out of cultivation;"

and General Jacqueminot, which "though constantly tried, have never been got to flower."

The Rev. H. Temple Frere honourably contributed an article entitled "Notes by an Old Fogey", which is more than most people would do. His memory went back to 1840, when communications impeded the smooth running of rose shows. "I shrink from imagining what Mr Harkness' flowers would be like if he had to give them a forty-eight hours journey, unsheltered from the full heat of July, on the top of a coach."

He remembers going to Paul's nursery at Cheshunt, where he saw Hardii (he calls it Berberidifolia Hardii) and learned to bud. And this gallant "Old Fogey" adds:

"Since then no hand but my own has ever budded Roses for me, till this year, when I found myself obliged to give it up when my stocks were half done."

Bless him! Cruel Anno Domini!

Mr Frere has a fascinating reminiscence of rose shows between 1840–1850; disbudding was not allowed, "to prevent anyone from thinning out to increase the size of the bloom, for this was not considered fair". Here is some more of Mr Frere:

"When that sensational Rose 'Géant des Batailles' came out ... a fresh gathered bloom looked wondrous well in a mass of black hair, the destination of the first bloom I cut ... But we have lost some colours. There is no Rose like Boula de Nanteuil, rich brown purple with crimson points: nor like that queer-coloured Rose, Majolin, dark slate with a fiery eye." He deplores also the abandonment of garden plants in favour of exhibition varieties: "While the individual blooms look well in the Show, there are no such glorious hills of colour as used to charm our eyes in an early morning in July in the old days ... Copper Austrian Briar, in the garden of a village shoemaker, as big as a small haystack, and a blaze like one of Turner's sunsets ... (We were promised a yellow some years ago, but it turned out as shameful a humbug as ever crossed the Channel, which is saying a great deal.)"

Perhaps Mr Frere was the first to record "the horse dealer's maxim that 'a good big one is better than a good little one'." On 'Horace Vernet': "A Rose that I cannot do without, and can do nothing with", and: "Remember that after all, Rose-growing is not the business but the recreation of life, and that it were better we should give it up than let it take the place of more serious duties."

I think the Rev. H. Temple Frere must have been a very admirable man.

His article is a joy to read. It is followed by an account by the Editor (the Rev. H. Honywood d'Ombrain) of "The Rose and the National Rose Society in 1889".

The unhappy consequences of the Shah of Persia's choice of 6.30 p.m. as a time to visit the Crystal Palace Show are again described. A large crowd came to see the Shah, so that it became difficult to move, and by the evening the condition of the roses was "most deplorable".

The Chiswick Conference is commended for its interest, but not for its organisation. "I fancy that the well-nigh general opinion was that the Conference was *not* a success." But the papers were successful, and he has a knock at the R.H.S. over them: "our members may hope to have the report of them when published in the Transactions of the Royal Horticultural Society, a process which is not now delayed as it used to be until the matter had lost well nigh all its interest".

A revealing frankness runs through the Year Book, showing our Victorian forebears rather more outspoken than perhaps we are. There is some of it in the Editor's comments on varieties and shows:

"Mrs John Laing (Bennett 1888) is valuable, constant and dependable, far superior to the over-praised Her Majesty." Clg. Niphetos is praised for its vigour, having "made even from budded plants, shoots of 15 or 20 ft in length", which is a lot more than we can make it do today. "Probably the Rose which attracted most attention, and which everyone (except those *lunatics* who can see nothing in a Rose except it be fit for exhibition) have been seeking after, is l'Ideale, a climbing Noisette of the William A. Richardson type. . . . Comte Rambaut has had a good record also; but it is simply, like Horace Vernet, an exhibition Rose, and only succeeds as a maiden." So now perhaps we know why the "Old Fogey" could no nothing with "Horace".

The "dressing" controversy is summed up as follows: "Talk of painting the lily, it is orthodoxy itself compared to turning a Rose inside out, and altering its character so thus a Marie Baumann figures as an A. K. Williams; and La France unlike any Rose we have."

Outspoken comment enlivens the article by Mr Alexander Hill Gray, entitled "Rose Jottings". He describes his visit to the Paris Exhibition where he saw 50,000 roses, planted specially by French nurserymen, including inferior sorts, and "Her Majesty, as represented, was overwhelmed with the original sin of mildew".

Mr Gray visited four gardens, (and named them without fear of libel), "to take note of miserable varieties of Roses, generally grown in each of these favourite resorts". He would have liked "to improve out of existence these 'holler chested and rupchered' specimens, many of them, as full of grief as of years".

But at two of those establishments were zoos, and ever searching for knowledge with single-minded zeal, Mr Gray turned his back on the roses, and made enquiries about the relative value of the zoo's exhibits as providers of manure. This interview between the French gardeners and an earnest Victorian gentleman has comic possibilities; and in view of the state of their roses, one might question the value of the Frenchmen's advice, which was:

Elephant	— least fertilising of all.
Lion, Tiger	— too heating.
Zebra, Camel, Ass	— more useful.
Dog	— injurious, too calorific, better mixed with cow dung.
Birds	— easily first, beyond all praise.

Back home, Mr Gray went to Bath Show, where the sight of sights was a collection of 'Niphetos'; but he disapproved of the "jaw-wagging" policemen, who were stationed in the tents, and who kept crying "move on there, move on". It was even worse at Gloucester Show, where a brass band "discoursed inside a moderate-sized hall, clashing and jingling enough to have satisfied a heathen Chinee".

A visit to Mr W. J. Grant's garden at Ledbury elicited a delightful remark from that gentleman, to the effect that unless standard stems were carefully selected, the garden next year would be "schwarming with absentees".

Mr John Harkness had the task of conducting "A Defence of Manetti as a Stock"; as against Briar. He is a canny advocate, saying "I do not recommend the adoption of either stock to the exclusion of the other, both should be employed; the blooming season will consequently be lengthened, and varieties not presentable on the Manetti on any given date may be had on the Briar, and *vice versa*."

Mr Harkness gives some interesting facts about the behaviour of roses in North Yorkshire. In an average season, he would expect to cut flowers from his Manetti cutbacks the first week in July; from cutting Briar nearly a week later; from seedling Briar a little later still, and from maidens few until the third week of July. The fact that roses on Manetti were shorter lived was indisputable, but not disastrous. Nine-tenths of the roses he had planted on Manetti eleven years previously were still to the fore. "This may be partly attributed to deep planting, which enables the rose to quickly become double-rooted . . . Every autumn a portion of our cutbacks are lifted and replanted, and give the most astonishing results the following two or three seasons." The article "Autumnal Roses" by Mr George Paul is a good study of the subject. The best to flower in autumn were Teas and Chinas, which he states were in full bloom as he wrote on 25 November. Next he places the Bourbon rose 'Souvenir de la Malmaison', as flowering all through October. Then a few Hybrid Teas, and after them the "Tea-scented"; it is useful to remember that expression, to remind us that it was the *scent* that was being described by the word "Tea".

By this time you may be wondering, like me, why Mr Paul started by putting Teas and Chinas first, and then introducing tea-scented at this stage. However he brings out the point that a good autumn rose has the greater need of resistance to mildew, to maintain healthy growth during cool autumn nights. He mentions one or two Noisettes, and then says "Perpetual Mosses are a delusion and a snare". Miniature Hybrid Polyantha (I thought the term dated from the Poulsen era) are commended, and their Tea blood is given as the reason for the late flowering of such as 'Perle d'Or'. Rugosas are continuous, and would be more so if they did not set seed.

Hybrid Perpetuals are a long way down the list, though Mr Paul does give credit to a few, including 'La France' (not yet a Hybrid Tea apparently) and then gives a list of 32, inconveniently omitting most of those he had specially commended. He mentions some species which flower in the autumn, and might have value to hybridisers, and politely bows out, trusting he has not been a bore. And we can assure him, I think, that he made an interesting job of his assignment.

I can't give Mr T. W. Girdlestone quite so much credit for his article on "Decorative Roses". It never quite recovers from a sentence 70 words long near the start. Yet careful study reveals some interesting points. His thesis is that none but exhibitors grows roses well, and since exhibition roses have become the best known, they are being wrongly planted by inexpert hands for garden display. He goes so far as to state that the effect of roses as garden plants is almost always incredibly poor. But beyond recommending that roses be planted in groups, rather than in singles of a variety, he does not solve the problem. He recommends some of the popular exhibition roses of the day which are most likely to thrive as garden plants—but leaves us asking, wherever were the *garden* varieties in 1890?

The last article is by Edward Mawley, F.R.Met.Soc., Hon. Secretary, National Rose Society. He and the Rev. Honywood d'Ombrain were joint Secretaries.

As F.R.Met.Soc., Mr Mawley regularly contributed a detailed article on "The Weather of the Past Rose Year". I daresay some people found it rather boring, but in fact there are many observations on the weather, and its subsequent effect on roses, which show the value of such a regular study.

He starts with the "Ripening Period"—August, September, October 1888. All went well until the night of 2 October, when the temperature suddenly descended to 20° F. The ripening process was thus abruptly interrupted; and when November turned out mild and wet, the plants started to grow again. The consequences of this appear at pruning time.

In the "Sleeping Period", of November to February, planting could be done only in early November, and new arrivals thereafter had to wait until nearly Christmas, because it was so wet.

In the "Awakening Period", that is March, April, May, the first discovery was that most of the late autumn growths had been destroyed by frost. Many plants had to be cut to the ground when pruning. An interesting observation is made about a few Tea roses: these were protected with gorse over winter, and before protecting them, Mr Mawley had transplanted some old plants. The transplanted ones were less affected by frost damage than those which had not been moved, and the reason suggested is that the move was a check to autumn growth, and therefore an assistance in ripening.

The "Blossoming Period"—June, July, August, proved to be an early one; it followed some late seasons, and Mr Mawley pointed out that we are apt to expect one year to be like the one before, which is not sensible. He gives the dates the flowers appeared, and describes a fairly normal June, until great heat brought the flowers out very quickly towards the end of the month. He even kept count of the number of caterpillars killed in his garden—1,643.

The Year Book gives the last word to Paul & Son, "THE" Rose Growers, The "Old" Nurseries, Cheshunt, Herts. They, perhaps from the privilege they might justly claim, occupied the back cover. And they advertised their new roses:—

H.P. Dowager Duchesse of Marlborough in Pots in May 7/6

H.P. Progress (Herr Rich Drögweller) in Pots in May 5/-

Which in delightful Victorian fashion supports the established order, by making a Dowager Duchess half as valuable again as Progress.

Fifty Years of Progress in Climbing and Rambling Roses

E. B. LE GRICE

(Rose nurseryman and breeder)

In the Rev. Dean Hole's *A Book about Roses* he recalls that Mr Rivers in 1834 issued the first Descriptive Catalogue of Roses. It lists by name 478 varieties. How many of them, he asks, are to be found in our recent lists (1896)? Eleven, eight of them climbing roses.

Although the last fifty years have seen many changes there are far more of the older roses surviving than in that previous century's list. But it is not my task to speak of the survivors from the pre-1920 era, but rather to speak of newcomers in the last fifty years.

Briefly, the period under consideration covered five types of climbing, rambling and similar roses. The first was closely related to the pre-1920s type of hardy, once-flowering ramblers. Two raisers left their impress here; Dr Van Fleet, with some of his late *R. wichuraiana* hybrids and Chaplin Bros. with their 'Paul's Scarlet Climber' crosses, with Barbier and Co. bringing out their last and best rambler, 'Albertine', in 1921.

The second type spread over the whole 50 years and is still appearing. This comprises the climbing sports, first of hybrid teas and later with the addition of floribunda roses. Parallel with these, but with growing momentum later, were the intermittent climbers.

A word should be said here about climbing types which flower more than once. They cannot be claimed to be perpetual; a few almost approach such standards, but as a whole they produce an appreciable number of blooms after the first flowering. As we shall see, some climbing sports may be placed in this category.

A special mention must be made of the Kordesii and it was an unforgettable memory to see the massive ranks of these rambler-climbers when they first flowered in full profusion in 1953 at Oaklands, St Albans. There were too many to be absorbed by the trade, but on the whole the best have remained, although a few of the better cultivars failed to become known. Their difficult names assured their early oblivion.

Finally came the large-flowered, very free climbers, first with Gregory's as important contributors, now succeeded by McGredy IV types.

There was always a need and desire for free flowering climbers with autumn bloom, but I think we must regard 'New Dawn', 1930, as the turning point in giving us a new concept of freedom of flowering and providing the means to attain it.

Looking back, I have but a hazy memory of masses of 'Dorothy Perkins', 'Crimson Rambler' and 'American Pillar' in every garden, the first and second being martyrs to mildew. There were many others of beauty, but not often grown so frequently. Possibly the gardens were more colourful then for a short period, but the present massed effect of floribunda roses was absent in those days, so the need for a brief, spectacular mass of colour has passed with their advent.

To go back to our list of raisers in their periods. The effect of the work of Capt. G. C. Thomas had already been felt and 'Bloomfield Abundance', like a very vigorous 'Climbing Cécile Brunner', just comes into this period, although his other twenty-six 'Bloomfield' progeny, seven of which were climbers, made little impression in Britain. His 'Dr Huey', which became the Shafta stock of America, has a greater reason to be remembered. Dr Van Fleet had also done his major work by that time, although 'Breeze Hill', a beautiful flesh tinted apricot seedling climber (1926) and 'Glenn Dale' (1927) come into our time. I fear the last has disappeared although I still consider it the best white rambler ever produced.

It was in this period that Chaplin Bros. were having considerable success and in their 'Royal Scarlet Hybrid' (1926) and 'Chaplin's Pink Climber' (1927) they produced two excellent roses. Indeed the latter still provides a spectacular mass when it can be placed to show to advantage its deep pink flowers with their almost mauve tint.

'Chaplin's Crimson Glow' (1930) was a more healthy grower than the previous red and, with its almost thornless wood and glossy leaves, was an advance in size of flower. Perhaps one should mention here 'Chaplin's Pink Companion', a softer pink with strong growth and semi-double flowers introduced too late (1961) to find a permanent place among its twice-flowering neighbours.

Another anachronism was 'Crimson Shower' (Norman 1951), an old type rambler partly redeemed by its late July flowering and excellence as a weeping standard.

To understand the climbing sports we find that there are two types. The rampant, once-flowering and the less vigorous but twice-flowering sorts. Both are 'sports' of their dwarf counterparts, but the vigorous are layer II chimeras, that is, the inner tissue has changed and so all budded plants climb; the layer III chimeras have changed in their centre part only and retain their

'Chaplin's Pink Climber' (once-flowering climber)
(see page 104)

'Pink Perpétue' (recurrent-flowering climber)
(see page 106)

'Schoolgirl' (recurrent-flowering climber)
(see page 108)

'Ritter von Barmstede' (Kordesii climber)
(see page 107).

In the garden of Old Roses at Nymans, Sussex (The National Trust)
(*see page 114*)

'Handel' (recurrent-flowering climber)
(see page 108)

'Mme. Gregoire Staechelin' (once-flowering climber)
(see page 105)

twice-flowering quality, but when budded give a proportion of dwarf bushes in proportion to their autumn flowering propensity. One cannot record all the 'sports'. A very large proportion of bush roses in hybrid teas and quite a number in floribundas have thrown climbing shoots. 'Mme. E. Herriot' (1921) and 'Talisman' (1930) were noteworthy for their early flowering, being often out some weeks before others. I remember with interest the popularity of 'Château de Clos Vougeot' (1920) in this form and I believe the firm of Henry Morse and Sons, who introduced it, received 15/- per pot plant, which makes the present price for a new rose look like a gift!

One of the best was 'Étoile de Hollande' (1931) which with its great vigour and sweet scent makes an ideal rose for a high wall where the hanging blooms may be seen to great advantage. A little later 'Lady Sylvia' (1933) sported to give us one of our most vigorous climbers. This needs space and time to mature, but given these its prodigality of bloom is amazing. I have grown and cut at one time 36 dozen choice disbudded flowers from one plant under glass. Outside it is equally effective while its sharp, penetrating perfume is quite heady. But, given room I would place 'Mrs Sam McGredy' at the head of the list. Admitted its flowers, with their rich coppery shades, fade to salmon on opening, but the rich red foliage of the young shoots equals the crop of flowers which it bears with striking prodigality in one wealth of blossom. 'Golden Dawn' and 'Shot Silk' are short in growth, covering up to 7 feet high, but give a number of sweetly-scented flowers in the autumn, as do 'Ellinor LeGrice' (1959) and 'Spek's Yellow' (1956) (the latter covering up to 12 feet). Of the many reds 'Crimson Glory' (1946), despite its mildew, and 'Ena Harkness' (1954) still offer a wealth of coverage, together with ample bloom.

There are fewer climbing 'sports' of floribundas, but most give a spectacular mass as their one contribution to the annual rose gala. Of these 'Allgold' must be given room, a warm spot and patience, when it will flower freely. 'Korona' is one of the most vivid, although 'Orangeade' may equal it. 'Masquerade' (1958) is unbelievably full with massive heads of multicoloured blooms, and one looks forward to 'Iceberg' which has at least two strains available.

One very lovely once-flowering climber should be mentioned. This was 'Mme. Grégoire Staechelin' (1927), later called 'Spanish Beauty'. It had a charm of its own with an attractive lightness of growth and flower, enhanced by a delicious perfume. The rich clear pink flower had the reverse stained crimson, as had the tip of each inner petal. But for its name it would have been one of our most popular climbers. How many good roses are spoiled by admirable local names which will not travel abroad!

Up to this point we have been looking back to links prior to and within the 50 years, but with the coming of 'New Dawn' (1930), a sport of 'Dr W. Van Fleet' which was almost continuous flowering, a new era in freedom of flower began. This was because one now saw the possibility of perpetual flowering climbers and—more important—seedlings of 'New Dawn' in many cases inherited the long-flowering characteristics. It became the most important parent until the 1960s in the production of this type of rose.

Before the potentialities of 'New Dawn' as a parent were apparent a few beautiful, short, free-flowering climbers appeared. I suppose many were not true climbers in so far as the terminal bud produced a flower head, but being tall and quick to break into new growth just below the first flower head, they soon attained the necessary height.

The first of these was 'Allen Chandler', single bright red and very free flowering. Then came 'Guinée', a vigorous true climber, deep maroon red with small hybrid tea type flowers which were often in clusters. Strongly fragrant, it is still unique in its depth of colour.

My own 'Soldier Boy' (TGC 1953) is extremely vigorous and flowers from June to October with large, bright red, single flowers. Then came 'Sweet Sultan' (1958), short and sturdy in growth, producing many large, deep red blooms with darker shading.

A very large and free-flowering cultivar was 'Parade' (1953). The deep carmine pink does not appeal to all but the perfume, growth and flowers are excellent. It became a very good parent. 'Danse du Feu' (1953) ('Spectacular' in U.S.A.) is still in the top half dozen. Its double, orange-red, full blooms are very freely borne, while it is sufficiently vigorous for most purposes. 'Danse des Sylphes' was missed by many, but as a larger 'Paul's Scarlet Climber' producing many autumn blooms it is extremely useful.

'Meg' (1954) caused quite a sensation when introduced. It is a lovely confection of coppery apricot suffused salmon pink. The large, semi-single blossoms are borne freely, often on tall, many-flowered stems. It is suitable as a short climber or, if used as a hedge, it needs little support. 'Royal Gold' (1957), probably the finest yellow of all when given a sheltered position, is aptly named, but it produces a second crop only after a long interval.

'Royal Lavender' (1961) of unusual shade seems to lack some quality needed for popularity. 1965 was a very special year, for then Gregory's introduced 'Pink Perpetue' which I think has all the good qualities of an excellent modern climber. Freedom of flower, a pleasing shape and colour, clear deep pink, perfume and excellent growth with good health. At the same time 'Autumn Sunlight' was introduced. An unusual colour, more golden than 'Super Star', it is more vigorous and less free than 'Pink Perpetue', but a useful change from the normal.

We must go back a few years to a remarkable break in rambler roses raised by Wilhelm Kordes.[1] Kordesii are described in the *Rose Annual* for 1965 and have the rare distinction of a group name given to them. Bred for hardiness and containing *Rosa rugosa* in its ancestry *R. kordesii* yielded a number of vigorous and short climbers which flowered in the autumn as well as providing a spectacular mass in the summer. Anyone seeing these at the old Trial Grounds at 'Oaklands' will remember the great array of the forty varieties which were planted in spring 1951 and came into flower during the two succeeding years. Never have so many cultivars come from one raiser with such resounding success. Unfortunately there was a surfeit of good things, but out of them some really outstanding varieties emerged, while others good in themselves failed to become known.

There is always a limit to what the market can absorb and doubtless those which came to the fore did so on merit. Of these the following are outstanding: 'Hamburger Phoenix' (1954), long pointed red buds in large clusters, tall and vigorous with recurrent bloom; 'Leverkusen' (1954), a real acquisition, with the characteristic vigour, health and deep green glossy foliage and some perfume. The double, sulphur-yellow flowers are carried in large clusters, and there are some autumn blooms. 'Dortmund' (1955) reminds one of a superior 'American Pillar'. Very prolific, the colour is deep red with a white eye and it is recurrent and vigorous. 'Ritter Von Barmstede' (1950) bears semi-double, deep rose-pink blooms of large size. 'Raymond Chenault' has proved both free and vigorous at the display garden at Bone Hill. Introduced in 1960 it has large, semi-double, bright red blooms which come in clusters and are fragrant. It is very vigorous and free.

Two varieties I have found very charming, but lacking the vigour attributed to them by *Modern Roses*. Approximating to the vigour of 'New Dawn' these are, in my estimation, two excellent semi-climbers which arrived just too late, for the fashion for large-flowered climbers was taking over. These were Morse introductions in 1962, salvaged from the many Kordesii which never were commercialised in Great Britain, and introduced by Morse's of Eaton. 'Norwich Pink' has large, semi-double, fragrant, deep

[1] He wrote on winter hardiness in the 1952 *Rose Annual*, page 26, and on page 32 speaks of the evolution of the Kordesii group and has an excellent article in the *Rose Annual* 1960, p. 45, on Repeat-flowering Climbers.

cerise pink blooms, while 'Norwich Salmon' has smaller hybrid tea type blooms in larger clusters, with a pleasing golden base. Both were moderate pillar roses in growth, but flowered over a long period.

'Golden Showers' (1956) was one of the larger flowered type producing a mass of bloom going up stage by stage until it reached about six feet. Deep yellow and sweetly scented, it became popular as a tall shrub or low pillar and remains so.

'Maigold' (1953) was another Kordes variety of unusual character and parentage[1] ('Poulsen's Pink' × 'Frühlingstag'). This has the thorny growth of the sweet briar with its hardiness, but the description in Modern Roses 7 hardly tallies with its performance here. Of considerable vigour, it bears a mass of semi-double, large, 4 in. flowers in June, after which it throws out strong growths often bearing flowers on their tips in August and September. I have found it sterile when seeking to cross it with tetraploids.

Lastly, turning to the hybrid tea type recurrent climbers, one of the first was 'Copenhagen' (1964). A large, shapely, hybrid tea type bloom produced on a strong cane, it flowered over a long period rather than producing a mass at one time. It is not profuse at any time.

Then came the McGredy IV climbing crosses which have proved themselves to be almost a separate class of large-flowered climbers, giving many flowers in the autumn.

Taken in chronological order 'Casino' was introduced in 1963. Scented, the full and shapely soft yellow blooms continue over a long period. The growth is suited to a wall or short pillar. In 1964 came 'Schoolgirl', a pleasing and unusual colour for a climber. The flowers are full and orange-apricot, with quite vigorous growth. In 1965 came what I think may be said to be the best in 'Handel'. Very free in growth and flower, the colours are unusual and attractive, creamy-white with a distinct carmine edge. The flowers are full and shapely. In 1966 came 'Galway Bay' with full, cerise pink blooms. It is vigorous, with deep green glossy foliage enlivened by the red young leaves and wood. In 1967 'Bantry Bay' appeared with semi-double, light flowers of a clear pink. The foliage, which is healthy and plentiful, is a light green with coppery young growths. Then 'Swan Lake' appeared in 1968. It is very free and vigorous. The flowers are large, very full and ivory white with a blush centre, set off by deep, olive-green foliage.

Possibly the reader may find this extended catalogue of varieties a bit boring, but the listing of such sorts over what is a fairly extended period

[1] Although this is the parentage given in Modern Roses 7 there is some doubt about it being correct. A reliable source gives the parentage as 'McGredy's Wonder' × 'Frühlingsgold'. Ed.

does show that trends have changed and, as with other types of roses, demand has produced supply.

Even so, I feel that there is still room for the spectacular mass of the rambler such as 'Albertine', which after its glorious but brief display modestly retires in its new dress of shining bronze-green leaves to keep watch, during high summer and autumn, over the more persistent neighbours which, lovely as they are, can never produce the brief glory of its brilliant hour.

(Dates of roses are taken from *Modern Roses 7.*)

Replacements in Established Rose Beds

Members are reminded that container-grown roses enable replacements to be made in rose beds and borders at any time of year. As there is no root disturbance, the operation may take place successfully even when the plants are in full flower.

It sometimes happens that an established plant collapses after pruning, when it may be too late in the spring to replace it with a bare root rose with much prospect of success. When this occurs, not only should the old plant be taken up, but the soil in which it was growing should be exchanged for soil from another part of the garden which has not grown roses. If possible obtain some old turf and chop this up into small pieces, incorporating them with the new soil, and also some garden compost or moist granulated peat and a sprinkling of bonemeal.

A container-grown plant of the desired variety may then be planted. First water the plant really thoroughly in its container and allow it to drain before planting. Cut down the sides of the container and make a hole amply large enough to accommodate the entire contents intact. Firm all round the ball of soil thoroughly and water in to consolidate. A top dressing of moist peat or compost 2 in thick will be helpful in conserving moisture during the ensuing few weeks, but watering may be necessary during very dry weather.—*Ed.*

Black Spot and Overhead Irrigation

PETER BEALES

(Rose nurseryman)

Not many years ago most nurserymen would have laughed at the idea of overhead irrigation on roses. In fact, any form of irrigation, except in very exceptional circumstances, would have been considered a complete and utter waste of money on a deep rooted, long term crop such as roses. I myself, only two years ago, failed to realize in time that one particular batch of roses was suffering from drought, on an exceptionally well drained part of the nursery. However, with farming crops becoming more diversified the need for modern irrigation equipment outdoors became an acceptable part of good husbandry. Various specialist manufacturers have made available quite sophisticated equipment for this purpose. Of course all this depends on whether a water supply is available within easy reach of the rose field; but here in the east of England I am convinced from experience that irrigation can make a considerable difference to the ratio between first and second size rose trees.

However, I am straying slightly from the point. My reason for writing this is to make known to both amateur and professional rose growers an observation I was able to make regarding the control of Black Spot as a direct result of overhead watering.

The soil here, a light deep loam over a sandy subsoil, is excellent for commercial rose growing in every respect, except in exceptionally dry seasons such as the summer of 1970. On one particular patch of some 3,000 maiden rose trees, unintentionally at first, I conducted an experiment on some fourteen varieties including 'Charleston', a notorious Black Spot addict.

The water was applied direct from the mains by a rotating sprinkler, and by placing the machine in the centre of the patch of roses the effect was a sort of "round peg in a square hole". Thus, at each and every watering all four corners, and about six feet at either end of the plot, remained dry; therefore every variety was part of the trial.

Watering was started about mid-June and with the exception of two wet weeks in August was done at weekly intervals of some eight hours per watering per week. 'Charleston', the ideal subject, remained completely free of Black Spot where the water was applied and by late September those plants of this variety in the dry area were infected to the point of losing their leaves. Other varieties were showing similar effects to a lesser extent. But the fact

110

that no Black Spot occurred on any variety in the wet zone proves without doubt that, for some reason, overhead irrigation is beneficial in its control.

It will take a more scientific brain than mine to establish reasons for this, and better controlled experiments before any exact conclusions can be reached.

My own feelings are that our mains water may have some beneficial ingredient, although the local Water Board tells me that chlorine is ·25 parts per million and the pH (lime content) is 7, with no appreciable amount of any other mineral or trace element.

Regular applications of water may be an influence for the good in that the resulting healthier plant would presumably be less likely to contract the disease.

Then, of course, there is the paradox of the disease being more prevalent in damp weather, which makes one wonder if perhaps temperature, or even sunlight combined with overhead watering are in fact the reasons for the control; after all, the sun seldom shines and the temperature usually drops when it is raining.

One swallow does not make a summer, so perhaps other members have noticed similar effects when their lawn sprinklers have been used regularly and the water has passed over part of a rose bed.

Editorial footnote:

Readers are referred to articles on this subject by Roy Hay in earlier editions of *The Rose Annual*:—

   1960 pp. 42–43
   1961 pp. 105–106
   1962 pp. 53–54

Mr Beales' experiment is interesting in that it is on a commercial scale covering maiden plants and bears out these earlier experiments which were conducted in a private garden on cut-back plants.

Whereas under Mr Beales' experiment watering was for eight hours *continuously* at weekly intervals by rotating sprinkler, Mr Hay used mist nozzles to give a fine spray for 35 seconds only at hourly intervals throughout the 24 hours.

Roses in the Gardens of The National Trust (2)

GRAHAM THOMAS, V.M.H.

(Authority on the "Old" roses and Gardens Adviser to The National Trust)

Roses subservient to the prevailing colour

Sometimes the rose is entirely subservient to the dictates of the colour of the house. I recall the choice of the yellow hybrid tea, 'Grandpa Dickson' which blends well with the strong red brick of Hanbury Hall, Worcestershire, built in 1701. A large planting of this persistent rose has been made in the strange forecourt with its Victorian-Indian arches and pavilions. Similarly a redder brick at Disraeli's home at Hughenden Manor, Buckinghamshire, influenced the choice of colours in the borders round the house. We used blue ceanothus for spring and summer, purple and lavender clematis, interspersed with the double yellow Banksian rose, 'Paul's Lemon Pillar', 'Mermaid' and 'Golden Showers'; between them these roses provide yellow for as long as the ceanothus and clematis are in flower—or rather longer. There is also a broad basal planting of *Senecio laxifolius*, lavenders, *Iris pallida dalmatica* and *Hypericum* 'Hidcote'. These light and cool colours help to tone down the overpowering red brick.

Under the long raised walk at Montacute House, Somerset, dating from 1588, a border of shrub roses was planted some 18 years ago, and they thrive in the heavy, limy soil, facing north. An underplanting of *Hosta fortunei* excludes all weeds and cultivation. Various Gallica and Alba varieties, *R. moyesii*, *R. villosa*, 'Pink Grootendorst' and many more are to be found. The famous honey-coloured stone from nearby Ham Hill was used throughout the building of the house and its garden walls and buildings, surmounted by finials as at Hardwick Hall, and this strong colouring and the similar colour of the gravel gives a very insistent background to the lawns and walks. So much so that only vivid, rich colours have any effect. The reliable 'Frensham' crops up again here enhanced by copper-leafed berberis, scarlet dahlias, *Salvia superba* and other richly coloured border flowers, while the Claret vine and *Clematis jackmanii* trail through the stone balustrade.

A new Victorian garden scheme

We seem fated to have most of our rose gardens on poor soils, either chalky, or sandy and acid. The latter occurs again at Shugborough, Staffordshire, a

'NATIONAL TRUST' (H.T.)
'Evelyn Fison' × *'King of Hearts'*
Raised by S. McGredy IV, N. Ireland
TRIAL GROUND CERTIFICATE 1970

See page 177

'ROSY MANTLE' (climber)
'New Dawn' × *'Prima Ballerina'*
Raised by J. Cocker & Sons Ltd
TRIAL GROUND CERTIFICATE 1970
See page 177

great grey house built in the 17th century by Admiral Lord Anson[1]; it has a series of shallow Victorian grass terraces to the west, punctuated by huge clipped golden yews. These are of a brilliant, brassy yellow tint when in their young growth from June onwards—a colour which shouts down all others except its own and blue and purple. This fact has caused us to plant the long terrace-beds with 'Golden Fleece' underplanted with white violas, and with violet-purple petunias used in a number of large stone boxes along the walks. A little way off is the rose garden itself, planted with a medley of soft colours as would have been the only choice in Victorian times. In the central beds are deep crimsons and rose pinks, 'Étoile de Hollande', 'Lady Sylvia', 'Josephine Bruce' and 'Wendy Cussons', complete with standards of the same varieties. A number of arches, swags and pillars will support mauve, purple, white, pink and crimson ramblers, and there are weeping standards of 'Crimson Shower'. These should flower with Clematis jackmanii 'Gipsy Queen', which are on separate supports. Beds of the constantly flowering bush type of 'Souvenir de la Malmaison', 'Kathleen Harrop', 'Ferdinand Pichard' and other Bourbon varieties have blending colours, while under the pillars and arches are some poly poms, 'Ellen Poulsen', 'Baby Faurax', 'Little White Pet', with repeating clumps of Santolina chamaecyparissus, the silvery cotton lavender.

A modern rose garden

One of the most interesting designs ever conceived for a rose garden is at Cliveden, Buckinghamshire. Designed by Mr G. A. Jellicoe in 1960 it may be described as three-dimensional. It has informal, flowing lines with graceful beds joined by pretty arches and the planting was arranged to echo above ground the curves of the ground plan. Thus the narrow portions of the beds have short bedding roses while much higher shrubs accentuate the wider portions. Species, old and new shrub roses and others all find a home, within a woodland setting. This garden had become considerably overgrown, but the trees overhanging it have been pruned or removed and this work has revealed the splendid growth of ramblers in the surrounding trees, including R. filipes 'Kiftsgate'. The roses in the beds will require a season or two to give of their best again.

Old fashioned roses

When I was busy collecting together all the old French roses still in cultiva-

---

[1]The Admiral was the introducer of Lathyrus magellanicus, known as Lord Anson's Blue Pea, a native of the southernmost part of South America. We should much like to grow this at Shugborough, but so far I have failed to locate a source of viable seeds. Will readers abroad please note?

tion some twenty years ago, one of the treasure-gardens was Nymans, Sussex. Had it not been for some half-dozen gardens like this where the old roses were appreciated, many would have gone out of cultivation. Recently at Nymans the old roses have received attention and a new planting has been made around the well in the upper garden and arches and pillars have been added; here we can enjoy Gallicas, Damasks, Centifolias and Albas once again, supplemented by *R. dupontii*, *R. multibracteata* and many more. Elsewhere in the garden *R. virginiana* produces its late pink flowers and splendid autumn colour, and the chestnut rose, *R. roxburghii normalis* thrives. Several roses ascend trees: *R. multiflora* to about 25 feet, hanging down in a fragrant curtain of white; *R. macrantha* whose large single pink flowers climb through a high apple, and R. 'Polyantha Grandiflora', a specially good hybrid with single creamy white flowers, richly fragrant, whose second beauty is the bunches of orange-red heps, lasting often through the winter. The old White Rose of York, 'Maidens Blush' and 'Félicité et Perpétue' grace the walls of the old home which was destroyed by fire but which adds so much romance to the main part of the garden.

Gardens where roses augment every scheme of planting

After Nymans we can suitably discuss the next little set of gardens, Hidcote, Gloucestershire, Sissinghurst Castle, Kent, and Tintinhull, Somerset. These are gardens where shrub roses and a few others become part of the general design, entering into almost every colour scheme. These gardens are, it is true, united into a group through one common character: they are divided into many areas or compartments, by walls and hedges. Particularly is this true of Hidcote which may be regarded as the prototype of this style of gardening, where plants of all kinds are used to furnish the different 'outdoor rooms'.

The Old French roses have always been favourites at Hidcote though originally only a limited number were grown, particularly the Bourbons 'Madame Pierre Oger', 'Madame Isaac Pereire' and 'Bourbon Queen', 'Prince Charles' and 'Blush Damask' in the Pillar Garden, while others were in the long borders in the kitchen garden. These borders were infested with weeds and suckering roses and over a period of some five years were cleared, fallowed, cleaned and replanted with a good selection of these old types. In addition there are some big shrubs of *R. multibracteata* and climbers on the stumps of old apple trees, and a hedge of 'Rosa Mundi'. This old striped rose is one of the most spectacular of sights at midsummer. Elsewhere there are hedges of 'Penelope' and 'Cornelia'; 'Blanc Double de Coubert' and

'Roseraie de l'Haÿ' flower profusely and more Rugosas are being established in the wild garden known as 'Westonbirt' (as it was principally planted for autumn colour) together with Burnet roses and high climbers for growing into trees. In the Maple garden 'Paul's Himalayan Musk' hangs out of a high yew tree, over the large single pink 'Complicata' and R. *californica plena*. In the courtyard are very old plants of 'Blairii No. 2' and also two climbing tea roses, 'Lady Hillingdon' in warm apricot and 'Vicomtesse Pierre du Fou' in coppery coral. The original plant of 'Lawrence Johnston' grows on a wall in the Old garden. (This was raised by Pernet-Ducher in France, a cross between 'Madame Eugène Verdier' and R. *foetida persiana*. Of the two resulting seedlings 'Le Rêve' was put on to the market in 1923, and has since just lingered in cultivation; the other was seen and admired by Lawrence Johnston about 1945, purchased by him and has since been planted widely. Thus a strange chance saved a worthy rose from extinction.) Here the tones are soft, and 'Magenta', 'Grey Pearl', pink and white roses are used; in the Red borders, assorting with copper foliage and purple and orange flowers, red floribundas and dahlias find a place with 'Scarlet Fire' climbing into a coppery purple maple. Above the rock garden 'Hidcote Gold' (R. *hugonis* × R. *sericea*) gives a marvellous spring display, overhung by the equally brilliant *Laburnum vossii*.

The old roses at Hidcote and Tintinhull are encouraged to grow fairly freely, but a different technique has been adopted at Sissinghurst where supports are provided. Each plant is carefully trained and pruned, so that the maximum quantity of blooms is presented over the bushes. The effect of 'Fantin Latour', 'Petite de Hollande', 'Cardinal de Richelieu', 'Hippolyte', 'Madame Hardy', 'Céleste' and the like treated in this way is superb. 'Ulrich Brunner', 'Baron Giraud de l'Ain' and 'Madame Lauriol de Barny' and others of their class flower all along their branches when bent down; again, this is most successfully done at Sissinghurst. The single 'Meg', coral pink with dark stamens, has ascended to 14 feet on a wall, and anyone who finds the little 'Cécile Brunner' weak should try 'Bloomfield Abundance' (9 ft high on a wall, but it is really a bush) which has flowers of the same extreme charm, size, and colouring, borne in sheaves throughout summer and autumn. Soft colours have always been appreciated at Sissinghurst and 'Lilac Charm', 'Rose-Marie Viaud', 'Veilchenblau' and 'Zigeuner Knabe', all mauve and purple, are used effectively. 'Goldfinch', that early flowering pale yellow rambler, and the sweet briar both provide a hedge effect and are exceedingly fragrant. In the main court the R. *moyesii* breed is much to the fore, the red flowers lighting the borders in June and the orange-red flagon-shaped heps contrasting with purple and blue clematis and monkshoods in late August. The white garden at Sissinghurst is very famous for its white and near-white flowers, displayed among plants with silvery foliage. One of the surprises is a grey stone statue nearly enveloped in the tresses of the silver weeping pear, while the foreground is given to *Stachys lanata*, *Lilium regale*, *Astrantia major*, white campanulas and foxgloves. The double white Burnet rose has made a large bush. The beds are edged with dark green fragrant box and down the long central walk are almond trees covered with festoons of white ramblers, *R. longicuspis*, 'Snowflake' and others. The old almonds are breaking beneath the weight of the roses and some other kind of support will soon have to be afforded. In sunshine this white garden is an inspiration, in dripping rain a cool refreshment and at dusk it is an ethereal delight. The backcloth is the east wall of the Priests' house on which are trained the single white *Rosa gigantea* 'Cooperi' and 'Madame Alfred Carrière'. This really great white climber with faint creamy blush in the centre of its full flowers, grows equally well on the south wall of South Cottage, proving yet again how adaptable and successful it is. The mass of blossom at midsummer is breathtaking, but the plants always provide a scattered display as well for the rest of the season.

One of the lessons to be learnt at Tintinhull is that the early flowering 'Mme Grégoire Staechelin', in rich warm pink, is a great success on a north wall. One plant covers about 35 ft length of wall by about 15 ft high. Various old roses like 'Céleste' and the Red Rose of Lancaster thrive in the borders, where the keyword is effect rather than rarity. The check lists of the borders which are on sale meet a ready demand with the public who are keen to repeat some of the colour schemes in their own borders. In a border of shrubs and plants principally of soft mauves, pinks and pale yellows, the old floribunda 'Holstein'—highly successful in the black-spot-ridden West country—grows and flowers well. The companion border opposite has a fantastic scheme of white, yellow and scarlet. The Rugosa 'Blanc Double de Coubert' and 'Frensham' are used with telling effect against verbascums, Spanish and Mount Etna brooms. These borders—two out of many—are rare creations and are made complementary to each other by the use of silvery foliage, ornamental grasses and a repetitive pattern of foreground planting. They are backed by yew hedges.

Old world gardens

While these three famous colour gardens may be considered in the forefront of deliberate design, the garden at Gunby, Lincolnshire, on limy soil, is what one likes to think of as having grown imperceptibly under the care of succeeding generations of a family devoted to flowers. Roses occur in every part of the garden. There are many old walls on which thrive 'Cupid', that superlative, large, single, light coral-pink with conspicuous heps in autumn; the silvery pink 'Madame Caroline Testout', and various good yellow roses such as 'Climbing Lady Hillingdon' and 'Easlea's Golden Rambler', which look particularly well on the soft-coloured brick. Many roses are grown in the flower borders alongside the paths in the kitchen garden, interspersed with old pyramid apples and pears; here we find 'Frau Karl Druschki' and the vigorous, single, orange-yellow 'Mrs Oakley Fisher'. So well does this and also 'Étoile de Hollande' grow that these varieties have been selected for beds on the lawn. While some of the single roses of this type, raised in the '20s of this century, are spindly in growth 'Mrs Oakley Fisher' is an excellent bush, always in flower; it grows equally well at Sissinghurst, where it reaches six feet in height. An assortment of Hybrid Musks, including 'Vanity', makes one of the walks colourful and fragrant through the season.

The historic walled garden at Wallington, Northumberland, has a similar rich selection of roses, some old and unidentified, others new, and the lichened walls make an ideal background for most climbers and ramblers. The dry, sunny top border is devoted to soft, pale colours and here *R. fedtschenkoana*, *R. soulieana*, *R. rubrifolia*, together with sea buckthorn and *Cytisus battandieri* augment the effect of grey foliaged plants: 'Natalie Nypels', a prolific rose-pink China floribunda always in flower, 'Iceberg' and the clear yellow 'Golden Wings' assort well elsewhere with bergenias and irises; while 'Scarlet Fire' and scarlet floribundas add weight to a border where much copper foliage and richly-coloured phloxes are used. 'Leverkusen' and 'Albéric Barbier' cover arches along borders devoted to blue and yellow flowers.

Roses in Northern Ireland

In Northern Ireland are two famous gardens, the one, Mount Stewart on the shores of Strangford Lough, on rich acid loam and experiencing very little frost, and the other, Rowallane, in colder conditions and on poor, stony, acid soil. *R. moyesii* has made an immense bush in the latter garden, and old French roses are being given prominence in the walled garden. 'Mary Queen of Scots', perhaps the richest-coloured variant of *R. spinosissima*, is a treasured possession; the petals are plum-crimson with creamy-grey reverses—resembling the modern 'Pigalle' but with more intensely contrasting colours. *R. mulliganii*, a musk rose closely related to *R. longicuspis*, is rarely seen elsewhere. The Kiftsgate *R. filipes* is growing with great abandon, slowly enveloping a large Japanese cherry and giving it a second period of blossom, and there is a large bush of the pretty, fringed, pink *R. rugosa* hybrid 'Fimbriata'. This has much larger and more beautiful flowers than 'Pink Grootendorst' and is sweetly scented.

It was an experience to go to Mount Stewart again last year and to find two very old and splendid plants of the Ayrshire rose, 'Dundee Rambler' on the south front of the great house, one covering something like 400 sq ft of wall. The intense fragrance of the double creamy white flowers flooded the air, and I could not help thinking what a joy it would be to awaken in the morning to that fragrance invading one's bedroom window, especially as nearby, but not so vigorous, are growing the Bourbon 'Boule de Neige' and two rare old Noisettes, seldom out of flower and possessing not only the lettuce-green leaves of the group, but their own amazing fragrance. These are 'Céline Forestier', a shapely, cupped double bloom in clear canary yellow, near to a Tea rose, and 'Desprez à Fleurs Jaunes' which is nearer to *R. moschata* (the other parent of this race) bearing smaller, loosely double flowers of peachy yellow, and smelling like a fruit salad. The most spectacular rose at Mount Stewart is *R. gigantea*, probably var. *macrocarpa*, with huge, single, lemon-white flowers, a grandparent of the Tea roses. It grows with blue ceanothuses and lavender *Solanum crispum* on a great wooden pergola (recently repaired at considerable cost) above a raised wall around a sunk garden. In due season this area displays fiery orange azaleas, blue camassias and hardy geraniums, honeysuckles and clematis, delphiniums and campanulas; other yellow climbing roses contribute. The Italian garden, a formal area below the steps on the south front, contains a pattern of formal beds augmented by avenues of cordylines. Old and new roses, dwarf shrubs and herbaceous plants keep up an uninterrupted display in this unique parterre; some of the most successful roses are the yellow 'Honeymoon', 'Shepherd's Delight', 'Korona', 'Rosemary Rose', 'Dainty Maid', 'Poulsen's Bedder'. It is like being transported to another world to find roses growing with things such as the New Zealand *Sophora tetraptera* and *Beschorneria yuccoides*, with a backcloth of *Eucalyptus globulus* whose bark peels like that of a plane tree, revealing pale green, grey and buff tones.

In some of our gardens are borders of herbaceous plants which do not really provide much colour until summer is well advanced, and some of the "Frühlings" shrub roses, with Rugosas and 'Nevada', help to bridge the gap suitably, as at Charlecote, Warwickshire, and also at Hardwick Hall, Derbyshire. There are many old roses on the original Elizabethan walls of this fine formal garden, including the old purple Boursault, 'Amadis', a thornless climber; 'Paul Ricault', one of the most sumptuous of hybrid Centifolias; these and the White Rose of York grow freely in this garden, 800 feet above sea level. In milder Herefordshire, at Croft Castle, the 'Kiftsgate' R. filipes did not take long to leap over the 25 ft high gothic curtain-wall at the entrance; R. brunonii is doing likewise and a fine old plant of this is supported by posts and cross rails at Clevedon Court, Somerset. The richest of the purple ramblers, 'Bleu Magenta' is well established on the old retaining wall of the terrace here.

Special roses and heirlooms

Wherever in the past people have gardened, there roses have been tried. Without doubt they grow better in the east rather than the west, though Bodnant and Mount Stewart are noted exceptions. At Killerton in Devon, an early arboretum of note, roses, apart from 'Frensham' and 'Allgold', suffer very much from Black Spot and a whole series of beds on the terrace have been given over to dwarf shrubs and plants which have thrived and give a year-long display of flowers or foliage. Two excellent plants of the Macartney rose, R. bracteata, are to be found in our Western gardens, at Penrhyn Castle, near Bangor, N. Wales, where it has covered a wall about 8 ft high in four years, and at Trelissick, Cornwall. The lemon-scented, substantial, single flowers are produced from midsummer onwards, with strange woolly calyces, and neat evergreen leaves. 'Plentiful' is a near failure at Saltram, Devon, but 'Lavender Lassie' is an unqualified success, likewise 'Penelope', R. soulieana and 'Sanders White' rambler, all in poor, shaly, acid soil, in a border of soft colours to tone with a blue cedar. Very vigorous hybrid teas give reasonable success at Trengwainton, in Westernmost Cornwall. There is much to be learned about the cultivation of roses and successful varieties in the wetter west and I hope this may be the subject for a collective article from growers in Cornwall and Devon in a future Rose Annual.

Favourites with succeeding generations are, as I have amply shown, well to the fore in our gardens and as a consequence our gardens are fortunate in having a number of heirlooms. The rare old conservatory Tea rose 'Niphetos' still gives its unique and splendid white blooms in an unheated greenhouse at Trelissick, Cornwall. High over a wall at Cliveden, Buckinghamshire, is a plant of the rambler 'Ayrshire Splendens'; I know of only one other in the country; it is unique in its fragrance and in its ability to thrive in shade from overhanging trees. R. sinowilsonii—the rose with the most handsome leaves of any variety or species, of glossy dark green above and crimson-purple beneath—grows well over an arch at Bodnant. At Melford Hall, Suffolk, is one again of only two specimens known to me of 'Gracilis' or 'Blush Boursault'. A rose of mystery, a soft pink China-Tea hybrid, grows at Killerton, Blickling and Trengwainton; I wish I could identify it. The ancient 'Scarlet Four Seasons' or 'Portland Rose' has long been grown at Blickling; this was an original hybrid between the China Roses and the Autumn Damask which paved the way for the Portland race, direct antecedents of the hybrid perpetuals, themselves the parents of the hybrid teas. Anyone who goes to Peckover, Cambridgeshire, or Oxburgh Hall, Norfolk, in August will note that the second crop of yolk-yellow fragrant blooms from 'Alister Stella Gray' is as good as the first. It is never out of bloom from June to November. The gorgeous crimson, fragrant 'Reine Marie Antoinette' is treasured at Gunby Hall, while at Sissinghurst are two heirlooms, the old, old Gallica known as 'Sissinghurst Castle', which reasserted itself in a derelict area after clearance many years ago, and also 'Souvenir du Dr Jamain', rescued from a local nursery. Lastly, nobody could fail to be impressed by the two annual crops of clear yellow blooms from 'Climbing Christine' at Beningborough Hall, Yorkshire. Many others of our gardens contain roses old and new, and all are tended by devoted head gardeners—devoted alike to their precious charges and to The National Trust and all its works.Without their interest and hard work the best of schemes would come to nought.

THE MAN WHO GAVE ME SIGHT

"They're red," he said. The vivid memory lingers,
Of how he found their perfume strong and fresh,
Then took them, and with gentle searching fingers
Caressed those petals delicate as flesh.

"Red roses!" Though his gaze seemed even duller,
He brightly claimed the roses as his prize.
He found them fragrant, vibrant ... Was there colour?
... I now see roses through a blind man's eyes.

MAURICE COX

The Use of Urea in Black Spot Sprays

J. H. BARTRAM, M.Sc.

To rose growers in the eastern half of the country and in industrial areas, the words "Black Spot" are just something they read in books about roses, but very few of them ever have experience of it. To growers in the humid south-west it is a continuing nightmare that lasts from early June to late October every year, and it is not an exaggeration to say that a rose grower's success in this area depends more on his ability to keep Black Spot at bay than his actual horticultural skill.

I have always sprayed with the best fungicides available every fortnight from early June to October, but even so, when the misty nights of September arrived, Black Spot always got out of control, and by early October the bushes were almost defoliated and flowering ceased. In a mild area such as this it is very irritating to have this happen, because if the leaves can be kept on it is easily possible to have quite nice blooms right up to Christmas; also, continuous early defoliation does the bushes no good at all.

In January 1967 I was reading in a horticultural journal about a three-year experiment[1] in which apple trees were sprayed with 5 per cent urea solution in autumn each year, in order to plump up their fruit buds and get a better apple crop the next season. The experiment was a success, but the item which caught my eye was a side effect noted by the authors. They had observed that the trees sprayed with urea in autumn suffered far less from scab the next season than the unsprayed trees, and the effect was cumulative.

Now scab is to apples as Black Spot is to roses and the same types of chemicals are used to control the two diseases. So I decided to try adding urea to the fungicide spray each time it was put on. What could I lose? If no good was done as far as increased Black Spot protection was concerned, at least the trees would have a regular foliar feed, because green growing tissues of all plants easily absorb urea, a nitrogen-containing compound.

I started at 3 per cent when the leaves were young and tender in early June, raised it to 4 per cent in late June and went up to 5 per cent from early July onwards.

[1] *Mr. E. F. Allen comments*: "This work at East Malling is still in progress and in the last (1969) Annual Report it is mentioned that there was a higher incidence of canker caused by *Nectria galligena* in the urea-treated area, particularly on the lower branches of trees damaged by a double application of the chemical. Hence the technique, although very promising, is not without its dangers on apple trees."

1967 was an average summer and I was able to spray pretty well to schedule. Black Spot appeared as usual in September, but progressed much more slowly and the leaves stayed on until the beginning of November. This was promising, but a single experiment means very little.

1968 was a vile summer in this area, more rain than had been recorded for years. As a result spraying was decidedly erratic. In October it rained every single day and I could not apply even one spray, but I did manage a last one in the first week of November. This year the Black Spot was obviously finding life difficult and the leaves stayed on until early December. I was very cheered.

1969 was, of course, a marvellous summer and all spraying went to schedule. There was no sign of Black Spot and the bushes had plenty of leaves and even a few half open flowers when I pruned them in February 1970, the first time this had happened. Incidentally, I always put on a Black Spot spray, (with urea) as soon as I have pruned.

In August 1970 despite a very warm and wet fortnight, Black Spot was conspicuous by its absence. The bushes were all growing very strongly with very good foliage, which was obviously the urea working.

During the first two weeks of September it rained at least part of every day and in the second two weeks there was bright sunshine, but with very thick mist at night which mostly lasted until 11 a.m. During the whole month it was very warm, thus providing four weeks of perfect Black Spot breeding weather. Unfortunately I had to be away from home from September 15–22, and the bushes went without a protective spray for $3\frac{1}{2}$ weeks at the worst possible time. Driving back through Somerset and Devon and observing the state of the roses along the way, I was not surprised to find that Black Spot had a hold on the lowest leaves of all my bushes. Just about the first thing I did was spray them, followed by another 10 days later and another 14 days after that. It has stopped the Black Spot dead.

It is now October 30th and October has been unusually warm and moist too. The bushes do not look quite as good as last year's at this time, but still have plenty of leaves and are still in bloom. Compared with the almost defoliated plants to be seen everywhere else I am doing very well indeed, and I am sure I shall once again find plenty of leaves and some buds still there at pruning time.

For those without the benefit of a scientific education, urea is a white crystalline solid, chemical name Carbamide, chemical formula $CO(NH_2)_2$. It contains no less than $46\frac{1}{2}$ per cent of Nitrogen, far more than any other available fertilizer, and if applied to the soil dry, must be used with some care, but it is very effective. It is now produced in very large quantities for plastics manufacture and manufacture of liquid feeds and foliar feeds, and costs £3 per cwt. It is one of a class of substances which causes water to get cooler as it dissolves and so it dissolves much more rapidly in a small quantity of hot water, which can then be added to the bulk of the spray liquid. It also has the effect of lessening the effectiveness of the "wetter" or "spreader" normally included in the spray materials, so last of all add one squirt of washing up liquid to each gallon of spray mixture. If you add it earlier you get masses of foam during the mixing. Three per cent is equivalent to 4¾ oz. urea per gallon, 4 per cent is 6½ oz., and 5 per cent is 8 oz. per gallon. I have tried these domestic detergents in sprays of all kinds, on all sorts of plants. They are very effective and never do any damage.

In case anyone thinks I am using a lot of nitrogen on my plants perhaps I had better show that this is not so. I use a one gallon Kestrel diaphragm pump knapsack sprayer and find that one gallon of spray fluid does on average 70 bushes. A 4 per cent urea solution contains approximately 6 oz. So each bush gets ·0855 oz. of urea. In my garden each bush has near enough 4 sq. ft. of space, so the fertilizer application is about 0·2 oz per sq. yard, which means 10 sprays are needed to equal the usual 2 oz. per sq. yd. normally applied as a dry fertilizer at one time. (If 5 per cent were used all the time it would need 8 sprays). As it is all nitrogen, on a very light sandy soil it might be wise to add a bit of extra potash to the soil in the spring, but not otherwise.

Editorial Note: Mr. Bartram used fungicide sprays based on maneb or zineb. Any member interested in this technique should write to the author at 25, Severn Road, Torquay for further details.

I sometimes think that never blows so red
The Rose as where some buried Caesar bled;
                    EDWARD FITZGERALD—*Rubaiyat*

A Motherly Touch

R. S. B. PINKS

(Amateur rose grower)

My wife's mother comes to stay at our cottage for a fortnight or so each summer; for her 85 years she is remarkably uneccentric save for an unfailing propensity wildly to confuse the Christian names of her many children, as well as those of their respective spouses. Our successes and failures, likes and dislikes, are similarly misattributed. It takes a little getting used to. She also likes roses.

Our garden is of rather less than an acre, and when we took it over some thirteen years ago from a very spry old countryman it seemed to hold no real terrors for a couple of comparative youngsters. As year followed year, however, it seemed that we were only just holding our own and never making any real progress. Although this was not altogether surprising—we had much to learn—we were most flattered from time to time to receive solicitous enquiries from members of the family, as well as from others, about the welfare of our roses. Wherever we went we were almost bound to hear of the excellence of our marvellous roses, and of their beautiful setting. It gradually became evident that we were the victims of another of mother's misattributions, but the identity of the master rosarian has eluded us completely over the years.

The psychological effect of all this was that we became ultra-sensitive about our roses. Poor things they were, too. There were some tall, scentless floribundas of reddish pink hue whose leaves fell off every summer; there were some tiny bushes which had been handed over to us as "Monthly Roses", together with half a dozen unlabelled varieties which we had hurriedly dug up prior to our removal and brought with us. In a desperate effort to make amends I bought a number of bushes of 'Peace', but as they refused to bloom until each August, possibly because moles gave them such a bad time earlier in the year, I let it be known that roses were not things for me but for other people, and even spread rumours that the soil here was quite unsuitable for them. Despite all this our visitors tended to make pointed remarks about how good the roses had been when mother was last here, even though at the time of speaking they were not quite all they had imagined them to be.

I suppose that it was fear that I should develop a syndrome of some sort that caused me to look more thoroughly than usual at the gardening weeklies, and in particular at the articles they contained on the subject of roses. It was at about that time that a rose called 'Fragrant Cloud' had burst on to an undeserving world and I was completely mesmerised by all that was written about it. It sounded all that a plant should be, so I dug up a bed of old perennials, forked it over and decided that it would hold a round dozen of these new bushes. It must have been the fact that I had to pay half a guinea each for them that turned them into the VIP category: certainly I had never lavished so much care on any plants before. They even got a sprinkling of bonemeal when I set them into position and I was supremely smug when I stood back after pruning them down to six inches. This would demonstrate once and for all whether we could grow roses or not. My private belief was that the whole thing would be a fiasco and that in a year or so the entire bed could go over to heather or some other nice ground cover which would enable me to pass those sunny summer days in a recumbent position on the lawn, freed for ever from the rosarian tyranny of spraying, disbudding, pruning *et al*.

During the winter months, whilst these gilt edged investments were frozen into their surroundings, I was busily consulting the available literature for guidance during the coming spring and summer, and I sped from volume to volume until I had almost exhausted the bibliography on the subject. When the first days of spring came along I casually noted where there were some odd spaces in the borders and began making surreptitious visits to a local nursery from which I rarely emerged without a twiggy bundle containing two or three bushes. 'Rumba', 'Wendy Cussons', 'Mischief' and 'Super Star' were early companions for my twelve 'Fragrant Cloud', but I took a little time selecting a suitable low white floribunda to plant in a bed in front of, and below them. 'Irene of Denmark' sounded as good as any of the others, so in went a dozen of these, right at the end of the planting season.

I think that spring and early summer was one of the most anxious periods I have spent—in the gardening sense, that is. "Irene" preceded the other roses by a week or so by flowering in the last week of May, but when my first 'Fragrant Cloud' opened their gorgeously perfumed blooms I realized that, whether I had a feel for roses or not, I should jolly well have to develop one. The sheer pleasure of these two rose beds that summer was worth so very much more than the cash, the work and the anxiety, and I began to realize just what a wonderful thing the modern rose has come to be. There are many who complain that it has no scent, that it wilts under the weather and that it gets every sort of disease. I had heard of all these complaints as I marvelled at Tantau's masterpiece and wondered when the news would get round.

Inevitably I planted more bushes at the end of that season and, because I wanted to get some colour above eye level, I constructed some pergolas and pillars and invested in numerous climbers and ramblers. Then came some standards and a couple of weeping standards. The more I planted, the greater was the anticipation for the following season, and the realisation that no plan can ever be the final one. There was always something not quite right about the display for this or that year, and that meant either cutting a new rose bed or digging up and burning some of the proven failures. A neighbouring farmer gave me access to his muck heap, having decided that it was not seemly for me to follow the riding school round the lanes with a bucket and shovel. The annual excursions to his field of plenty now give me lots of exercise just as the evenings are beginning to lengthen, and as we unload the bulging bags from the boot of the car and tip their reeking contents on to the rose beds we tell ourselves fervently that the ultimate reward is great.

Regardless of the counsel of some of the pundits I maintain a permanent cutting bed and stick likely looking rose prunings into it, especially if the parent plants are new varieties. Many cuttings have made better plants than their original budded parents and make excellent fillers of any gaps in the ranks of varieties which are difficult to obtain. It is certainly a joy not to have to de-sucker cuttings, as this is part of the art I have never really mastered.

The garden has thus, over just a few years, taken on a quite different appearance, and the change has been a distinctly favourable one. Our programme, anyway, was to introduce labour-saving features in order that we could devote what spare time we had to plants which particularly pleased us. Our heathers and dwarf conifers have contributed greatly to this and I have experimented with pegging down clematis and roses for enhanced colour effects at ground level. Since I developed something of an aptitude for clematis at about the same time as we were converted to roses, many of the climbers and ramblers have suitable large flowered clematis as partners, and most of these have come from cuttings. In the English climate, and against the colour of its countryside, the white clematis are particularly effective in company with roses. I have found 'Henryi' and 'Mme Le Coultre' ('Marie Boisselot') grievously subject to wilt and therefore the white form of 'Jackmanii' (J. Alba) is rather more reliable for the beginner.

The soul-destroying slavery of the rose has become rather less of a problem than I expected it to be. It is quite true that spraying is essential—just try going for a whole season without it—but the rewards of regular fortnightly treatment during the growing season are incalculable. If you use a combined Mildew and Black Spot fungicide, a foliar spray and an insecticide you will find your plants both looking well and keeping free from trouble, though Mildew does seem to rise even above this at times. The application of sulphate of potash to the rose beds in August really does seem to help toughen new growth against the worst excesses of the winter, since our established bushes, treated, always seem less troubled than newly-planted bushes straight from nurseries where, normally, no potash treatment is given to them.

We have become a little wiser about the selection of roses for next year, and for the years after that. Instead of reading the catalogues we visit the nurseries or public gardens after heavy rain or gales and make a note of anything that, however remotely, looks healthy and unscarred. I am pleasantly surprised how some of my earlier fancies have given consistently good results as garden flowers, despite comparatively low ratings by the statisticians and popularity pollsters. If I had to make a choice unseen I would go for something by Kordes or Tantau, whose creations have done better here than any others. I seldom buy a rose which is highly recommended for exhibition, for as garden roses most seem horrible frauds and crumple away to a wet mess in the average English summer with its generous quota of rain.

The following varieties have done particularly well in our Gloucestershire garden:

Hybrid Teas: 'Fragrant Cloud', 'Doreen', 'Whisky Mac', 'Colour Wonder', 'Mischief'.

Floribundas: 'Elizabeth of Glamis', 'Evelyn Fison', 'Gypsy Moth', 'Orange Sensation', 'Orangeade', 'My Girl', 'City of Leeds', 'Diablotin', 'Iceberg'.

Climbers: 'Orfeo', 'Zéphirine Drouhin', 'Orangeade', 'Mrs Sam McGredy', 'Handel', 'Schoolgirl', 'Maigold', 'Leverkusen', 'Hamburger Phoenix'.

Shrub Type: 'Fred Loads', 'Heidelberg', 'Joseph's Coat'.

The following clematis have been associated with them most successfully. The happiest undoubtedly is the combination of 'Ascotiensis' with 'Maigold'. 'Jackmanii Alba', 'Sieboldii Ramona', 'Xerxes', 'Ascotiensis', 'Mrs Hope', 'Ernest Markham', 'Jackmanii Superba,' 'Ville De Lyon', 'President', 'Lasurstern', 'Mrs Cholmondley'.

Looking round the garden as summer wears on we begin to think again whether we can fit a few more bushes in here, or perhaps a climber there.

Perhaps we have been bitten by some sort of bug, but whatever it is, it is an agreeable enough feeling and there doesn't seem to be any particular sort of harm in it. It seems a long time since mother said all those things about our roses. Of course, nobody now enquires after them, even after mother has been staying with us, as she goes straight home and misattributes them to most other members of the family. If they react as I did—and the odds are that they will—then the great hybridists and nurseries will be provided with excellent business for years to come. If, therefore, mother gets a rose named after her for services rendered to the increased prosperity of the trade, this would only seem to be the true fulfilment of justice.

Plant Breeders' Rights and Roses

In 1964 an Act of Parliament set up the Plant Variety Rights Office to encourage, protect and reward innovation in plant breeding. In so doing it enabled breeders to obtain an exclusive right in their new varieties and to collect royalties in return for licences to reproduce the varieties they have raised.

Our Society plays a part in the scheme[1] by assisting the P.V.R.O. during growing trials of rose varieties submitted for plant breeders' rights—and by maintaining a reference collection of "patented" roses at St Albans. Currently they number 169.

In July 1970 the P.V.R.O. staged a Plant Breeding Display[2] to mark the first five years of operation. It was extremely well presented but the show—including as it did wheat, barley, tomatoes, red delphiniums, chrysanthemums, freesias and potatoes—was stolen by the roses, the more so when at dusk the wonderful chandeliers of the historic Banqueting House in Whitehall were lighted.

The rose blooms for the central display were provided by the hybridists having plant variety rights and their display was a co-operative effort by a team led by Mr John Mattock Jnr.

The Society showed blooms of the ancestral varieties to which 'Grandpa Dickson' (the first "patented" rose) owed its being.

Mr Leslie J. Smith, Controller of Plant Variety Rights, and his staff must be congratulated on a fine piece of organisation and publicity.

[1] Rose Annual 1964 pp 122/126.
[2] For members really interested copies of the programme "Plant Breeding Display, July 1970" can be obtained from the P.V.R.O., Murray House, 3 Vandon St., London, S.W.1.

'ESTHER OFARIM' (floribunda – H.T. type)
'Colour Wonder' × *'Zorina'*
Raised by W. Kordes & Sons, Germany
TRIAL GROUND CERTIFICATE 1970
See page 176

'MEGIDDO' (floribunda – H.T. type)
'*Coup de Foudre*' × '*S'Agaro*'
Raised by Gandy's Roses Ltd
TRIAL GROUND CERTIFICATE 1970
See page 177
(These blooms were grown under glass. The colour is slightly deeper in the open.)

Rose Seed Germination in relation to Stock Production

J. B. BLUNDELL AND G. A. D. JACKSON
(*School of Plant Biology, University College of North Wales, Bangor*)

Introduction

The rose "pip" or "seed" is technically speaking an achene, i.e. a one seeded fruit, which consists of an apparently mature embryo enclosed in a thin papery testa (to give the seed proper) which in turn is surrounded by a thick pericarp (fruit wall). The texture of the pericarp varies from species to species; for example, it is relatively soft in *Rosa rugosa* but extremely hard and "bony" in *R. canina*.

Although the achenes of most rose species are dormant when mature and require a period of low-temperature after-ripening before germination is possible, species with soft pericarps are generally less dormant than those with hard. This has led to the suggestion that the pericarp imposes dormancy in the mature achene, either by preventing water and gaseous exchange or by acting as a strait-jacket to the growth of the embryo. Thus, early attempts to break the dormancy of achenes centred around methods of improving their permeability to water and gases, and ways of reducing the strait-jacket effect of the pericarp. Pre-treatments such as prolonged soaking in water, exposure to 100 per cent oxygen, scarification and treating with acid were all tried with little success (Tincker, 1935). Some success with acid treatment has, however, been achieved by Popcov and Buč (1967).

The strait-jacket effect of the pericarp on germination is at first sight supported by the fact that, when embryos are excised from testa and pericarp, they will usually germinate within a few days if placed in a germinator (Barton, 1961; Blundell, 1965). However, it has been shown that any physical repression of germination by the pericarp is combined with the presence, in both pericarp and testa, of the water-soluble growth-inhibitor abscisic acid which probably plays a major role in dormancy. Its effects in delaying germination of excised embryos and seeds can be counteracted by the use of gibberellic acid and benzyl adenine, and it has been suggested that the state of the embryo is determined by the internal balance between certain growth inhibiting and promoting hormones (Jackson and Blundell, 1963; Jackson, 1968).

Unfortunately, the response of entire achenes to growth promoters is variable, and low-temperature stratification is still the only practical method of breaking dormancy. Rowley (1956) obtained the best germination for *R. canina* in the first year after sowing by using achenes taken from firm, red hips and stratifying them in moist vermiculite for two months in a warm greenhouse, followed by two months at approximately freezing.

One of our aims at Bangor is to find a method of stratification, suitable for general use, which will give consistently good germination under field conditions. The following gives an account of some of the progress made towards this goal.

Experimental and Discussion

Firm red hips of a particularly dormant variety of *Rosa canina* were collected from an experimental bush in the Bangor area. The achenes were immediately removed from the hips and immersed in water. Achenes which did not sink were discarded, since such light achenes generally have aborted or immature embryos. The achenes were dried and a proportion of them treated with acid (Popcov and Buč, 1967). In these first experiments the entire and acid-treated achenes were stratified in moist vermiculite and kept in plastic pots at either 26° C. or 2° C. After 3 months at 26° C. some of the pots were transferred to the cold. At intervals during the stratification process the contents of each pot were examined and achenes in which the root could be seen protruding through the pericarp were counted and removed; ungerminated ones were then returned to the pot for a further period of stratification.

TABLE 1. **The germination of entire and acid-treated achenes of**
R. *canina* under different conditions of stratification

| Pre-treatment | Percentage Germination after Months at 2° C. | | | | | | | | | |
	6	7	8	9	10	11	12	13	14	15
Entire achenes 3 months warm	0	0	2	3	5	8			17	
Acid-treated 3 months warm	8	57	84	94	96					
Acid-treated no warm	0	0	3	11	28	38	44	54	58	62

Entire and acid-treated achenes failed to germinate when subjected to 15 months of continuous warm treatment.

It is clear from the results that the one essential factor in achene germination is a period of low-temperature after-ripening (which probably induces the production of growth-promoting hormones in the embryo) since cold treatment alone, if of sufficient duration, will bring about germination.

The warm period on its own, although unable to promote germination of the embryo, does have a beneficial effect on achene germination when used immediately prior to the cold period. The precise way in which the warm period has its effect is still unknown, though evidence from other experiments suggests that water uptake in the early stages of stratification is improved and that the suture of the pericarp is weakened, thereby reducing mechanical resistance to the growth of the embryo during any subsequent cold period. Both of these processes proceed only slowly at low temperatures and the better germination observed in acid-treated achenes may also be attributed to an improvement in these factors. Another possibility is that the acid and warm treatments accelerate the overall breakdown of the pericarp and the leaching away of the inhibitor it contains; this reduces the cold requirement necessary for the embryo to produce sufficient promoter to counteract any of the remaining inhibitor.

On occasion embryos excised from achenes stratified in pots were found to be dead due to waterlogged conditions and poor aeration. In later experiments, in order to prevent this, the achenes were stratified in nylon knitmesh bags loosely filled with moist vermiculite. The bags were placed on a layer of moist vermiculite in seed trays and the whole tray loosely enclosed in a large polythene bag. The main function of the polythene bag was to cut down water loss during the stratification period and it was found that, if the bag was not sealed, this was still accomplished whilst at the same time permitting adequate aeration. The trays of achenes were stored at either 26° C. or 5° C., an all-purpose temperature more likely to satisfy the range of cold requirements of the different commercial species and varieties. At intervals during the stratification process the contents of the bags were shaken up and, if necessary, watered. Using this modified stratification technique it was found that, in the species tested, where comparison was made, a shorter period of cold treatment was required to initiate germination.

Having investigated the condition of stratification and the pattern of germination of a number of wild varieties of R. *canina*, under controlled conditions, a start was made to relate these findings to the production of rose rootstocks in the field.

A supply of four commercially important varieties of rose achenes ('Inermis', 'Laxa', 'Pfänder' and R. *rugosa*) was obtained from Old Farm Nurseries, Boskoop, Holland, and samples of entire and acid-treated achenes were stratified in nylon bags in the way already described. Some of the entire achenes were sown in the field on 18 December, 1969 and the remainder, together with the acid-treated ones, were sown on 16 March, 1970. To facilitate hand sowing, the stratified achenes were mixed with dry vermiculite and planted at a density of about 100 per yard and at a depth of $\frac{1}{2}$ in.

The autumn-sown achenes at the time of planting had received 2 days of stratification at 26° C. to speed up imbibition of the achenes followed by 3 months at 5° C. A longer period at 26° C. was not given since it was thought that, with an autumn sowing, there was a possibility that premature germination might occur resulting in frost damage to the young seedlings during the winter months. Furthermore, it was hoped that the non-sterile conditions in the field would eventually break down the pericarp. Thus, at the time of sowing, the achenes were showing no signs of germination. The spring-sown achenes at the time of sowing had received 2 months of preliminary warm treatment plus 5 months of cold.

On March 17, half of the autumn and spring-sown samples were covered with polythene tunnels to provide some protection against frost damage for the emerging seedlings. Since no severe frosts were recorded during the subsequent germination period, there was very little difference between the protected and unprotected samples and only the results of the protected ones are shown in Table 2.

TABLE 2. **The overall germination (based on emergence of seedlings above soil level) of entire and acid-treated achenes of four varieties of rose under field conditions**

	Final Percentage Germination		
Variety	Autumn-sown	Spring-sown	Spring-sown, acid-treated
'Inermis'	41	22	63
'Laxa'	68	16	73
R. rugosa	51	50	82
'Pfänder'	5	2	37

Stratification pre-treatment before sowing:
Autumn-sown—2 days at 26° C. plus 3 months at 5° C.
Spring-sown—2 months at 26° C. plus 5 months at 5° C.

Counts of the number of seedlings emerging, made at intervals during the period February–June, showed that with autumn-sown achenes, R. rugosa began to germinate on February 25, 'Laxa' and 'Inermis' on March 19 and 'Pfänder' on April 8. The rate of germination in all varieties steadily increased for a number of months. With R. rugosa the peak-rate of germination, under our conditions,[1] was reached by the first week of April and was followed about 4–5 weeks later by 'Laxa' and 'Inermis'. 'Pfänder' never reached a peak of germination and from this it was assumed that the amount of preliminary cold received before sowing was inadequate for after-ripening

[1] Meteorological data for the field site gave an average day temperature of 5° C. during the December–March period.

purposes. Thus the amount of cold experienced by *R. rugosa* at the time of peak germination was approximately 7 months and for 'Laxa' and 'Inermis' 8 months (3 months preliminary cold plus 4 or 5 months respectively in the field).

Although the spring-planted achenes had received an additional 2 months of warm pre-treatment, it is interesting to note that the peak-rate of germination in *R. rugosa* occurred after the achenes had experienced a roughly similar amount of cold to those planted in the autumn. Thus, the expected peak of germination in 'Laxa' and 'Inermis' would have been 4–5 weeks later in mid-June but, because temperatures at this time were too high to permit after-ripening, the peak was never reached. 'Pfänder', for the same reasons, represents an even more extreme case.

With the acid-treated achenes, those of *R. rugosa* and 'Laxa' were beginning to germinate at the time of sowing, whilst 'Inermis' and 'Pfänder' were still dormant. Since it has already been shown that acid-treatment reduces the cold requirement (see Table 1), it was possible for a high proportion of the treated achenes to complete their after-ripening before the higher temperatures in late May–June interrupted the process. Thus, even with 'Pfänder' 37 per cent germination had occurred by the end of May.

Practical Problems of Rose Stock Production

The grower seeking a good percentage of seed germination is faced by a number of dilemmas, some of which arise because of a lack of information, and some of which are beyond his control (such as spring frosts) for which amelioration may be sought. In even a given sample of rose achenes the individuals of the "population" vary in the number of months of cold they require for germination, and the variability is even greater when trying to cater for different species. Because of this spread in germination, for spring sowing in February or early March, the best germination will be obtained if the *peak* is reached by the after-ripening effect of the subsequent $2-2\frac{1}{2}$ months of cold in the field. This would mean that the early germinators would be damaged and must be sacrificed during planting, and the achenes demanding a longer cold period would also be lost. For complete success, the grower thus needs to know for each batch of seed (since the requirements may be different from year to year) how and when to stratify. Acid treatment (if this is commercially viable) certainly seems to reduce the cold-requirement and may iron out some of the differences.

Autumn-sowing has, superficially, one great attraction. By using a reduced amount of preliminary after-ripening, insufficient to start germination, a longer period of cold in the field is able to satisfy the varying demands of a much bigger proportion of the population of the achenes as they lie *in situ*. Unfortunately, the early germinators would be subject to damage if temperatures fell below about 8° F. This could possibly be minimised by deeper planting or protection with polythene tunnels.

Literature relating to the density of sowing and germination of achenes under commercial field conditions is scant. One has the impression that the density of sowing necessary to yield 200,000 saleable stocks per acre is of the order of 200–300 pounds per acre. For example, Krause (1960) states that, in Holland, using *R. canina,* one pound of seed containing approximately 30,000 achenes produces about 825 seedlings. Of these about 30 per cent have crooked necks and must be down-graded so that only some 2 per cent of the achenes sown produce good quality stocks. It may be of interest to growers to know that, in our experiments, the approximate number of achenes per pound was: *R. rugosa* = 78,000; 'Inermis' = 36,000; 'Laxa' = 30,000 and 'Pfänder' = 20,000. Based on the results obtained from our most successful acid-treated, spring-sown achenes, the density of sowing necessary to produce 200,000 stocks per acre was 4 pounds per acre for *R. rugosa,* 10 pounds for 'Inermis' and 'Laxa' and 20 pounds for 'Pfänder'. In the case of 'Laxa', even allowing for a poor germination of 20 per cent and a further loss of 30 per cent due to down-grading of stocks, the saving in the cost of seed alone would be in the region of £500 per acre.

About three-quarters of a million pounds is being spent each year in importing stocks from Europe, even though there appears to be no fundamental reason why stocks cannot be produced in certain parts of this country. It is hoped that, once a reliable method for determining the optimum stratification conditions for each variety has been developed, it will be possible to raise our own stocks and in this way make a small contribution to the balance of payments problem (Jackson, 1970).

Summary

1. Dormancy is imposed on the rose embryo by the surrounding testa and pericarp.
2. The one essential factor necessary for rose achene germination is a period of low-temperature after-ripening.
3. A warm treatment alone does not promote after-ripening of the embryo.
4. A preliminary warm period reduces the cold requirement necessary for achene germination.

5. Acid treatment of achenes reduces their cold requirement for similar reasons.

6. Stratification in moist vermiculite contained in nylon bags, at a temperature of 5° C., proved to be more effective than stratification in plastic pots at 2° C.

7. A comparison was made of spring and autumn sowing of entire achenes (using four commercial varieties) and the latter gave the better germination. Acid-treated achenes, however, when spring sown, gave the best results.

Acknowledgements

The authors wish to express their appreciation of the technical assistance given by Mrs M. Higgins and Mr C. Ellis and for the grants given by The Royal National Rose Society, Association of British Rose Producers and Rose Distribution Ltd. in support of this work.

References

BARTON, L. V. (1961). Experimental seed physiology at the Boyce Thompson Institute. *Proc. Intern. Seed Testing Assoc.*, **26**, 561.

BLUNDELL, J. B. (1965). Studies of flower development, fruit development and germination in *Rosa*. Ph.D. thesis, Univ. of Wales.

JACKSON, G. A. D. (1968). Hormonal control of fruit development, seed dormancy and germination with particular reference to *Rosa*. S.C.I. Monogr., **31**, 127.

JACKSON, G. A. D. (1970). Broadcast interview B.B.C. 4 (Wales). See University College of North Wales Gazette, **9**, No. 2, 14.

JACKSON, G. A. D. and BLUNDELL, J. B. (1963). Germination in *Rosa*. *J. Hort. Sci.*, **38**, 310.

KRAUSE, W. G. C. (1960). Rose root stocks, problems and research. *Hort. Trade Journal*, Aug. 11, 13.

POPCOV and BUČ (1967). Horticultural Abstracts, **37**, 3427.

ROWLEY, G. D. (1956). Germination in *Rosa canina*. *Am. Rose Annual*, **41**, 70.

TINCKER, M. A. H. (1935). Rose seeds: their after-ripening and germination. *Jl. R. Hort. Soc.*, **60**, 399.

Early 19th Century Climbing Roses in New Zealand

NANCY STEEN

(Collector of Old Roses and Author)

Let us take you back a century and a half and introduce you to some splendid old climbing roses—roses that still grace a number of modern gardens and parks. Some are summer-flowering only. Others bloom as freely as the best of the modern roses, and all have fine luxuriant foliage—extremely healthy too and a real boon to hard-working gardeners. Some of these are actually wild species while others are the earliest hybrids bred from them, mostly in the United States, Great Britain and France. A number of them graced the garden at Malmaison where the Empress Joséphine established her famous collection of roses. Because of this historic association, we find they fascinate visitors when they see such roses for the first time.

For many years, there has been in the garden a healthy plant of *R. noisettiana* or 'Blush Noisette'. We found this rose in the centre of the North Island, where the winters can be extremely cold. One plant, bushy in form, grew near a roadside in very tough conditions, while the other had established itself happily in a moist area at the base of some native trees. Under these conditions it flourished and, when we saw it festooning down from the top of the trees, we actually thought we had discovered still another rose. Redouté painted *R. noisettiana* at Malmaison and we often marvel at the accuracy and charm of this picture. As the smooth green stems are almost thornless, we have trained 'Blush Noisette' along a low trellis beside a pathway—an ideal site as the lovely, pink-budded sprays of scented, semi-double, blush-lavender flowers can be enjoyed at all seasons.

Nearly three hundred miles farther north, on a fishing trip and a rose hunting expedition, a bright flash of colour met our eyes as we motored along a winding country road beside a stream. It was obvious that we had just missed a flood, for the steep banks of the creek were heavily silted, so we had to slide and slither down through blackberry, bracken and a tall white eupatorium to see what we felt sure was a rose. And what a find it was! None other than the true 'Seven Sisters Rose' or *R. multiflora platyphylla*—a rose we had been searching for far and wide. Though rare today, this rose created a sensation in Europe when it was introduced there from the Far East at the very beginning of the last century. The sprays of small flowers

'Lamarque' at the rear of a yellow and white border (*see page* 140)

Borders at Hidcote, Glos. (The National Trust) (*see page* 114)

Rome. The display garden with the Palatine ruins in the background (*see page* 180)
Geneva. The beautiful rose garden is located near the Leman Lake (*see page* 180)

'Dundee Rambler' adorns a pergola in Mrs. Nancy Steen's garden in New Zealand (*see page* 137)

have the look of gay posies, as the blooms range in tone from blush through to crimson-purple. Add to this large handsome leaves—an inheritance from a Rugosa ancestor—and you have an exceptional rose.

When roads were scarce or non-existent, these narrow waterways were much used by the earliest settlers, and naturally they built their tiny homes along the banks. Even in those stirring times, when the Maoris were still hostile, they bravely planted gardens, though how they acquired so many rose rarities in those far off days is a mystery. A mile farther on, where emerald mosses and bullrushes adorned the river bank, we saw the loveliest sight. A large, prostrate plant of R. *multiflora carnea* trailed over the damp moss, studding the ground with clear pink posies. This was the first of the wild multifloras to be introduced into Europe; and it must have arrived out here at an early date. It is featured also amongst the accurate and exquisite paintings by Redouté and is thought to have been one parent of the 'Seven Sisters Rose'—the other having been a wild Rugosa. An extremely hardy rose, we found it once in the middle of a swamp where it had been burnt over in the summer and flooded in the winter. Yet the following year, fresh growth shot up from the base of the maltreated plant.

The lovely, bush clad, far north of New Zealand, with its glorious coast-line and off-shore islands, had become the haunt of whalers and traders even before the first missionaries and their families arrived about 1814. With the missionaries came skilled tradesmen and farmers; and, before long little cottages had been erected along the sheltered bay. Seed germinated easily in that rich, virgin soil, and soon hedges of 'Sweet Briar' and 'Dog Rose' were springing up round the new homes. Archdeacon Henry Williams, who had done so much for both pakeha and maori in his large diocese, built, a few miles inland, a lovely early colonial home to retire to in 1853. In the spacious garden of "The Retreat", we first saw the 'Dundee Rambler'. It was a fantastic sight to see the flower-laden branches swaying down from the top of a tall tree, with 'Cloth of Gold' in all its glory, nearby. By sheer good luck, we planted a minute cutting of the 'Dundee Rambler' by our pergola. This rooted and grew at a tremendous pace—the rose now covering the top of a slatted shelter over the centre of the pergola. As one parent of this rampant rose was R. *arvensis*, the 'Field Rose of England', we were not surprised to find that it preferred to lie flat over its support, as R. *arvensis* is a trailer that winds along grass verges and through hedges. The flowers of the 'Dundee Rambler' resemble those of the other parent, 'Blush Noisette', being semi-double with pink-tinted buds, though the white blooms are larger and come in enormous sprays. As soon as the flowers fade, the heavily laden branches which covered the pergola are cut out at once and surprisingly vigorous, healthy new growth soon sprouts in all directions. Because of prevailing westerly winds, we do tie branches down to some of the slats; but otherwise, the plant is left severely alone until the next season.

Not far away from "The Retreat" are the lovely Haruru Falls above which, in the early days, an hotel was built. This no longer exists but the rampageous Sempervirens hybrid,[1] 'Félicité et Perpétue', not only climbs through many old trees on the deserted property, but has forced its way up through a metalled roadway. We put up with this vigorous rose for a few years but found, in the end, that the rose was taking charge, not only of the garden, but of us. So, reluctantly, it was relegated once more to the country. We find that its close relative, 'Adélaïde d'Orléans', is even lovelier and certainly much easier to manage. The semi-double, rosy tinted flowers have a cherry like appearance—not at all like the closely petalled blooms of its sister plant, 'Félicité et Perpétue'. An added attraction is the fact that it does produce some flowers quite late in the season. Through the courtesy of our Parks Department, we acquired cuttings of this rose from the Grafton Cemetery in the heart of Auckland. Recently, a great deal of this area has been cleared to make way for motorway extensions, so we are relieved that a number of the fine old roses that grew there have been saved. There were two extensive patches of 'Adélaïde d'Orléans' in the cemetery. One plant was consorting very happily with R. gallica officinalis or the Red Rose of Lancaster, and both were thriving in a tangle of dog-daisies, periwinkle and bracken. A little farther over 'Adélaïde d'Orléans' had a most unusual companion in the form of a wild rose from North America. This was the double form of R. carolina— a rare rose, even in the United States. How it found its way, in 1881, to this part of the world is a mystery we have not been able to unravel. One other plant has been located, more recently, on the wild West Coast of the South Island of New Zealand.

Not far from the two roses just mentioned, we came across a small plant of the Alpine Rose of Europe, R. pendulina. The foliage had coloured brilliantly in the autumn, so it stood out quite dramatically. From a tiny cutting placed alongside the tennis court, it has now grown to the top of a high fence. We found the medium sized, rosy-purple flowers to be semi-double, so the form is R. pendulina plena. This healthy, vigorous rose has attractive foliage for use indoors, and it has proved its worth as a garden plant.

The Prairie Rose of North America, R. setigera, is the only species on that continent to be a natural climber and many garden plants have been raised

---

[1] Modern Roses 7 describes this as a sport from R. sempervirens. Ed.

from it. We did grow, for a time, 'American Pillar', one of its progeny; but it mildewed badly here so had to be discarded. Give it a swamp or a moist ditch to live in, and mildew will never attack it. Fortunately, one of its parents, R. setigera, is absolutely trouble-free. Its pale green leaves resemble those of the wild blackberry in shape, so it is frequently referred to as the 'Bramble-leaved Rose'. A hardy rose this for a tough situation, the only attention it receives being the thinning out of old branches immediately after flowering. Its gay, cherry-pink sprays of bloom appear when the flowers of most summer climbers are over, a valuable trait, as they certainly brighten up the garden in February.

Fortunately for the rose amateur, a few rose families have very marked characteristics. One of these is R. sempervirens or the Evergreen Rose whose foliage persists right into the winter. In fact, in some instances, new growth is appearing before the old has all fallen. An unusual rose, found semi-wild in a country district, is 'Banksiaeflora'. It has vivid green young foliage, and sprays of medium-sized flowers that open from a bright yellow bud. The creamy flowers deepen to yellow at the base of the petals. The thin, wiry, thorny branches are lightly tipped at pruning time, old tired stems being removed right at the base. We would prefer this Sempervirens hybrid to bloom a little later—it is in a hot, sunny corner—when the garden is at its best; but even now, in late winter, a few touches of yellow are visible along the branches.

Looking down from our terrace, past a long lawn, we can see a tall Yellow Guava tree. Its branches are so beautiful that we clear away any needless basal foliage. At its foot, we put in cuttings of a white climbing rose that was sent to us from a sheep station in the far south of New Zealand. They rooted well, and the rose has now travelled up through the guava. Lovely, long sprays of medium sized, white flowers hang down to delight the eye for several weeks. It has all the hall marks of a form of R. sempervirens, and we think it is 'Donna Marie'. If it bloomed perpetually, it could prove a serious rival to the great 'Lamarque'.

R. laevigata or R. sinica alba is a very popular rose species that came originally from China, and is to be found in many parts of the country. Commonly called the Cherokee Rose, the three to five shiny leaflets, the bristle-covered buds, and the large, single white flowers coming from each leaf axil, make this a distinctive rose; but its thorns are a menace and branches must be handled with due respect. One year our Cherokee Rose leapt across a driveway into a neighbour's oak tree. The offending branches were removed as soon as we noticed what was happening—to our neighbour's sorrow, as she was really enjoying the intrusion. The Cherokee Rose, the violet-scented, 'Double White Banksia', and their offspring, *R. fortuneana*, are all grown in the white garden, all flower early, and all were grown from tiny cuttings collected in northern districts.

Mr G. S. Thomas covered the Musk Rose family very fully in a recent article, so we shall not describe our finds in old milling and mining areas, except to say that they were exciting and varied. Forms of *R. moschata* certainly flourish in New Zealand.

It was in an old Northland garden that we saw for the first time the famous Tea-Noisette of 1830, 'Général Lamarque'. Miss Clarke-Walker, an elderly rosarian and a niece of the owner of one of Auckland's earliest nurseries, led us out into her orchard proudly pointing up into the trees. Masses of white and yellow roses could be seen amongst the branches, creating a charming picture against a clear blue sky. The white ones were blooms of 'Lamarque'— as it is generally called—and the yellow ones were the slightly larger flowers of 'Cloth of Gold' or 'Chromatella'. Later, we saw these two roses trained in a similar manner in the South of France and Italy. They both love warmth and plenty of sunshine. 'Lamarque', particularly, is a rose for warmer areas, though it will grow in cooler climates if given warm and sheltered positions. A number of older roses seem to have deteriorated somewhat over the years, but 'Lamarque', after one hundred and forty years of popularity in many countries, still had a fresh, vigorous look.

'Lamarque' and 'Desprez à Fleurs Jaunes'—another delightful noisette we grow—were bred in France at the same time and from the same parents. Over the years, there has been much speculation as to the exact parentage of these roses; but it is generally conceded now that the early, cluster-flowered noisette, *Rosa noisettiana*, must have been one parent used by the amateur breeder, Maréchal. The other parent, because of the yellow tones in these roses, is considered to have been 'Park's Yellow Tea-Scented China' which had arrived in Europe by 1824. Before long, these two beauties produced other yellow Tea-Noisettes—charming roses that are listed still. They are 'Céline Forestier', 'Cloth of Gold' or 'Chromatella' and 'Solfaterre'. In the next generation, two other popular descendants were to appear—'Gloire de Dijon' or 'Old Glory' and 'Maréchal Niel'.

We were given cuttings of 'Lamarque' in Whangarei, and later, in Ohaupo, but were unsuccessful in persuading them to root. It was known to be notoriously difficult in this respect, so more cuttings were generously provided. Some we gave to Miss Pat Mason of Manurewa who produced a fine budded plant for us. The others we took out to Mr Hunter—who was

President then of the Auckland Rose Society—and he placed them under glass for us at the Plant Diseases Division of the D.S.I.R. A mist spray was used, and later a plant of 'Lamarque' on its own roots was sent in to us. Even under those perfect conditions, this noisette proved difficult to root.

The budded plant and the one on its own roots now grow against a green trellis at the rear of a yellow and white border. Both plants have flowered well, and have given us and others tremendous pleasure over the years. But it is the plant on its own roots which has grown in a truly spectacular manner. From the fence, of its own accord, it hooked itself up on to a nearby silver birch, and, from there, it continued to climb into two other birches. From the top of these trees, long, flexible branches hung down nearly to ground level. In early summer masses of blooms appear, and even now, in mid-winter, flowers are appearing at all levels. These subtly scented, lemon-white blooms come in sprays, often at the end of long, swaying branches. This habit makes them ideal for use indoors. Add to this the fact that 'Lamarque' is a healthy rose, and you have a real garden treasure. Naturally, it is the plant on its own roots which produces the finest basal shoots. Where possible, we remove any old or tired wood. We have a young and interested helper who, with the aid of a sturdy orchard ladder, is able to cope with this situation, so we are indeed fortunate. I doubt if any newly introduced climbers will stand the test of time as well as has our own lovely 'Général Lamarque'.

Many fine climbing roses were introduced into New Zealand by its early settlers. We found many by the roadsides in the vicinity of derelict or burnt out homes; but, as we retrace our steps, we find that the need for wider roads and the activities of the bulldozer have rapidly eliminated many of these gay plants from our rural districts.

At Christmas I no more desire a rose
Than wish the snow in May's new-fangled mirth,
But like of each thing that in season grows.
                    SHAKESPEARE—*Love's Labour's Lost*

Pegged Down Roses

S. M. GAULT, M.B.E., V.M.H.

Pegging down of roses is frequently advocated as a means of inducing strong-growing cultivars to produce more flowers, and has indeed been carried out for many years, particularly in some of our public gardens. In the past many of the stronger growing hybrid perpetuals, such as 'Hugh Dickson' and 'Frau Karl Druschki', have had their exuberance curbed by this method, several breaks being induced along the pegged down stems, resulting in many flowers and a much improved garden display.

My first recollection of pegged down roses was in the 'twenties in a Scottish garden in the days before I had hit the high, or was it the low road south of the Tweed. So far as I can remember the sloping bank was ten to twelve feet wide, with roses planted at three feet intervals top and bottom. I remember the cultivars well, all of the R. wichuraiana type, the old favourite 'Dorothy Perkins' and its white sport, 'White Dorothy', 'Excelsa' and one which at that time I gave a higher rating called 'Minnehaha', mainly I think, because it had larger trusses of flowers. The young growths were trained and pegged up and down the bank so as to cover it and made a wonderful splash of colour. Alas, this has disappeared, as so many garden features have from various causes which are only too well known.

More up to date and certainly still to be seen is an adaptation of this system at the end of the lake in Queen Mary's Garden, Regent's Park. In this garden the young growths are pegged into the bank around the plants in such a way that they resemble loops which, when festooned with bloom, are most effective, especially so when reflected in the somewhat murky water of the lake. The murk, by the way, is the inevitable result caused by the activities of the attractive diving ducks, a source of additional interest to the many visitors. 'Lady Godiva' is another old cultivar still growing there.

Another example of this technique with this type of rose is to be seen in the walled garden at our Society headquarters at Bone Hill. This time the cultivars used are rather later in flowering, being the lovely scented 'Sanders' White' complemented by 'Crimson Shower', a seedling from 'Excelsa'. Both gave a tremendous display in 1969, not quite so good in 1970, the very dry weather for several weeks previously having a deleterious effect.

Visitors to the famous and magnificent Savill Garden in the Great Park, Windsor may have noticed 'Albertine' pegged down, covering quite a large space under a tree, a space without doubt difficult to fill because of the numerous roots, but by this adaptation covered ornamentally and effectively, particularly when this popular rose was in full bloom.

The Royal Botanic Gardens at Kew have for many years been a favourite haunt of mine; unfortunately I have never been able to visit these famous gardens as frequently as I would have wished. Among the most pleasing of my recollections were the large beds of pegged down roses in the rose garden there, in particular that sumptuous old rose 'Hugh Dickson' with its wonderful scent, the large flowered salmon-pink climbing rose 'Lady Waterlow' and the Pemberton musk 'Vanity'. Few roses continue to bloom so late as the latter and its somewhat thin, straggly habit can be overcome by this method. I have not been to Kew for a couple of seasons, and I am informed that the famous old bed of 'Mme Caroline Testout' has been removed, but I hope it has been found possible to retain some of the pegged down beds. The method employed was to tie the long growths down to wooden pegs some twelve inches or so above ground level.

The Royal Horticultural Society's Garden at Wisley provides two examples of pegging down modern cultivars in the rose borders leading up to the Bowes-Lyon Pavilion. Both are rumbustious growers, 'Chinatown' and 'Uncle Walter', and both flower freely when their exuberance has been curbed in this manner. Similar treatment has been meted out to 'Uncle Walter' in Queen Mary's Garden at a somewhat higher level, but at least it has proved effective.

Those who have not tried this method and have a suitable site such as a sloping bank, may like to try it out but may be worried about pruning. This need not cause any headache where *R. wichuraiana* types are used because generally enough growths are produced annually from the base of the plant to replace the old flowering growths, which can be removed when flowering has ceased. The young growths can then be pegged down in such a way as to cover the allotted space. Similarly, cultivars such as 'Uncle Walter' will produce sufficient young growths from near the base, or where the growths are bent over, to replace older wood which should be removed together with any weak growths. More care is required when tying down hybrid perpetual or hybrid tea roses, as the young growths are not so flexible as are the hybrids of *R. wichuraiana* in particular. I am sure if space were available some of the Kordesii would be very effective treated in this way, even as specimens on the lawn.

Some of the sprawlers also, such as *R.* × *paulii* and somewhat easier *R.* × *paulii rosea* could be restricted to an area by pegging down, but are not very easy to handle, their thorns being quite formidable. Much more prostrate, naturally, is *R. wichuraiana* itself, with its attractive glossy foliage and its white, single, very fragrant flowers produced generally in August. These trails may be pegged into position where desired and could be used to fill blanks in shrub borders.

A new cultivar from Japan called 'Nozomi', which has just received a Trial Ground Certificate in our trials, could also be treated in this way. In the Belfast trials I saw it growing most attractively as a pillar rose, producing a large crop of small, single pink flowers. Unfortunately it does not seem to repeat, but a combination of plants on short pillars with pegged down growth between and around would, I think, be worth trying, especially as the foliage is attractive. In our trials it was allowed to grow naturally and proved an interesting and decorative low growing rose with slightly arching growths some three feet in length.

Did I but have the magic touch
To describe thee, beauteous Rose
I could not praise thee overmuch
In verse or even prose.
For how in printed word portray
Leaves kissed by golden sun,
Or beauty massed in bright array
In truth words have I none.
I'll write of petals gold or red
Or pink with orange merging,
Or stout green stems that from the bed
Grow fast with sap upsurging.
But I cannot here in black and white
(Again in verse or prose)
Express my very soul's delight
In thee my lovely Rose.

G. J. BAILEY

'LAGOON' (floribunda)
'Lilac Charm' × 'Sterling Silver'
Raised by R. Harkness & Co. Ltd
TRIAL GROUND CERTIFICATE 1969

'ROAMING' (H.T.)
'*Vera Dalton*' × '*Super Star*'
Raised by John Sanday (Roses) Ltd
TRIAL GROUND CERTIFICATE 1970
See page 177

An Alternative to DDT

E. V. ELWES, F.R.I.C.

For the past ten years, an insecticide known as Carbaryl has been used in agriculture and horticulture in place of DDT which has the disadvantage of being very persistent, taking a very long time to decompose and disappear so that it can be passed on through natural food chains and can adversely affect beneficial insects and predators. Carbaryl has now been made available to the amateur gardener as a 5 per cent dust under the registered name of Sevin, marketed by The Murphy Chemical Co. Ltd., to whom I am indebted for much technical information. I am informed that Sevin rapidly breaks down in the soil, having an average half-life of 9 days compared with a half-life for DDT of 3 to 6 years. Sevin is also considerably less toxic to domestic and farm animals, birds and fish than is DDT.

During the summer of 1970 I made controlled comparative trials on roses between DDT and Sevin, using the former as a 5 per cent dust and leaving some trees untreated by any insecticide. Space does not permit detailed results to be given but in brief, no difference in insecticidal effect was found between the two compounds. The pests that were observed on the untreated bushes were leaf miners, leaf-rolling sawfly caterpillars, capsid bugs and an unusually heavy infestation of thrips on two separate occasions; earwigs were also often present in the opened blooms. Neither group of treated bushes was affected by any of these pests but aphides appeared on all of them. DDT is, of course, ineffective against aphides and Sevin behaved similarly. No damage to foliage dusted with Sevin was noticed.

It has been reported that the repeated use of DDT can increase the incidence of rose red spider mite and Sevin may have the same effect, but I was not able to confirm this as no red spider mites appeared on the rose trees used in the trial.

I understand, too, that commercial growers have used Sevin as a fruit-thinning spray when the set of apples has been high. This would indicate that hybridists should avoid the use of either DDT or Sevin after pollination as this might result in the loss of heps.

To summarise, it would seem that Sevin Dust is as effective as DDT for the control of the common rose pests and it has the added advantage of much lower toxicity and persistence.

Notes From My Files

E. F. ALLEN, M.A., Dip. Agric. (Cantab.), A.I.C.T.A.

(*Gardener, Naturalist, Agronomist and Fruit-Grower*)

Boron deficiency

In November, 1967, I had given a talk to the Enfield Rose Society and, towards the end of the question period, a member at the back of the hall asked me what was causing the abnormal tip growth on some of his roses, the terminal leaves being distorted, brittle, rough to the touch and with corky patches on some of the midribs. This puzzled me at the time but, turning the problem over in my mind during the journey home, it occurred to me that there was a strong possibility that the symptoms were those of boron deficiency. I therefore sent to the member concerned the advice that he should dress part of his rose beds with not more than $\frac{1}{2}$ oz per 10 sq. yd. of either borax or boracic acid. Since a slight excess can be harmful I advised that great care should be taken to ensure uniform distribution and that this would be facilitated by mixing the chemical beforehand with a small quantity of soil. The best time of application would be in the spring, when other fertilizers were given.

At the following Summer Rose Show the member told me that my diagnosis had been correct and that the treated roses had recovered. Apparently his soil was a very sandy one which he manured with Hoof and Horn meal at pruning and with Tonk's in May and June. He had not limed it recently. I then suggested that he would be well advised to use each year a proprietary fertilizer which contains a trace of boron, PBI's Toprose Fertilizer being one that does.

It is never easy to prove the existence of a boron deficiency and, previous to this, I had been able to do so on only one occasion, that being when such a deficiency appeared in a mild form in some of my pot roses which I force for the Spring Show. These had not been repotted for about five years and I had relied on an annual application of 1 or 2 oz per pot of dried seaweed meal as a source of trace elements. However, this material contains only about one part per million of boron and this had evidently been insufficient to prevent a deficiency from building up. It showed up by puckering of the leaflets and an application of one gram (about $\frac{1}{28}$ oz) of boracic acid per pot cleared up the symptoms within one year. One very interesting feature about this occurrence was that I then had three large pots of 'Silver Lining', all of the same age and all of which had been treated identically. However, the boron deficiency symptoms were much more severe on the one plant which had been budded on to R. *rugosa* rootstock than on the other two plants on R. *multiflora* stock.

The simplest way to prevent a trace element deficiency in the garden is to give the rose beds a mulch of old cattle manure in the spring. However, this practice is less suited to pot cultivation because of the introduction of weed seeds.

Foliar Sprays

One rosarian, who likes to make up his own foliar feed, has had extreme difficulty in obtaining potassium acid phosphate. He had approached numerous chemists, both large and small concerns, but none could supply him.

There are a number of different potassium phosphates but none is normally used as a fertilizer. They can be obtained from specialist medical or laboratory suppliers and are pure chemicals which are hence very expensive. For this reason I do not consider them to be suitable for use as fertilizers. However, it is always possible to buy fertilizer grades of urea, potassium nitrate and ammonium phosphate. The last is a crude form of mono-ammonium phosphate and usually contains about 11 and 48 per cent of N and P_2O_5 as compared with 12 and 60 per cent for the pure chemical. The fertilizer grade of potassium nitrate usually contains about 13 per cent N and 44 per cent potash.

All these three chemicals are readily soluble in water and compatible. By varying the content of each one can make up an excellent liquid fertilizer with a wide range of nutrient content. A little seaweed liquid can be added to colour the solution. Unfortunately magnesium sulphate cannot be added as it precipitates out the phosphate. One answer is to make up two solutions, one NPK and the other NKMg.

Pea Gall on Rose Rootstocks

In August 1969, I was interested to receive from Mr W. D. Gobbee, who is a keen amateur rose breeder, a piece of 'Laxa' rootstock with what looked like several green peas attached to the foliage. These had been made by the small gall-wasp, *Rhodites eglanteriae* which, as the specific name suggests, is most often found on the Sweet Briar. I have never seen it on hybrid roses. It is quite unnecessary to spray against it since virtually no damage is caused to the host. Very little seems to be known about the insect's life history.

The natural history of these gall wasps is often very complicated and interesting. Thus the common Bedeguar Gall, or Robin's Pin Cushion, caused by the related *Rhodites rosae*, may harbour as many as seven different insects, only one being the gall-causer, the others being three parasites, one predator, one guest or lodger (inquiline) and one hyperparasite. Details of this astonishing relationship are given by A. D. Imms in his *Insect Natural History* (New Naturalist series), p. 175–176. In the same book there is also a good illustration of the Pea Gall, opposite p. 202, but no other details.

Silver Grey Stem Blotch

One member from Victoria, British Columbia, has written to me to enquire what causes the irregular silver-grey stem blotches on the canes of the cultivar 'Prima Ballerina' and, to a lesser degree, of 'Little Darling' and 'Sabine'.

These grey blotches on the maturing stems of 'Prima Ballerina' in my own garden are much more conspicuous when the bed is viewed from the southwest than from the north-east. Since there is a tall hedge on the north east side this suggests that this discoloration, which is associated with vertical cracking of the bark, may be caused by a mild form of sun scorch. As against this hypothesis I know that this cultivar does well both in India and in Sabah, so it must be quite well adapted to growth in hot countries. A somewhat cursory examination under the microscope has not shown the presence of any pathogen so the verdict at present must be that it is a physiological response to some undetermined condition of growth. Since the condition appears not to be harmful I do not think that research to find out more about its cause would be justified.

Ultra Hardy Cultivars in Finland

Rosarians from Finland, Canada, Russia and northern United States can teach us a great deal about winter hardiness so I am always pleased to receive a letter from Mr G. W. Hackman, who gardens east of Helsingfors, close to the town of Borgå. Apparently hybrid teas do not thrive but the hybrid perpetuals 'Mrs John Laing' and 'Ulrich Brunner Fils' do well. 'Betty Uprichard' and 'Mme. Caroline Testout' are equally hardy but do not flower well. Some of the single or semi-double-flowered floribundas which are successful are 'Betty Prior', 'Frensham', 'Jiminy Cricket', 'Rudolf Timm', 'Käthe Duvigneau', 'Sarabande', 'Buismann's Triumph' and 'Queen Elizabeth'. The shrub 'Sparrieshoop' does well but grows no taller than an average floribunda. Of the climbers 'Hamburger Phoenix', 'Leverkusen' and 'Clair Matin' have done well—also the non-recurrent 'Flammentanz'.

In the UK winter hardiness cannot be equated with resistance to late spring frosts. In our garden we have a bush of 'Yellow Curls', one of Dr W. D. Brownell's so-called sub-zero cultivars from Canada. However, experience has shown that it is just as susceptible to damage from May frosts as perhaps 90 per cent of the other cultivars in general cultivation. 'Golden Wings' is probably the hardiest rose in our garden: even in the 1962–63 winter, when the ground temperature fell to −1° F., this cultivar suffered no die back.

Black Spot and Tar Spot

In the autumn of a bad year for disease Mr L. G. Turner was asked if there was any relationship between Black Spot of roses and the similar leaf spot to be seen in wet autumns on the Sycamore and other Maples.

Tar Spot of Maples is caused by the fungus *Rhytisma acerinum*. It does little harm to the trees and has no relation to Black Spot of the rose.

Growing Roses by the Sea

JOHN R. WINSHIP
(Amateur rose grower)

The rose gardens of the convalescent home of which I am the Superintendent, overlook the sea on the north Yorkshire coast, the lower garden being a few feet only above sea level and within a stone's throw of the sea itself. The top garden is a further 150 ft. higher up the cliff face and is of the sunken variety; it is sheltered from the prevailing north-east wind by an adjacent border of large old trees, which unfortunately also shelter it from the sunshine and, in addition, their roots steal most of the food from the nearby rose bushes.

We are fortunate to have a very experienced head gardener and over the past seven years he and I have re-planned the 16 beds of hybrid tea and 6 beds of floribunda roses in this garden, throwing out most of the older varieties and bringing in newer and more vigorous ones and, at long last, we seem to have a rose-garden which pleases all who see it, except we two that is. The queen of the hybrid teas, despite being in the worst situated bed of all, is 'Wendy Cussons' (a great garden rose in our opinion); whilst of the floribundas 'Anna Wheatcroft' consistently stands out year after year.

The lower garden is entirely devoted to floribundas, and a large circular bed of 'Iceberg' is flanked by half a dozen rectangular beds, of which 'Orange-ade' and 'Circus' are the most admired every year.

We are all in favour of autumn pruning, for various reasons including: (a) to minimise damage by the gale-force easterly winds which abound on this coast during winter; (b) because it suits the head gardener's work plan to get pruning over before the spring; (c) being so near the salty air we are not very much troubled by frost and thus our newly-pruned bushes do not suffer much from dieback; (d) by pruning early we are thus able to make good use of the prunings by turning them into cuttings.

During the past three years we have produced hundreds of new rose bushes by this method and warmly recommend it to anyone wishing to increase their stock of existing varieties at little or no cost. Last November we took 400 cuttings and, as I write in August, over 75 per cent of them appear to have taken and will soon be ready for planting out in a large new bed which is being prepared for them. Our method is simply to make a hole with a dibber, half fill the hole with sharp sea sand, dip the end of the cutting in rooting powder and plant it in the usual manner. There the cutting stays until twelve months later, with no further attention except for an occasional watering during any very dry spells during the summer. Although we usually concentrate on floribunda cuttings, with 'Masquerade' and 'Anna Wheatcroft' being our most successful, with almost a hundred per cent "take", we have had very good results from the more vigorous hybrid teas. In fact this year (1969) we have experienced a 75 per cent success with a bundle of cuttings from 'Wendy Cussons' and 'Rose Gaujard' which had been heeled-in from November to April before we were able to plant them, because of the shocking weather.

Two years ago I planted a few bushes in a cold greenhouse, some in pots and some in the greenhouse soil, and when they began flowering during June I tried my hand at hybridising. After much trial and error I now have a few seedlings under observation and a nice crop of ripening heps, which would have been bigger but for that scourge of breeders, botrytis. The disease has not affected the pot-grown heps nearly as much as those on the bushes planted in the greenhouse soil. I feel there is a lesson to be learned from this. Perhaps someone of the calibre and experience of Mr J. Harkness could draw a conclusion from it.

Whilst on the subject of disease, I might mention here that we never see Black Spot in our rose gardens and very little Mildew, and then only on those two arch-villains 'Frau Karl Druschki' and 'Frensham'.

Yet another compensation, perhaps, for growing roses by the sea.

The Provincial Display Gardens

S. M. GAULT

Judging at flower shows has been for several years one of my "extra-mural", or should I say "extra-parochial" occupations, which has brought additional pleasure to me since in some instances I can combine this activity with that of visiting our Provincial Display Gardens. This year I started in the first week of June with the Bath and West and Southern Counties Show at Shepton Mallet, followed by a visit to Vivary Park, Taunton, in the same county. It was too early to see hybrid teas or floribundas in full bloom—indeed the only award winner showing flowers was the lovely blood red, single-flowered 'Altissimo'—but not too early to see the remarkable growth made by most of the award winning cultivars there.

The next opportunity arose in conjunction with Leeds Flower Show, where, of course, we also have our Northern Rose Show. Few will want reminding of the disastrous weather of the first day of this event. However, the following day proved more reasonable so in the company of our Secretary, Mr Turner, I went to Harlow Car. In spite of gale force wind and torrential rain the previous day, the roses contrived to make a brave show, although some cultivars were not so impressive when a close scrutiny was made. Having missed Geoffrey Smith, the Superintendent of Harlow Car Gardens on my visit last year, it was a great pleasure to meet him on this occasion, even without his white Alsatian. Naturally, the merits and demerits of the new roses were a subject of discussion; indeed, inspection and discussion went to some length and as a result I fear Mr Smith had a very cold lunch awaiting him.

A month later the next chance was provided by Southport and its famous Flower Show. After the early morning activities had been resolved, Mr Roscoe took Mr Turner and me by car to the Botanic Gardens. Mr Gibson, who continues to have a great interest in this garden, did not accompany us this time, feeling it was better to take things more quietly after his recent illness. Weather was considerably improved, and the roses with one exception were giving a fine display and obviously providing interest and pleasure for many visitors. The exception referred to was 'Herself', the sole victim of Black Spot in this garden, an attack so obvious that we felt instant removal was called for and this was carried out by a member of Mr Patrick's staff in exemplary fashion. Mr Patrick himself was, of course, too busy with his manifold duties to come with us on the visit, but found time for a short discussion on the subject. We are grateful for his continued interest.

The following week found me in Bristol and its fine Flower Show on the Downs and from there, my duties completed, I headed west via the Severn Bridge, the prospective port of call being Roath Park, Cardiff. On arrival I met Mr Nelmes who has succeeded his father (formerly a member of Council) as Director of Parks, and Mr Rees who was associated with the late Mr Whitney in the supervision and maintenance of the rose garden. I found these gentlemen somewhat perturbed because, in spite of a well conducted spraying programme and a very successful early display of roses, an attack of Black Spot had presented them with a problem, especially as Rust was also appearing on some cultivars. This disease was not, of course, confined to the new roses, but also prevailed in the rose garden itself with, in some cases, fairly disastrous consequences. I hope it may be found possible to suggest alternative alleviatory measures which may provide greater control.

Having come to the end of combined activities I proceeded north to Edinburgh to inspect the roses at Saughton Park, Edinburgh. Mr Strachan, Director of Parks was away, but I hoped to meet the Deputy Director Mr MacBean, particularly as I had known his father for many years. Unfortunately, through an urgent engagement, he was detained and I learned by telephone he had come through one gate as I had left by another! However, Mr Paterson and two enthusiastic members of his staff conducted me round our display garden and also the main rose garden in the Park. Here I was delighted to see 'Shot Silk' looking as I knew it in its heyday, but, alas, it has lost this vigour farther south. I have never seen 'Dearest' better anywhere in spite of rain; it is a lovely rose when in such good condition. The weather was far from kind, and I found writing notes under a wind tossed umbrella, accompanied by a steady downpour of rain not an altogether pleasing activity, but at least it made me realise why in this display garden it had been found necessary to plant 'Fred Loads' and other shrub roses in a more sheltered position than that provided by the display garden. This was a practice I didn't favour until I fully understood why it was necessary in this situation; a gale rocked shrub is unlikely to have much garden value. For this reason also tall growers such as 'Santa Fé', 'Caramba' and 'Ville de Zurich' seem unlikely to be good garden roses under such conditions.

From Edinburgh by motor-way to Glasgow, there is little inclination to dally en route, as there is more beauty elsewhere in Scotland. In Glasgow I met Mr Oldham, the very active Director of Parks, and also member of Council Dr Dick, both of whom are intensely interested in the display garden which is being constructed in the grounds of Pollok House. Their interest augurs well for the success of this project and will provide a good comparison of cultivar behaviour with the garden in Edinburgh.

Coming back south a stop was made at Harrogate and a second visit to Harlow Car followed, this time after breakfast on the Sunday morning. A number of visitors were enjoying the roses which were looking well in spite of a gale the previous day which had wrenched out strong young basal growths from the base of some of the plants. 'City of Belfast' was looking impressive and fully justifying its high award in 1967 and 'Merlin' also was growing well and flowering profusely.

As in 1969 the weather in late September was the English climate at its best, so the first day of October found me making my way by cross country routes to Taunton to finish up my visits where they had commenced some months previously. By this time the remarkable growth referred to on my previous visit had become something of a problem in some cases. 'Fred Loads', for instance, was so exuberant, as indeed it was in 1969, that 'City of Belfast' planted alongside was to some extent overwhelmed, so that this fine bedding rose suffered somewhat in comparison with other gardens. I met Mr Wyatt, Deputy Surveyor, Mr Taylor, Superintendent of Parks and his deputy Mr Verrier, also the head gardener who takes a keen interest in these new roses and keeps a comprehensive record of their performance. The Borough Surveyor, Mr Tyzack, was otherwise engaged, but I am grateful to him for allowing me to have a very full discussion with his staff, in which it was agreed to give additional room between rows in future plantings to allow cultivars to be more easily distinguished and also help to lessen the spread of Black Spot late in the season, a problem in this area. 'Pharaoh' in particular had suffered badly.

To all those already mentioned my thanks are due for all their help; also to Messrs. Fairbrother, Shotter and Raban for their assistance in sending on reports and other useful information concerning the roses at these display gardens.

(See details overleaf)

AWARDS 1967	Southport	Taunton	Cardiff	Harlow Car	Edinburgh
Gold Medal					
'City of Belfast'	1	2	2	1	1
'Fred Loads'	1	1	2	1	1
Certificate of Merit					
'Bantry Bay'	2	1	1	2	1 SBS
'Escapade'	1	1	2 BS	1	1
'Irish Mist'	1	1 BS	3 BS	1	3
'Peer Gynt'	1	2 M	2 BS M	1	1
'Santa Fé'	1	3	2		1 very tall
Tril Ground Certificate					
'Brasilia'	1	1	1	1	1
'Cappa Magna'	2 (1969)	1 SM	2	2	2
'Caramba'	2	2	2	1	1 very tall
'Elida'	2	2 BS M	3 BS M	2	2
'Gallant'	2	2	2	3	1
'Merlin'	1	2	1	1	1
'Moonraker'	2	2 BS	3 BS	1	1 SBS
'Orange Silk'	2	2 BS	3 BS	2	1
'Pharaoh'	2 (1968)	3 BS M	3 M	2	2
'Princess Paola'	2	3	2 BS	3	2
'Silva'	1	3 BS	2 BS	2	2
'Vesper'		2 fades	3 fades	3	
'Ville de Zurich'	3	2 M	3 BS M	3	2 very tall

1	Very good	SBS	Slight Black Spot
2	Good	BS	Black Spot
3	Fair	SM	Slight Mildew
		M	Mildew

Dates 1968, 1969 = year planted.

May'st thou long, sweet crimson gem,
Richly deck thy native stem;
Till some evening, sober, calm,
Dropping dews, and breathing balm,
While all around the woodland rings,
And every bird thy requiem sings;
Thou amid the dirgeful sound,
Shed thy dying honours round,
And resign to Parent Earth,
The loveliest form she e'er gave birth.

ROBERT BURNS

The Decorative Classes

JULIA CLEMENTS
(International judge, lecturer and author)

Surely there is no sight more magnificent than that provided by the Royal National Rose Society's Summer Show at Alexandra Palace. I believe that I actually did see more potential prizewinners in the Alexandra Trophy Table Arrangements class this year than I have ever seen before. They were all so well staged, with cleverly coloured cloths and accessories to interpret the title "A Buffet Arrangement for a Special Occasion".

Mrs E. Woodcock, of Westcliff, won the coveted Queen Alexandra Memorial Trophy with her table decoration entitled "Teen-age Birthday Party". It was outstanding. The tablecloth was a bright candy pink colour, with accessories of mauve glass. The tall, modern triangular arrangement was composed of orange, mauve and cerise-coloured roses, with black grapes and *Rosa rubrifolia* foliage. Fruit glasses were filled with bright 'Super Star' roses, with plums and purple grapes cascading over the edges. A modern multi-coloured birthday card completed the scheme.

She also took a first with "Pair of Arrangements suitable for a Church", making two asymmetrical arrangements of roses in gold and white, using 'Spek's Yellow' with 'Pascali' and 'Iceberg' roses, with golden privet and Aucuba leaves. These designs were staged in brass vases on a raised platform against a pale gold lamé background.

Class 94 was an innovation. Exhibitors were asked to make an arrangement of any roses, with any rose foliage, to illustrate the name of the variety used. Accessories were allowed. When you think of the hundreds of ingeniously named roses, the scope was vast, and I hope this class is repeated. Mrs Wells, of Dover, took first prize here with "Masquerade". She grouped 'Masquerade' roses around two tall red and yellow black spashed candles, making an asymmetrical line into which was tucked a tortoiseshell fan. Accessories were two black masked ball eye masks on gold sticks, one of which was placed in the arrangement, the other low in the foreground. All this on a yellow satin backdrape.

The men are not being left out of the artistic classes, and certainly this year's first prize in the Men Only Class was very worthily won by W. Field, of Camberley, Surrey, whose exhibit in the novices class last year I wrongly attributed to his wife. This time he made a lovely loose triangular arrangement in a copper coloured container using 'Super Star' roses with pale green poppy seed heads, green *Iris siberica* seed heads, variegated Vinca and blue-green Cupressus. Obviously a keen gardener and a colourist, for all were staged on a moss green velvet base. I am sure he will go far.

Mrs M. Brooker, of Swindon in Wiltshire, is another talented rose arranger, and this time she took a number of prizes among which was her first for an arrangement of roses displayed on a natural base, i.e. wood, slate, stone, wicker, etc. Using a wicker base standing on a soft grey-green back drape, she gained height with sprays of the ornamental thornbush, and grouped the 'Super Star' roses in a slanting design with other rose species and large tomato red heps of the Rugosas. The play on the different textures was noticeable to complement the coarseness of the wicker.

She also did well with her frontal arrangement of roses with any rose foliage, by making an asymmetrical arrangement of 'Orangeade', 'Orange Sensation' and 'Elizabeth of Glamis' roses in a bronze figurine container, which stood against an olive green velvet drape with an apricot nylon stream running through it.

The Autumn Show

I was refreshed at the sight of the talented exhibits at the Autumn Show for I could detect a certain freedom of expression that was not visible at the Summer Show. Perhaps the experience of the season had made the entrants more carefree.

Mrs K. Wells, of Dover, excelled herself in the Harvest Supper Class, using a tall bronze figurine with outstretched hand filled with a group of roses, fruit and leaves, the statue itself standing on a base, being surrounded at the right with roses, peony leaves, blackberries, and dock and wheat, completed with fruit and leaves low down on the base, with a separate grouping of bread and cheese and glasses by a beer mug filled with wild clematis seed heads to simulate froth.

Apart from other prize winning exhibits, Mrs Wells came second with her interpretation of "Fire" in Class 58. She used swerved dry burnt blackened branches with red and flame coloured roses ('Paul Crampel', 'Super Star' and 'Baccara') arranged low on bark with red shot back drapes, and two straw miniature brushes as accessories. It was the best interpretative piece in the show.

I discovered Mrs Wells had entered every class, also that she travelled up from Dover the night before the show, and after setting up her backgrounds and mechanics, she dozed in the Hall, then started to arrange at 2 a.m. and finished all her eight entries by 10 a.m. the next morning, in time for judging.

Mrs D. Scanlon, of Guildford, took first prize in the "Fire" class with a beautiful low triangular arrangement of 'Baccara' roses, reddish Croton and Dracaena leaves in a shallow pewter tray, with shot silk back drape. It was almost too formal to represent an interpretation of "Fire", for in interpretative work it is the *meaning* of the title which should speak to the judges, and not only the perfection of the arrangement. In such classes the arranger can break away from formality and allow flair and imagination to enter.

However, I thought Mrs Scanlon's design of seven yellow roses in Class 53 was superbly staged in a white and gold vase on a gold velvet base, against an acid green background. It took a second. I had picked it as first. In this class I noticed that some competitors needed to use a bigger drape (if they want to use one at all) and they must ensure that the material has no crease. If the drape is rolled round newspaper or corrugated cardboard, creasing during travel can be avoided.

Mrs W. Crabb is another keen exhibitor. Entering every class she was up at 4 a.m. on the day of the show, and worked right through to judging time. She was rewarded with many prizes. I liked her seven 'Super Star' roses in Class 53 for five or seven roses, and her first prize-winning pedestal was outstanding. In this she used 'Pink Sensation' roses with variegated Weigelia sprays, with berries tucked in the centre. Many pedestal arrangers are today adopting a style allowing the lower flowers to point downwards unnaturally, but Mrs Crabb did not fall into this trap. A pedestal arrangement should flow loosely outwards and forwards.

Mrs W. Porteous, of London S.E.22, composes well. She used 'Diorama' roses, the flame peach 'Bettina' and coppery-orange 'Vienna Charm' roses grouped around a bottle of cider. In this composition to represent "Harvest Supper", she also included a cane cornucopia full of fruit and vegetables, corn on the cob and purple aubergines, together with a low side placement of bread and cheese and cider. Colouring and idea were good, but the space needed to be more filled. Exhibitors should not forget that the space given in the schedule represents the frame and the contents displayed should at least two-thirds fill the frame.

A newcomer to the show, Mrs L. Sturdy, of Luton, made an excellent arrangement in the "Fire" Class, abiding strictly by the rules of the schedule which stated that accessories, driftwood and dried material would be allowed only when specifically stated. Many used these items even though it was not stated that they could be used. However, Mrs Sturdy, living up to her name, was not deterred by not winning this time, and I am sure we shall see a lot of her work in the future. Some who had used driftwood explained that the wood was fixed to the container and was therefore part of the container. This is an arguable point, but the regulations as printed in the Schedule should be watched by competitors and judges alike.

I would have liked to see more entries in the Novices Class, for there must be many dying to have a go. Nevertheless, the entries were good, Mrs Scanlon taking first prize with a well staged arrangement of 'Pink Sensation' roses in a pewter figurine vase placed on two covered and braided cake boards; and I liked Miss A. Mascall's second prize arrangement very much. She also used 'Pink Sensation' roses in a green ormolu vase placed on a green velvet base. It was delicate and free-flowing.

I noticed on a number of occasions that the wooden base or slab was too narrow or small for the arrangement placed on it. If unable to obtain a larger base (this gives better balance), I would suggest using two placed slightly crosswise, or even bring a tray into operation. Another point which should be watched by all exhibitors at this important show is the use of Oasis. A piece large enough to contain sufficient water for the roses should always be employed and space somewhere should be left for topping up. If Oasis is placed in or on top of a bottle, it should be made sure the bottle is filled with water, otherwise the Oasis will dry out. Nothing is more disappointing to second day visitors to the show, than to see a first prize arrangement drooping through lack of water.

Certainly the Autumn Show with its class for Foliage and Heps is always a delight, and the decorative classes seem to draw more comments from visitors each year. As I stood taking my notes one well-known rosarian said to me, "What do you think of it?" "Wonderful," I answered, "there is a lot of talent here." He then went on to say he wasn't quite sure where it was going, for he'd recently seen an arrangement which featured a tall branch and three roses. "That's not flower arrangement," he added. "Why not?" I said, and suggested we must look at, and give room to all styles, just as in other creative arts, such as painting or the dance. If you like landscape painting, you cannot say modern art is not painting; just as if you enjoy the Waltz, you cannot say that Tap dancing or Ballet is not dancing. They are all different expressions of the particular art. And so it is with flower arranging.

The Summer Show

J. P. WOOD, N.D.H.

Despite a cold and miserable spring, which contrasted with very high temperatures in June, the Summer Show at Alexandra Palace on July 1 and 2 was a great success. The nurserymen's stands in the Great Hall created a wonderful spectacle and there were many outstanding amateur exhibits in the adjacent Palm Court.

There seems to be a trend among the nurserymen to allow visitors a closer look at the roses they are showing. Cant's, for instance, had an island centrepiece of roses, around which one could walk, and two separate groups at either end of blooms in bowls at varying heights stood on the floor of the hall. They received a Large Gold Medal. I liked the look of several of their new varieties, including 'Solitaire', a new pink floribunda; 'Naughty Nancy', another floribunda having single blooms in a cheerful shade of coral and orange; and 'Red Dragon', a deep crimson floribunda. They also showed 'Alec's Red', a crimson hybrid tea that was prominent throughout the show.

Samuel McGredy & Son Ltd. also allowed visitors to walk among their roses. These were arranged around the centres of what looked like huge white trumpets stood on end. The staging certainly allowed one to take a close look at the roses, but the white "trumpets" were rather overpowering. There were many new roses here, including 'National Trust', a fine red hybrid tea; 'Kathleen Joyce', a pink floribunda; 'Satchmo', a bright red floribunda; and 'Irish Rover', a salmon pink hybrid tea. A Silver Medal was awarded.

John Mattock Ltd. repeated their success of 1969 and took both the Championship Trophy and the Queen Mary Trophy, as well as a Large Gold Medal for a magnificent exhibit along a large section of wall. Here could be found the latest hybrid teas and floribundas rubbing shoulders with old-fashioned and shrub roses—types of every shape and form. It was an exhibit from which one could learn a great deal about garden-worthy roses.

Bees Ltd. staged their roses in large bowls and tall pillars against backgrounds of white trellis and brickwork. It was certainly one of the most spectacular exhibits in the show and took the Coronation Trophy and a Large Gold Medal for the best island exhibit. Among the varieties here were 'Grandpa Dickson', 'Zambra', 'Wendy Cussons', 'Milord' and 'Cologne Carnival'.

C. Gregory & Son Ltd. put up an exhibit which was almost a show in itself and it won a well-deserved Large Gold Medal. The roses were effectively displayed in large bowls at different levels against black metal screens, and included golden yellow and apricot 'Whisky Mac', one of the most prominent varieties in the show, 'Manuela', a new deep pink hybrid tea, 'Red Planet', a dark red hybrid tea but showing signs of weather damage, 'Alec's Red' and 'Ice White'.

The quality of the blooms in Harkness's wall exhibit was superb and a Large Gold Medal was given. Here the blooms were staged in traditional fashion against a black background. Some of the newer floribundas displayed included 'Moonraker', 'Arakan', 'Fairy Dancers' and the very popular hybrid tea 'Alec's Red'.

The China Trophy, for the best island exhibit not exceeding 200 sq. ft., and a Gold Medal, went once again to Warley Rose Gardens Ltd. On a pale blue base bowls of blooms were staged on white pedestals. 'Whisky Mac' was looking good and so were 'Princess Michiko', 'Red Devil', 'Pharaoh' and 'Manuela' among many fine blooms.

Gold Medals were awarded to both Waterer's and Dickson's of Hawlmark. On a black and white tile base Waterer's showed their blooms in large copper bowls and included many popular varieties—'Grandpa Dickson', 'Red Devil', 'Arthur Bell' and the floribunda 'Red Gold' were well shown. Dickson's used a light-coloured imitation wood base for their stand and the blooms were displayed on white shelving fixed to black uprights. Once again 'Whisky Mac' was good and I was also impressed with 'Mr Chips', an orange-flowered hybrid tea bicolour; 'Illumination', a yellow floribunda and 'Heartbeat', a salmon-orange floribunda.

The Norman Rogers Cup for the best exhibit not exceeding 100 sq. ft. against a background, and a Gold Medal, went to F. Carter & Sons. Among their varieties were 'Alec's Red', 'King's Ransom', 'Grandpa Dickson' and 'Whisky Mac', shown in black containers against a black background. In contrast the Gold Medal group of Blaby Rose Gardens consisted of wrought iron white stands and hanging baskets set against screens of lap fencing on a grey and white base. Among their varieties were 'Summer Holiday', 'Pink Peace', 'Gigi' and 'Alison Wheatcroft'.

The blooms of Wheatcroft Roses Ltd. were also effectively shown in black bowls, each standing on three slender legs. The base was black and white and the centrepiece consisted of a display of 'Queen Elizabeth' on a white pillar. 'Whisky Mac' was prominent, as well as 'Miss Harp', a deep gold hybrid tea. A Silver Gilt Medal was awarded.

First Prize entries at the 1970 Autumn Show –
Above: Class 8. A box of 12 specimen blooms, distinct
Below: Class 12. Bowl of H.T. roses, not more than 18 stems,
6 or more varieties

'LORNA DOONE' (floribunda)
'Red Dandy' × *'Lilli Marlene'*
Raised by R. Harkness & Co. Ltd
TRIAL GROUND CERTIFICATE 1969

Fryer's, who were also awarded a Silver Gilt Medal, made use of light stained wooden uprights for the staging of their roses, together with white slatted tables on a blue tiled base. Popular varieties here included 'Princess Michiko', 'Alec's Red', 'Red Gold', 'Duke of Windsor' and 'Diorama'.

The William E. Harkness Memorial Trophy for a bowl of roses was won by Mark Court Nurseries, who also took the box classes for the John Hart Memorial Cup (48 blooms) and the Kilbee Stuart Memorial Cup (24 blooms). They finally added to their successes the A. C. Turner Challenge Cup for 15 distinct varieties in vases.

Amateurs

The amateur section of the show was arranged as usual in the Palm Court and generally the quality of blooms was superb. One of the highlights for me was the six vases shown by Mrs F. A. Pugh in Class 36 and which took the H. R. Darlington Memorial Cup. 'Red Devil', 'Grandpa Dickson', 'Bonsoir', 'Perfecta', 'Pink Favourite' and 'Fred Gibson' were the varieties she used. They were all superb blooms and I noticed that Mrs Pugh also had a wonderful bowl of 'Fred Gibson' which came first in Class 27.

Another delight of the show was the vase of six blooms shown by T. J. Vale in Class 58 which took the Cocker Cup. His variety was 'Red Devil' and they were some of the best of this variety I have seen.

An outstanding box in Class 26 took the Lindsell Cup for F. E. Owen. It is not an easy class—24 specimen blooms are required—but Mr Owen had superbly matched blooms. He used most of the best show varieties which included 'Charlie's Aunt', 'Grandpa Dickson', 'Fragrant Cloud', 'Silver Lining', 'Shannon', 'Norman Hartnell', 'Ann Letts', 'Dorothy Peach', 'Brilliant', 'Stella', 'Super Star', 'Royal Highness', 'Kronenbourg', 'Akebono', 'Princess', 'Red Devil', 'Isabel de Ortiz', 'Memoriam', 'Red Lion', 'Gavotte', 'Peace', 'Peaceful', 'Montezuma' and 'Perfecta'.

Mr Owen also scored a success in Class 31 for a box of six specimen blooms which took the Brayfort Challenge Cup. He had a really thrilling bloom of 'Perfecta' as well as 'Princess', 'Stella', 'Royal Highness', 'Dorothy Peach' and an excellent bloom of 'Norman Hartnell'.

Another fine box which could hardly be faulted was shown by L. E. J. Wood in Class 30. Among his superb blooms were 'Pink Favourite', 'Gail Borden', 'Femina', 'Show Girl', 'Chicago Peace', 'Peace' (a little on the small side), 'Fred Gibson', 'Bonsoir', 'Brilliant', 'Montezuma', 'Kronenbourg' and 'Red Devil'. This fine box took the Nicholson Challenge Cup.

Dr T. M. Cullingworth was successful in two important classes. His box of 12 specimen blooms in Class 16 won the Edward Mawley Challenge Cup and he had exceptionally good blooms of 'Perfecta' and 'Karl Herbst', as well as 'Ernest H. Morse', 'Rose Gaujard', 'Stella', 'Isabel de Ortiz', 'Brilliant', 'Pink Favourite', 'Montezuma', 'Memoriam', 'Dorothy Peach' and 'Christian Dior'. He also won the S. W. Burgess Memorial Cup in Class 22 for six vases of hybrid teas which included 'Super Star', 'Wendy Cussons', 'Perfecta', 'Rose Gaujard', 'Stella' and 'Montezuma'. All the blooms were excellent and evenly matched.

F. Wiltshire is usually a prominent name among the prize-winners. This year he came second in the difficult box class for the Lindsell Cup, which I have already discussed, but he also won Class 23 for a R.N.R.S. Trophy. Three vases of floribundas in separate varieties are required. The three he chose were 'Europeana', 'Iceberg' and 'Fireworks'—all nice, clean blooms and well matched.

It is not uncommon for Capt. C. A. E. Stanfield R.N. to put up a good bowl of roses. He did so again in Class 35 and took the Alfred Hewlett Memorial Class with superb blooms of 'Red Devil', 'Anne Letts', 'Silver Lining', 'Peer Gynt', 'Princess', 'Bonsoir' and 'Isabel de Ortiz'. He also won the Rev. H. Honywood D'Ombrain Memorial Cup for the best bowl of floribunda roses in Classes 25, 39 and 46.

Division C is restricted to amateurs who do not grow more than 500 rose trees, and H. W. Palmer took the Sam McGredy Challenge Cup in Class 40 for a box of 12 specimen blooms. The blooms were superb and 'Gavotte', 'Golden Giant' and 'Montezuma' were particularly good. In the same division D. M. Scott took the Edward J. Holland Memorial Cup with three vases of hybrid teas which, although good, were showing signs of weather damage. The three varieties were 'Isabel de Ortiz', 'Gavotte' and 'Red Devil'. He also had the highest number of aggregate points in this division and was awarded the Edward Mawley Memorial Medal.

R. West took the Gilbert Burch Memorial Class in Division D, where exhibitors must not have more than 250 rose trees. His box of six blooms comprised 'Honey Favourite', 'Margaret', 'Grandpa Dickson', 'Red Devil', 'Fred Gibson' and 'Pink Favourite'. The blooms were well matched but on the small side.

'Pink Favourite' was the best variety shown by Mrs M. Short in Class 53 for the Slaughter Memorial Cup. Her other two varieties in this three vase class included 'Red Devil' and 'Honey Favourite'. The Charles Rigg Cup for a box of six specimen blooms was won by D. M. Cowderoy with 'Peer Gynt' (2), rather small blooms, 'Perfecta', 'Stella' and 'Show Girl' (2). B.

Cover won the Kathleen Louise Mahaffy Class for a box of six blooms. They were all pinkish blooms—'Anne Letts' (2), 'Perfecta', 'Winston Churchill', 'Silver Lining'—except for the pale-yellow and pink 'My Choice', which looked a little out of place.

The blooms in the vase shown by Miss E. Metherell were rather small but all the same they took the Albert E. Griffith Memorial Class. This is in Division G, for amateurs who grow no more than 50 rose trees. The Worcester Park Horticultural Society were the worthy winners of the Hereford Centenary Cup in the Affiliated Societies section. This was their third win in a row and their bowls and baskets of hybrid teas and floribundas were superbly staged against black and green drapes. Although the colour blending of the blooms was most pleasing, the shade of the green drape, to my eye, was discordant.

Finally, two really wonderful bowls of hybrid teas and floribundas were shown by the Birchington Horticultural Society. They won the Franklin Dennison Memorial Cup in Class 91. Their floribundas included 'Hobby', 'Europeana', 'Banbridge'. 'Iceberg' and 'Ohlala'. The hybrid teas they used were 'Honey Favourite', 'Princess', 'Silver Lining', 'Perfecta', 'Isabel de Ortiz', 'Pink Favourite', 'Red Devil', 'Wendy Cussons' and 'Anne Letts'.

The Best Bloom in the Show award went to 'Fragrant Cloud', which was shown by R. P. Bathe in a vase of three blooms in Class 77.

Members are invited to write to the editor, indicating which five articles they liked best in this edition of *The Rose Annual*, and placing them in order of preference. They are also asked to state which, if any, of the regular features they find of little interest and to suggest subjects for papers they would like to see in future editions.

Articles for *The Rose Annual* should be submitted to the editor by the end of August, addressed to him at The Royal National Rose Society's Offices, Bone Hill, Chiswell Green Lane, St Albans, Herts. They should be the author's own work, should not have been accepted by any other publication and should be typed in double spacing or, if hand-written, the lines should be well spaced. Black and white photographs of good definition, featuring items of general interest to members, are also welcomed.

The Northern Rose Show, 1970

R. C. BALFOUR

After weeks of sunshine, the weather broke on the first day of the Northern
Rose Show, which was again held in Roundhay Park in association with the
Leeds Flower Show, but those who braved the rain were well rewarded.

Nurserymen

The outstanding exhibit was staged by Fryer's of Knutsford, who not only
won the Brotherton Trophy for the best rose exhibit and a Large Gold
Medal, but also the Roundhay (Leeds) Horticultural Society's Trophy for
the best in the whole Leeds Show. Staged on pale blue tiles, with some bowls
raised on wooden stools, the roses were of high quality and were very well
arranged. At one corner the dark red of 'Europeana' contrasted with the rich
colouring of 'Ideal Home' and at another the orange-salmon of 'Irish Mist'
with the cherry-red 'Manuela'. That splendid rose for the herbaceous border,
'Ballerina', and the delicate-coloured climber 'Handel' looked charming:
others to stand out were 'Caramba', a crimson and silver bicolour, and aptly
named 'Redgold'.

Gregory's showed their roses in black bowls, raised on black metal tables
of varying shapes, on a black base and well earned a Large Gold Medal.
Especially attractive was one table of miniature roses, including white
'Easter Morning', 'Scarlet Gem' and pale red 'Beauty Secret'. Two climbers
caught the eye, 'Swan Lake', with its large white blooms with a blush tinge,
and Etude, whose many-petalled flowers, changing from red to pink,
are perhaps loveliest when fully out. The deep vermilion shrub rose 'Fred
Loads' and 'Peer Gynt', the frilly petalled yellow hybrid tea with a slight red
tinge, must have attracted many rose lovers.

Le Grice's first ever Large Gold Medal was well deserved. Their roses
were beautifully staged on a pale blue base with a triangular centrepiece
raised on laddered steps, featuring 'Lilac Charm' and 'News' at the base,
ascending through 'Goldgleam' and 'White Spray' to a pinnacle of 'Spek's
Yellow'. Many of their home-bred roses are curiously coloured, with a
special appeal to flower arrangers, and typical of these is 'Tom Brown',
which was well shown.

A local success was achieved by Charles Kershaw who were awarded a

164

Gold Medal for a very attractively arranged display of high quality roses in white bowls, with white painted wrought iron on green velvet. It is rare at shows to see a bowl of 'Zéphirine Drouhin', which looked very bright and which, with 'Ballerina', was offset by a raised bowl of 'Iceberg'. In contrast were startlingly bright 'Charleston' and 'Telstar'.

Another fine exhibit was staged by Lowe's, winning them the Society's Cup, on a base of rush mats, using black bowls, some raised on wire stands. The brighter coloured floribunda roses stood out, coppery-salmon 'Fairlight', tangerine 'Princess Michiko' and the bicoloured 'Sea Pearl'. Among their hybrid tea roses were another bicolour, 'Colour Wonder', and golden amber 'Whisky Mac'.

McGredy's limited their roses to sixteen varieties, on their usual large white stands. The quality was good; some appeared to have been grown under glass. Outstanding were 'Kathleen Joyce', a blush pink floribunda which opens attractively to show an orange centre, red hybrid tea 'National Trust' and bright salmon-pink floribunda with H.T. type blooms, 'Charles Dickens'.

Centrepiece of Wheatcroft Roses exhibit was a huge bowl of red 'Dorothy Wheatcroft' raised on a white column on black and white floor tiles. A new red shrub rose 'Fountain', yellow 'Miss Harp' and the frilly-petalled 'My Fair Lady' were attractive—but the many damaged blooms of 'Royal Air Force' detracted from the display and cannot have endeared that variety to flying rosarians.

The mixed bowls of shrub, dwarf polyantha and miniature roses were a feature of H. Robinson's stand, which also included Gandy's new orange-red floribunda 'Megiddo' and 'Coral Star'. De Ruiter's included rosy-salmon floribunda 'Michelle' and 'Scarlet Sunset', a new 'Orange Sensation' seedling, in their display on a green, grass-like base with a black background. The local nurseryman, David Lister, used deep red 'Lilli Marlene' and that splendid low-growing red floribunda 'Marlena' to good effect.

New Seedlings

New seedling floribundas shown by Le Grice included his Gold Medal winner, 'News', with clusters of semi-single rich purple flowers; 'Ripples', pale mauve, with pale green foliage and two as yet unnamed, a deep pink, with large hybrid tea shaped flowers especially attractive in bud, and a deep yellow with good foliage.

Gandy's new seedlings were attractively displayed. 'Megiddo' is a dazzling orange-red floribunda with shiny green foliage and is named after the biblical battleground in Israel. A deep, yellow-ochre sport of 'Woburn Abbey' is appropriately named 'Woburn Gold'. The last of their trio, 'Saul', bred by Gandy's from 'Super Star', has large, deep pink blooms with a touch of silver on the reverse and is a tall grower.

It was encouraging to see the large increase in new seedlings from amateur breeders. Two shown by D. Bracegirdle of Kneesall, Newark, were selected for trial, both with strong scent and bred from 'Fragrant Cloud', one with 'Wendy Cussons', whose colour it resembles and the other with 'Piccadilly'. Also selected was a red semi-double sport of 'Iceberg' shown by G. D. Spenceley of Penistone, and a peach floribunda from 'Rumba' × 'Apricot Nectar'. I particularly liked one floribunda not selected for trial from D. Melody of Cookridge, bred from 'Daily Sketch' and 'Masquerade', with blooms of varying shades from white to somewhat the colouring of 'Handel' and deepening to a rich red.

Amateurs

In the Amateur classes the winner of the Jubilee Trophy for the exhibitor with the highest aggregate points in Divisions A or B was F. E. Owen of Tamworth, whose many first prizes included the boxes of twelve in which 'Anne Letts' and 'Chicago Peace' were outstanding, and of six in which the 'Gavotte' pair were very fine. Among his floribunda successes was a bowl of 'Europeana' and 'Lilli Marlene'.

Another successful exhibitor was Mrs Iddon of Hesketh Bank, whose winning box of twelve included richly coloured 'Liberty Bell' and 'Avon'. Four 'Royal Highness' were especially fine in a mixed bowl and 'Fred Loads' and 'Evelyn Fison' in her bowl of floribundas.

Winner again of the Roundhay (Leeds) Cup for local exhibitors was J. Hardaker of Leeds, who used some fine blooms of 'Royal Highness' to good effect. Among other Yorkshire successes were two from Halifax, J. Pyrah and S. Walker, who produced six huge 'Stella' of very rich colour. 'Perfecta' was prominent in the vases of G. J. Abrahams of Alwoodley and L. Moorhouse of Meltham. Among the floribunda winners were J. I. Naylor of Seacroft, Mrs M. Anderson of York and G. Medley of Cottingley, whose bowl of 'Atlantic' with large trusses of semi-double light red flowers with yellow stamens was most striking.

The Northern Show usually attracts exhibitors from far away and it was especially gratifying to see that J. K. Stephens' journey from Reading had been rewarded by successes, for which his 'Princess' was mainly responsible.

From the North came the best bloom among the amateur classes, 'Grandpa Dickson', shown by Lakeland exhibitor, A. D. Robinson.

The Congleton Horticultural Society are always great supporters of the Northern Show and this year they again won both the Affiliated Societies classes, with splendid displays which included 'Dorothy Wheatcroft', 'Katharine Worsley' and 'Red Favourite'. Their members also had many individual successes.

The standard in the classes for those who had not previously won a first prize was unusually high, with outstanding exhibits by R. Beckett of Thornton Cleveleys and J. Done of Blackpool.

Floral Arrangement Classes

It is most encouraging that the floral arrangements classes at the Northern Show have improved so much in quality and in numbers. An unusual feature of this show was that the best exhibit was in the miniature class, in which Mrs V. Riley of Harrogate won the Balfour Cup with a beautiful triangular arrangement using carmine red 'Perla de Alcanada'.

Perhaps even more surprising was that in three classes a man, G. H. Tingle of Keighley, stole the honours. His twin arrangements in silver candlesticks for a church altar, using pink floribundas with dark green ivy, were most attractive. The red floribunda roses he used in the single roses class were set off against blue velvet and driftwood. It would be most helpful to visitors if he would name the roses he uses.

Another successful arranger was Miss Yardsley of Adel, who used grey foliage to set off 'Baccara' and 'Lady Sylvia' in a marble vase and, in another class, 'Junior Miss' roses against a pink satin drape, with two tiny dolls and trailing ribbon, to illustrate that variety.

The Rose Group from Harlow Car used Walter de la Mare's "Through what wild centuries roves back the rose" as the theme for their most attractive display on a dark blue base, which included a beautiful arrangement of red roses of different hues.

I cannot close this report without paying tribute to the officials of the Roundhay (Leeds) Horticultural Society, our hosts, who do so much to make the Leeds Show such a friendly occasion.

The Autumn Rose Show

GORDON FORSYTH

In spite of the somewhat wild weather in many parts of the country during the preceding week, there was no lack of top quality blooms at the Society's Autumn Show, which occupied both of the Royal Horticultural Society's Halls at Westminster on September 15 and 16. It was indeed a great success and again was magnificently supported by the trade growers, who filled the Greycoat Street Hall with some really glorious displays, while many fine specimen blooms were to be seen in the amateurs' competitive section. Well contested floral arrangement classes provided without question one of the major attractions of the show.

Star exhibit in the nurserymen's section, awarded the Society's Roses Challenge Cup, together with the D'Escofet Cup for the best island group, and Large Gold Medal, was that of Bees of Chester, who really excelled themselves with a large island group of top-class varieties for general garden planting. Large, beautifully arranged bowls of blooms displayed the charms of each variety, and the corner columns of rich silvery rose hybrid tea 'Rosenella' and orange-gold floribunda 'Zambra' were certainly the inspiration of an artist.

So, too, were their large mounds, with not a bloom out of place, of scarlet floribunda 'Evelyn Fison' and hybrid tea dark vermilion 'Fragrant Cloud.' Other hybrid teas noted especially in this exhibit were 'Summer Sunshine', ivory 'Message', pale yellow and pink 'My Choice', 'Piccadilly' as brilliant as ever, 'Gold Crown', lavender "blue" 'Cologne Carnival', shapely deep red 'Milord', light vermilion 'Aventure' and vermilion 'Duke of Windsor'.

As we have come to expect, John Mattock of Nuneham Courtenay again excelled by winning the Lewis Levy Memorial Cup for an exhibit against a background, a glorious display of all types, ancient and modern, including the pick of the hybrid teas and floribundas. Of the former I noted especially Cocker's International Trophy-winner 'Alec's Red', crimson-red 'National Trust', 'Peer Gynt', 'Diorama' and superb 'Fragrant Cloud'. Top quality floribundas included their new 'Moon Maiden', crimson-scarlet 'Franklin Engelmann', 'City of Leeds', 'Molly McGredy' and 'Arthur Bell'. I also admired particularly their climbers 'Schoolgirl' and 'Pink Perpetue', the

168

deep rosy-pink Rugosa variety 'F. J. Grootendorst', repeat-flowering single red climbing rose 'Altissimo', and the small pink-flowered shrub variety 'Ballerina'.

High quality was the keynote of the display against a background for which R. Harkness & Co. were awarded the Jubilee Trophy and Gold Medal, with floribundas particularly strong, especially 'Orange Sensation', the brilliant 'Anne Cocker', which should I think prove popular for cutting; light vermilion 'Lively Lady', rich cream 'Moonraker', which seems to be a valuable bad weather rose; full-petalled, very free 'Yellow Cushion'; 'Pink Parfait' and rich salmon pink 'King Arthur'. Of the hybrid teas 'Alec's Red' in perfect condition was certainly the most conspicuous; indeed, I considered this to be the rose of the show.

Hybrid teas were shown remarkably well in the island group of Warley Rose Gardens, awarded the R.N.R.S. Challenge Cup and Gold Medal. Outstanding varieties for quality were 'Blue Moon', 'Beauté', 'Alec's Red', 'Diorama', 'Rose Gaujard' and 'Grandpa Dickson,' and the pick of their floribundas were 'Elizabeth of Glamis', 'Evelyn Fison', light red 'Alec Rose', 'Scarlet Queen Elizabeth' and 'Arabian Nights'.

The Large Gold Medal group of C. Gregory and Son of Chilwell was most beautifully arranged and embraced good selections of hybrid teas and floribundas in grand condition, with outstanding climbers including their 'Pink Perpetue', and a generous selection of miniatures. Of the hybrid teas, rich vermilion-red, full petalled 'Summer Holiday' was shown in perfect condition, and so, too, were their rich coral pink 'Blessings', golden-orange, pink-flushed 'Whisky Mac', and such winners as 'Mullard Jubilee', 'King's Ransom', superb 'Apricot Silk', 'Mischief', 'Peer Gynt' and 'Grandpa Dickson'. Eye-catching floribundas for colour were orange-pink 'My Girl', 'Elizabeth of Glamis', their new H.T.-type 'Orange Silk', 'City of Leeds' and the floribunda shrub rose, light vermilion 'Fred Loads'.

Hybrid teas were strongly in evidence in the colourful Gold Medal group, arranged by Cants of Colchester, with 'Alec's Red' most conspicuous. Others I noted specially for autumn quality were richly fragrant 'Wendy Cussons', 'Red Devil', 'Summer Holiday', scarlet 'Ernest H. Morse', 'Super Star' at its best, rich rose pink 'Prima Ballerina', 'Duke of Windsor' and 'Royal Highness'.

Needless to say, interesting selections of modern roses were shown in Gold Medal exhibits by Geo. de Ruiter, Wm. Lowe and Son and the Waterhouse Nurseries, who had notable hybrid teas in 'Blessings', 'Wendy Cussons', light vermilion with pale reverse 'Miss Ireland', 'Beauté', 'Apricot Nectar',

'Josephine Bruce' still as good as ever; 'Red Devil'—how popular this is; 'King's Ransom', with the scarlet floribunda 'Jack of Hearts', which I admit was a stranger to me.

Noteworthy floribundas in the grouping by Fryer's Nurseries included one of my special favourites, the very long flowering H.T.-type 'Redgold', with 'Dearest', 'Orange Sensation', invaluable 'Elizabeth of Glamis' and 'Fred Loads'. The new large orange-flame floribunda 'Chorus Girl', salmon-pink 'Michelle', and H.T.-type very generous 'Golden Pride' were noteworthy in a good selection shown by Herbert Robinson, together with the hybrid teas rich pink 'Ballet', dark-foliaged 'Mellow Yellow' and 'Gold Crown'.

Noteworthy hybrid teas in the Harry Wheatcroft selection were pink 'Manuela', rose-red 'Peter Frankenfeld', 'Beauté' in grand form and the new golden 'Sunblest', with blooms of ideal size for cutting, which should appeal to the flower arrangement enthusiast. Needless to say the house of Meilland had some very interesting productions to show, notably the hybrid teas soft salmon-flushed 'Sweet Promise', crimson 'Lovita', rich pink 'Maria Callas', 'Pink Wonder' and light vermilion 'Interflora', already a favourite commercial rose for cutting. C. Newberry showed a delightful selection of the shapely, small-flowered 'Garnette' roses.

As we have come to expect, Geo. Longley dominated the nurserymen's competitive classes for specimen blooms. He again won the A. C. Turner Challenge Cup for 15 vases of distinct varieties which included grand 'Stella', 'Grand'mère Jenny', rose-scarlet 'Helene Schoen', 'Fragrant Cloud', 'Blue Moon', 'Peace', the vivid cerise-pink French 'Can-Can' and 'McGredy's Yellow'. He also won first prizes in the rather disappointing classes for specimen blooms in boxes, in which most of the blooms were weather battered.

Coming to the amateurs' section, which occupied the old horticultural hall, in view of the bad weather entries were thin in some classes, though competition generally was keen and plenty of good quality blooms were shown.

A really glorious spray of the large-flowered beautiful pink hybrid tea 'Paris Match', shown naturally with no disbudding, won first prize in the special open class for a single inflorescence, for W. D. Gobbee, London. F. W. Marston, Leominster, was a deserving winner of the Challenge Cup and first prize for a box of twelve blooms, distinct. For the record his varieties were light red 'Liebestraum', large pink 'Peaceful', pink-tinted 'Honey Favourite', 'Montezuma', 'Sam McGredy', soft pink 'Gavotte', 'Red Devil', 'Pink Favourite', 'Isabel de Ortiz', white 'Royal Highness', 'Vienna Charm' and pink 'City of Bath'.

In the class for 6 specimen blooms F. E. Owen, Tamworth, scored with 2 blooms each of 'Memoriam', light pink 'Gavotte' and 'Red Devil', a really lovely set. The best bloom of the show, of 'Gold Crown', was to be seen in the second prize exhibit of L. E. J. Wood, Waddesdon.

Women exhibitors took the lead in several of the open classes. Mrs F. A. Pugh, for instance, had the best vase of two varieties, three blooms of each, with grand 'Red Devil' and 'City of Bath', and she was also first for three vases of distinct varieties, 'Red Devil', 'Fred Gibson' and 'Pink Favourite'. In the class for a box of six blooms of four or more varieties, Mrs Iddon, Hesketh Park, had especially good 'Grandpa Dickson', 'Ernest H. Morse' and the popular 'Red Devil'.

One of the loveliest classes in the show was that for a bowl of up to 18 stems, won by Capt. C. A. E. Stanfield R.N. Walmer, with a really glorious arrangement, and for top quality I admired the first prize bowl of not more than 12 stems arranged by L. E. J. Wood, Waddesdon, varieties 'Gail Borden', 'Bonsoir', 'Gavotte', 'Peace', 'Gold Crown', 'Femina' and 'Karl Herbst'.

In the section for growers of not more than 500 trees, M. L. Watts, Northampton, was certainly the winner for a box of six blooms, varieties 'Fred Gibson', 'Fragrant Cloud', 'Isabel de Ortiz', 'Memoriam', pink 'Charlie's Aunt' and deep pink 'Red Lion'. Other specially noteworthy exhibits were the Society's trophy winning exhibit of three vases of hybrid teas, glorious 'Gavotte', 'Isabel de Ortiz' and 'Perfecta', by D. H. Scott, Beaconsfield and F. M. Bowen s bowl of floribundas.

Finally, special congratulations to B. S. Pearce, Sutton Coldfield, who as an amateur had never won a first prize at any of the R.N.R.S. shows; on this occasion he was first for a box of six specimen blooms, and for a vase of six

Change of Variety Name

To conform with the International Agreement under the Plant Varieties and Seeds Act, the following alterations to names have been made and the International Rose Register has been amended accordingly:

'Interflora' changed to 'Interview'

'Liebestraum' changed to 'Red Queen'.

The Trial Ground and Display Garden, 1970

L. G. TURNER

The completion of the Edland Memorial Pavilion was a significant landmark in the development of the Display Garden. It has established a further focal point and opened another fascinating vista across the garden, contrasting well with the floribunda walk and pond. The building, designed by Mr Harry Clacy, who has done so much for the Society, is raised above ground level and follows a line similar to the main building. It is a noble piece of architecture and a fitting tribute to my predecessor, who so loyally served the Society for more than 42 years until his untimely death in 1964.

The five pairs of echelon beds, each containing over 100 trees, make a bold sweep to the pavilion; the varieties—'Mischief', 'Evelyn Fison', 'Iceberg', 'City of Leeds' and 'Pink Parfait'—contrast well with 'Escapade' and 'Yvonne Rabier' that embellish the Pavilion terrace. It is a coincidence that the latter variety was one particularly favoured by Harry Edland, and I well remember it growing in his garden at Sidcup.

The Pavilion was formally opened by Mr E. J. Baldwin, assisted by Mrs Edland, on the occasion of the Council meeting in June, when the roses were just coming into bloom. On the same day the Society's flag was unfurled and in future will fly at the entrance to the gardens on appropriate occasions. The Society is grateful to Mr John Clarke, then President and now Hon. Treasurer of the Society, for the most generous gift of flag and mast. The design for the flag has been debated in Council for more than a year and the one that was finally accepted was the work of Captain E. M. C. Barraclough, C.B.E., R.N., who is Adviser to the Ministry of Defence, Navy Department, on flags and badges for H.M. ships. The thanks of Council are also extended to Mr L. A. Anstiss, Vice-President, who has kindly presented a seat for the garden.

The hawthorn hedge, which was the original boundary hedge of the property before the additional land was purchased, has now been removed and replaced by a hedge of 'Schneezwerg' and 'Roseraie de l'Haÿ.'

During the year considerable progress has been made in the establishment of the beds of historical roses, planned by Mr Graham Thomas, but, unfortunately, the winter weather turned against us and it proved quite impossible to complete the work in the spring. Beds to the south of the Pavilion were prepared and a number of Hybrid Perpetuals, Bourbons and ground cover varieties were planted. The remaining beds to the north are now ready (November) for planting and the major part of this collection will be in flower next summer. The perimeter bed around the Trial Ground, which contains every variety that has received an award since 1963, is one of the most popular attractions for visitors. It is interesting to compare the newer varieties and I am sure it has helped many members to decide on the most suitable to order, without being unduly influenced by a pretty picture in the nurseryman's catalogue.

Bone Hill, in company with the remainder of the south and east, suffered from lack of rain during the summer months and this, undoubtedly, had a pronounced effect on the growth—particularly that of the newly-planted trees. The comparison in rainfall over the past five years, for the period April to September, may be seen from the following chart:

	1966	1967	1968	1969	1970
April	3·68	2·01	1·78	1·16	2·72
May	2·35	4·29	2·15	2·00	1·03
June	3·49	1·83	2·68	1·21	·68
July	2·93	1·88	2·38	2·12	1·99
August	3·48	1·71	3·44	1·86	2·08
September	1·8	2·78	5·32	0·20	2·1
Total	17·73	14·50	17·75	8·55	10·60
Total 12 months	32·91	29·86	29·23	21·51	

Although the rainfall for the six months was higher than in 1969 it will be observed that during the crucial growing period, May–July, it was in fact 1·63 inches lower. Irrigation of roses has always been a contentious matter, but there seems little doubt that if the roots are starved of moisture they cannot produce top growth. Unfortunately the soil in the gardens here is, in the main, of a gravelly nature and tends to dry out very quickly, a fact that will undoubtedly have been observed by visitors. Accordingly, consideration is being given to the possibility of installing irrigation for use in emergency. Certainly in the last two years the use of a reliable system during the early part of the summer would have been of great benefit to the spring-planted trees. I must, however, emphasize that the type of irrigation to which I refer is the application of a controlled amount of water for a given period. It is certainly not my wish to give the impression that the Society is recommending the haphazard splashing around of water from a hose pipe or watering can—unless such operations are carried out regularly they can do more harm than good.

In spite of the dry weather most of the varieties in the display gardens grew well and throughout July, and again in September, the garden was a feast of colour. Visitors from all parts of the country and from overseas expressed appreciation, but I am a little disappointed that more of our 100,000 members do not attend. The 13,000 visitors, representing as it does no fewer than 4,000 non-members, is not a very high percentage of our entire membership, for whose enjoyment and interest the Display Garden was established.

Much has been said in the press regarding the awards made at the Trial Ground, but I cannot allow this report to be written without reference to the wonderful achievement of Alec Cocker, raiser of 'Alec's Red', which received the President's International Trophy and a Gold Medal. The trees on trial did quite well during the first and second years and were worthy of the Certificate of Merit, but in the third year they were superb and justly deserved the premier award. The sturdy stems were laden with shapely, fragrant blooms for weeks at a time. Congratulations are also extended to E. B. LeGrice on the colour break achieved in his novelty 'News'. The greatest problem appears to be for the printer to produce a truly representative colour illustration of this variety; I have yet to see one that can be considered identical. So often with new colour breaks the constitution of the variety suffers, but 'News' grew well throughout its three year trial and well deserved the Gold Medal.

For some considerable time there has been a demand for a bush rose larger than the miniature roses but not as big as the normal floribunda. It would appear that the hybridists are now responding to this demand and beginning to concentrate their energies in producing such low growing varieties. These will undoubtedly be popular for the smaller garden and also for 'ground cover' in front of floribundas. 'Kim' from Jack Harkness, 'Esther Ofarim' from Reimer Kordes and 'Sunday Times' from Sam McGredy are the forerunners. Mr McGredy has also a fascinating break in his 'Picasso' which is already being followed by others, as I have noted that he has one or two varieties in the first year trial creating a similar effect.

The Awards to New Roses in 1970

The President's International Trophy for the Best New Seedling Rose of the year and Gold Medal were awarded to:

*ALEC'S RED (H.T.). 'Fragrant Cloud' × 'Dame de Coeur'. Trial Ground No. 1618. Reg. No. 1372. *Raiser and distributor:* J. Cocker & Sons Ltd., Aberdeen. Bloom: cherry red, very full (45 petals), large, borne singly and several together. Very fragrant. Growth: upright and vigorous. Foliage: light to medium green, matt.

A Gold Medal was awarded to:

*NEWS (Flori.). 'Lilac Charm' × 'Tuscany Superb'. Trial Ground No. 1630. Reg. No. 1174. *Raiser: and distributor:* E. B. Le Grice (Hybridisers) Ltd., N. Walsham. Bloom: beetroot purple, moderately full. (18 petals), borne in trusses. Growth: bushy and compact. Foliage: medium green, matt.

Certificates of Merit were awarded to:

CHORUS GIRL (Flori.). 'Highlight' × seedling. Trial Ground No. 1743. Reg. No. 1421. *Raiser:* H. Robinson, Hinckley. Bloom: vermilion red, moderately full (18 petals), borne in trusses. Growth: Bushy and compact. Foliage: medium green, matt.

*GOLDEN CHERSONESE (Shrub.). *R. ecae* × 'Canary Bird'. Trial Ground No. S.111. Reg. No. 1055. *Raiser:* E. F. Allen, Copdock, Suffolk. *Distributor:* Hillier & Sons, Winchester. Bloom: yellow, single (5 petals), small, borne along flowering shoots early in season (May/June). Growth: very bushy. Foliage: extremely plentiful, small, medium green, matt. Reddish wood.

KIM (Dwarf Flori.). ('Orange Sensation' × 'Allgold') × 'Elizabeth of Glamis'. Trial Ground No. 1746. Reg. No. 1446. *Raiser and distributor:* R. Harkness & Co. Ltd., Hitchin. Bloom: canary yellow, full (35 petals), borne several together and in trusses. Growth: dwarf, compact and bushy. Foliage: small, medium to light green, matt.

*PICASSO (Flori.). 'Marlena' × ['Evelyn Fison' × ('Orange Sweetheart' × 'Frühlingsmorgen')]. Trial Ground No. 1786. Reg. No. 1343. *Raiser:* S. McGredy IV. *Distributor:* S. McGredy & Son Ltd., N. Ireland. Bloom: carmine with deeper blotches, silvery reverse, moderately full (25 petals), borne several together and in trusses. Growth: bushy and compact. Foliage: small, medium green, matt.

SUNDAY TIMES (Flori.). ('Little Darling' × 'Goldilocks') × 'Munchen'. Trial Ground No. 1793. Reg. No. 1452. *Raiser:* S. McGredy IV. *Distributor:* S. McGredy & Son Ltd., N. Ireland. Bloom: deep pink, lighter reverse, full (28 petals), borne several together and in trusses. Growth: dwarf, bushy and compact. Foliage: small, dark green, semi-glossy.

Trial Ground Certificates were awarded to:

*CHARLES DICKENS (Flori./H.T. type.) 'Paddy McGredy' × 'Elizabeth of Glamis'. Trial Ground No. 1549. Reg. No. 1361. *Raiser:* S. McGredy IV. *Distributor:* S. McGredy & Son Ltd., N. Ireland. Bloom: rosy salmon, darker reverse, moderately full (22 petals), borne several together and in trusses. Growth: upright, vigorous and compact. Foliage: dark green, semi-glossy.

*CITY OF GLOUCESTER (H.T.). 'Gavotte' × 'Buccaneer'. Trial Ground No. 1922. Reg. No. 1272. *Raiser and distributor:* John Sanday (Roses) Ltd., Bristol. Bloom: saffron yellow shaded gold, full (37 petals) borne singly and several together. Growth: tall and branching. Foliage: medium green, matt.

COLOUR SERGEANT (Flori./H.T. type.) 'Queen Elizabeth' × ('Ann Elizabeth' × 'Circus'). Trial Ground No. 1755. Reg. No. 1462. *Raiser and distributor:* R. Harkness & Co. Ltd., Hitchin. Bloom: vermilion-scarlet, moderately full (20 petals), borne singly, several together and in trusses. Growth: upright and bushy. Foliage: dark green, matt.

DORRIT (Flori.) seedling × 'Folie d'Espagne'. Trial Ground No. 1571. Reg. No. 1242. *Raiser:* O. Sonderhousen, Denmark. Bloom: Deep orange, fading to orange-yellow, very full (66 petals), borne in trusses. Growth: vigorous and upright. Foliage: medium green, semi-glossy.

*ESTHER OFARIM (Flori./H.T. type.). 'Colour Wonder' × 'Zorina'. Trial Ground No. 1844. Reg. No. 1464. *Raiser:* W. Kordes & Sons, Germany. *Distributor:* S. McGredy & Son Ltd., N. Ireland. Bloom: orange-red and yellow, full (30 petals), borne several together and in trusses. Growth: dwarf, bushy and compact. Foliage: medium green, matt.

GOLD COIN (Min.) 'Golden Glow' × 'Magic Wand'. Trial Ground No. 1712. Reg. A.R.S. *Raiser:* R. Moore, U.S.A. *Distributor:* C. Gregory & Son Ltd., Nottingham. Bloom: canary yellow, very full (52 petals), borne in trusses. Growth: compact and bushy. Foliage: small, light green, matt.

GOLDEN TIMES (H.T.) 'Fragrant Cloud' × 'Golden Splendour'. Trial Ground No. 1927. Reg. No. 1396. *Raiser:* J. Cocker and Sons Ltd., Aberdeen. *Distributor:* Harry Wheatcroft & Sons Ltd., Nottingham. Bloom: golden yellow, very full (51 petals), borne singly and several together. Fragrant. Growth: tall and upright. Foliage: large, medium green, matt.

GRACE ABOUNDING (Flori.) 'Pink Parfait' × 'Circus'. Trial Ground No. 1535. Reg. No. 1167. *Raiser and distributor:* R. Harkness & Co. Ltd., Hitchin. Bloom: creamy white, semi-double (14 petals), borne in trusses. Growth: bushy and uniform. Foliage: light green, semi-glossy.

GYPSY MOTH (Flori./H.T. type) seedling × seedling. Trial Ground No. 1586. Reg. No. 1136. *Raiser:* M. Tantau, Germany. *Distributor:* Harry Wheatcroft & Sons Ltd., Nottingham. Bloom: rosy-salmon, full (30 petals), borne several together. Fragrant. Growth: vigorous and branching. Foliage: dark green, glossy.

LAVENDER LACE (Min.), 'Ellen Poulsen' × 'Debbie'. Trial Ground No. 1713. Reg. A.R.S. *Raiser:* R. Moore, U.S.A. *Distributor:* C. Gregory and Son Ltd., Nottingham.

'DORRIT' (floribunda)
Seedling × *'Folie d'Espagne'*
Raised by O. Sonderhousen, Denmark
TRIAL GROUND CERTIFICATE 1970
See page 176

'SUNDAY TIMES' (floribunda)
(*'Little Darling'* × *'Goldilocks'*) × *'Munchen'*
Raised by S. McGredy IV, N. Ireland
CERTIFICATE OF MERIT 1970
See page 175

Bloom: lavender, very full (53 petals), borne in trusses. Growth: bushy and compact. Foliage: small, light green. matt.

MEGIDDO (Flori./H.T. type). 'Coup de Foudre' × 'S'Agaro'. Trial Ground No. 1947. Reg. No. 1386. *Raiser and distributor*: Gandy's Roses Ltd., North Kilworth. Bloom: scarlet red, moderately full (22 petals), borne several together and in trusses. Growth: tall and upright. Foliage: dark green, glossy.

*NATIONAL TRUST (H.T.) 'Evelyn Fison' × 'King of Hearts'. Trial Ground No. 1552. Reg. No. 1370. *Raiser*: S. McGredy IV. *Distributor*: S. McGredy & Son Ltd., N. Ireland. Bloom: red, very full (60 petals) borne singly and several together. Growth: upright and compact. Foliage: dark green, matt.

NOZOMI (Clg.Min.). 'Fairy Princess' × 'Sweet Fairy'. Trial Ground No. 1587. Reg. No. 1184. *Raiser*: T. Onodera, Japan. *Distributor*: C. Gregory and Son Ltd., Nottingham. Bloom: pearl pink, single (5 petals), borne in trusses. Growth: spreading. Foliage: small, pointed, medium green, glossy.

ROAMING (H.T.). 'Vera Dalton' × 'Super Star'. Trial Ground No. 1923. Reg. No. 1401. *Raiser and distributor*: John Sanday (Roses) Ltd., Bristol. Bloom: reddish-pink, moderately full (22 petals), borne singly and several together. Growth: upright and bushy. Foliage: dark green, matt.

ROSY MANTLE (Clr.). 'New Dawn' × 'Prima Ballerina'. Trial Ground No. C113. Reg. No. 1232. *Raiser and distributor*: J. Cocker & Sons Ltd., Aberdeen. Bloom: deep rose pink, moderately full (25 petals), borne several together. Slightly fragrant. Growth: vigorous. Foliage: dark green, glossy.

SEVEN SEAS (Flori.) 'Lilac Charm' × 'Sterling Silver'. Trial Ground No. 1538. Reg. No. 1463. *Raiser and distributor*: R. Harkness & Co. Ltd., Hitchin. Bloom: lilac, very full (48 petals), borne several together and in trusses. Growth: bushy and compact. Foliage: dark green, matt.

*SNOWLINE (Flori.). Trial Ground No. 1801. Reg. No. 1355. *Raiser*: N. D. Poulsen, Denmark. *Distributor*: S. McGredy & Son Ltd., N. Ireland. Bloom: white, very full (42 petals), borne several together and in trusses. Growth: bushy and compact. Foliage: dark green, semi-glossy.

*STEPHEN LANGDON (Flori./H.T. type). 'Karl Herbst' × 'Sarabande'. Trial Ground No. 1924. Reg. No. 850. *Raiser and distributor*: John Sanday (Roses) Ltd., Bristol. Bloom: deep scarlet, moderately full (20 petals), borne several together and in trusses. Growth: upright and bushy. Foliage: dark green, matt.

TAORA (Flori.) seedling × 'Super Star' seedling. Trial Ground No. 1407. Reg. A.R.S. *Raiser*: M. Tantau, Germany. Bloom: signal red, reverse cherry, full (32 petals), borne in trusses. Growth: bushy and compact. Foliage: medium green, semi-glossy.

European Rose Trials

STELVIO COGGIATTI

(Horticultural writer; President Garden Club of Rome; Vice President Italian Rose Society; member of Jury in continental rose competitions)

Every year in spring and early summer panels of rose judges assemble at the twelve rose trial grounds in various European countries. These experts make awards to new cultivars sent by breeders from all over the world who wish to test the adaptability of their seedlings to different climatic conditions.

The awards made normally comprise a gold medal, a silver medal and/or certificates, both for hybrid teas and for floribundas of sufficient merit. The aims are similar to those of the R.N.R.S. rose trials, but there are differences in the way the juries are organised and in the methods of making awards. Thus, the final score for bush roses is assessed in the second spring after planting, while climbers and ramblers are inspected a year later. Throughout the period of the trials a local board of judges inspects the seedlings and awards points, these being finally integrated by an international jury which looks at the seedlings on one occasion only, at the height of the flowering season. The local board judges such matters as resistance to disease, recurrence and floriferousness. On the other hand the international jury is usually asked to award points for colour, fragrance, shape of flower, vigour of growth and foliage.

This system may be vulnerable to criticism, because some good seedlings may be overlooked if they are out of flower when the international jury inspects them. On the other hand a moderate performer may be over-pointed if it happens to be at its best on the day of the inspection. There are also inconsistencies in the methods used as between the twelve rose trial grounds, so that comparisons may be unreliable. It has been suggested that the same international jury should visit each trial ground for an inspection and to integrate the points awarded by the local boards of judges. This excellent proposal would involve considerable expense, but it may be that a fund out of which this could be met could be raised by charging entrance fees for each seedling sent by a breeder.

Display Gardens and Trial Grounds on the Continent

The first international outdoor rose competition was held in 1907 at Bagatelle Gardens in the Bois de Boulogne, on the outskirts of Paris. The name

"Bagatelle" is derived from a mansion where French dignitaries were in the habit of spending their holidays many years ago.

The Gold Medal of the first *Concours Internationale de Roses Nouvelles* was awarded to 'Marquise de Sinéty', a hybrid tea raised by Pernet-Ducher which is rarely seen today.

The Bagatelle competition's rules were largely adopted for similar trials held in other parts of Europe, in particular the two years check on the plants by a local board of rose judges, supplemented by foreign experts at the final inspection. Year after year the Bagatelle trial ground has been in the forefront, as well as the adjacent display garden, thanks to the foresight of J. C. N. Forestier, *Conservateur en Chef des Jardins de Paris*, entrusted with the work of planning and planting the *Roseraie*. Subsequently the Bagatelle gardens have been managed efficiently by such keen technicians as Robert Joffet, André Leroy and finally by J. M. Chasseraud who is in charge at present.

Anyone visiting Paris in early summer should not miss a day at the Roseraie de Bagatelle where the roses are at their peak in mid-June.

Only for Remontant Cultivars

Since September, 1958 the municipality of Orléans, represented by M. Roger Secrétain, Mayor of the town, and by M. Albert Poyet, Parks Department Superintendent, has sponsored a special international competition with the primary object of finding floribundas and climbers with very remontant qualities. The municipality has also equipped and opened to the public the "Parc Floral de la Source" in which there are no less than 250,000 rose bushes; it is a permanent display garden beautifully situated near the source of the Loiret river.

The Finest French Rose

A traditional, but special competition, sponsored by the French Rose Society, is held annually at Lyon "the rose capital of France", and the birthplace of world-famous rosarians, starting with the Pernet-Duchers, the Guillots and now represented by the Croix, the Gaujards, the Laperrières, the Meillands, the Richardiers and others whose roses have helped to establish the pre-eminence of the French rose nurserymen.

Entries for the Lyon competition are restricted to French seedlings aspiring to the "most beautiful rose of France" award. The modern display garden, covering 10 acres and comprising some 100,000 rose bushes, has already earned a high reputation.

Before leaving France mention must be made of the competition held at

Saverne (Alsace) since 1925 by the *Societé Alsacienne et Lorennaise des Amis de la Rose*. It is mainly through the efforts of the President in office, M. Alfred Dietrich, that this worthy Society is continuing to function.

Rome

Rome was the second European city to sponsor an international rose competition, with the main object of finding seedlings which do well in the long, hot and dry summer, typical of many parts of Italy. From 1933 until 1940 the trial ground and display garden were located near Nero's Domus Aurea on the Oppian Hill. Thereafter the competition was suspended for the duration of the war. In 1950 the plants were removed to a magnificent site on the slope of the Aventine Hill, just in front of the Palatine ruins.

Madrid Rosaleda

There is perhaps the most outstanding rose garden in Europe at the Parque de l'Oeste in Madrid, with its geometrical stylised parterres crossing each other and framed by a ten foot high wall of climbing roses which runs along the Rosaleda.

The first gold medal was awarded to the Spanish breeder Pedro Dot for his seedling 'Condesa de Mayalde', thus keeping to the tradition in evidence at Bagatelle, Rome, Saverne and Monza of awarding the first gold medal to one of the country's own breeders.

The Madrid rose garden is dedicated to its founder and first Director, Señor Ramon Ortiz Ferré. He was succeeded in 1965 by another first class rosarian, Señor Luis Pita Romero.

Geneva

Geneva is a town that owes its magnificent rose garden to the outbreak of mass unemployment in Switzerland at the end of the war. Realising that an investment encouraging tourists would soon be rewarded, the municipality hired all unemployed hodmen and set them to work at the La Grange Park. Eighteen months later the rose garden was completed, and the following year saw the start of the international competition which reserves a special award for the most fragrant seedling of the year. M. Armand Auberson, Garden Department Superintendent and President of the Geneva Horticultural Society, is responsible for the organisation of the competition.

Baden-Baden

Baden-Baden, in Germany, is a well-known and sophisticated spa where the usual competitions and display gardens are under the efficient management of Dr Walter Rieger. The jury for the international competition meets in mid-July or even later. While this may be on the late side for roses compared with some other European countries, the tourist season is then only just starting.

Belgium and Holland
In Belgium a flourishing *Societé Nationale des Amis de la Rose*, headed by the charming and keen Baroness Gaston de Gerlache de Gomery, is encouraging rose enthusiasts in addition to two autonomous international competitions. The first one, presided over by dynamic Mme L. Gillon, is located at Courtrai, West Flanders. The other enjoys a remarkable site near the old Roeulx Castle and is directed by the well-known landscape architect, René Pechère.

From Belgium it is an easy journey to the Westbroekpark on the outskirts of The Hague, Holland. The well cared for trial ground is in a glade of this magnificent park and surrounded by display gardens laid out in settings of lawns and shrubberies. Provision is made there for a number of awards for new seedlings of hybrid teas, floribundas, shrubs and climbers as well as for cultivars already in commerce and for the most fragrant rose of the year.

Peak Blooming Periods at the Rose Gardens Described
Rome: first half of May
Madrid: end of May and early June
Lyon: mid-June
Paris (Bagatelle): mid-June
Saverne: mid-June
Geneva: last ten days of June
Courtrai: beginning of July
Roeulx: beginning of July
The Hague: beginning of July
Baden-Baden: first half of July
Orléans: (remontant roses trial): mid-September

International Awards 1970

ROME

LARGE FLOWERS

Gold Medal	'Vol de Nuit'	M. Delbard, France
First Certificate	Unnamed	Q. Mansuino, Italy
Certificates	'Mme. Philibert Tsiranana'	Paul Croix, France
	'Asa-Gumo'	Keisi Rose Nursery, Japan

SMALL FLOWERS

Gold Medal	'Climbing Diablotin'	M. Delbard, France
First Certificate	'Pironti Tournedos'	N. Pironti, Italy
Certificates	Unnamed	A. Meilland, France
	Unnamed	L. Meilland, France

PARIS—BAGATELLE

Gold Medal	'Climbing Diablotin' (Climber)	Delbard-Chabert, France
Silver Medal	'Porthos' (flori.)	Laperrière, France
Certificates	Unnamed	A. Meilland, France
	Unnamed	G. de Ruiter, Holland
	Unnamed	Benjamin Williams, U.S.A.

MADRID

Gold Medal and Prize of the City of Madrid	'Crépe de Chine' (H.T.)	Delbard-Chabert, France
First Certificates	'Interflora' (H.T.)	Louisette Meilland, France
	'Climbing Firecrest' (Clr.)	E. B. Le Grice, England
Second Certificates	'Mullard Jubilee' (H.T.)	Sam McGredy, N. Ireland
	'Reda' (H.T.)	P. Gaujard, France
	'Sweet Home' (flori.)	Louisette Meilland, France

LYON

HYBRID TEA

Gold Medal and title "La Plus Belle Rose de France"	'Illisca'	Laperrière, France
Silver-Gilt Medal	'Interflora'	Meilland, France
First Certificate	'Arthuro Toscanini'	Meilland, France
Second Certificate	'Crépe de Chine'	Delbard-Chabert, France

POLYANTHA/FLORIBUNDA

First Certificate	'Sweet Home'	L. Meilland, France
Second Certificate	Unnamed	A. Meilland, France
Third Certificate	'Porthos'	Laperrière, France

CLIMBER

First Certificate	'Gothard'	A. Combe, France

THE MOST FRAGRANT ROSE

First Certificate	'Salopin'	A. Combe, France

THE HAGUE

HYBRID TEA

Gold Medal	'Mullard Jubilee'	S. McGredy & Son Ltd., N. Ireland
First Certificates	Unnamed	W. Kordes Söhne, Germany
	Unnamed	Meilland, France

FLORIBUNDA

Gold Medal	'Satchmo'	S. McGredy & Son Ltd., N. Ireland
First Certificate	Unnamed	G. de Ruiter, Holland
Second Certificates	Unnamed	Rijksstation voor Sierplantenteelt, Belgium
	'Valfleury'	Paul Croix, France

CLIMBER

First Certificate	'Climbing Diablotin'	G. Delbard, France

In the beds of roses planted out in the Westbroekpark the International Jury awarded the *Golden Rose of the Hague* to 'Jan Spek' (flori.) raised by S. McGredy & Son Ltd., Northern Ireland; *First Class Certificate* to 'Tombola' (flori.) raised by G. de Ruiter, Holland; *Second Class Certificate* to 'Europeana' (flori.) raised by G. de Ruiter, Holland; Challenge Prize of Dutch Rose Association to 'New Dawn' (climber) raised by Somerset Rose Nursery, U.S.A. and *Silver Medal* for the most fragrant rose of 1969 to 'Lady Seton' (H.T.) raised by S. McGredy & Son Ltd., Northern Ireland.

COURTRAI

Gold Medal	Unnamed (H.T.)	L. Meilland, France
Silver Medal and		
Friends of the		
Rose Prize	'National Trust' (H.T.)	S. McGredy & Son Ltd., N. Ireland
Silver Medals	Unnamed (flori.)	L. Meilland, France
	'Porthos' (flori.)	Laperrière, France
	'Mullard Jubilee' (H.T.)	S. McGredy & Son Ltd., N. Ireland
	Unnamed (flori.)	A. Meilland, France
	'John Waterer' (H.T.)	S. McGredy & Son Ltd., N. Ireland
	Unnamed (flori.)	Rijksstation voor Sierplantenteelt, Belgium
	Unnamed (flori.)	A. Meilland, France

BADEN-BADEN

Bronze Medals	'Merlin' (flori.)	R. Harkness & Co. Ltd., England
	'Hilde Heinemann' (flori.)	Meilland, France
	'Prins Wilhelm Alexander'	Verschuren, Holland
	(The remainder of the awards went to unnamed seedlings)	

ROEULX

LARGE FLOWERS

Gold Medal	'Femme'	G. Delbard, France
Silver Medals	'Mullard Jubilee'	S. McGredy & Son Ltd., N. Ireland
	Unnamed	U. R. S. Meilland, France

SMALL FLOWERS

Gold Medals	'Satchmo'	S. McGredy & Son Ltd., N. Ireland
	'Echo'	Louis Lens, Belgium
	Unnamed	U. R. S. Meilland, France
Silver Medals	'Courvoisier'	S. McGredy & Son Ltd., N. Ireland
	'White Spray'	E. B. Le Grice, England
	'Golden Flame'	J. Laperrière, France
	'Susan Massu'	W. Kordes Söhne, Germany
Certificates	Unnamed	U. R. S. Meilland, France
	'Neue Revue'	W. Kordes Söhne, Germany

CLIMBER

Certificate	'Golden Parfum'	Jan Leenders, Holland
Prize for the most		
fragrant rose	'Mullard Jubilee'	S. McGredy & Son Ltd., N. Ireland

GENEVA

LARGE FLOWERS

Gold Medal and		
Prize of the City		
of Geneva	'Aquarius'	David L. Armstrong, U.S.A.
Silver Medal	Unnamed	A. Meilland, France
Certificate	'Interflora'	Louisette Meilland, France

SMALL FLOWERS

Gold Medal and Prize	Unnamed	A. Meilland, France
Silver Medal	'Sable Chaud'	M. Delbard, France
Certificates	Unnamed	G. de Ruiter, Holland
	'Porthos'	Laperrière, France

CLIMBERS

Silver Medal and Prize	'Climbing Diablotin'	M. Delbard, France
Certificate	'Murmure'	P. Croix, France

PERFUME CUP 1970

'Duftzauber' (H.T.)	W. Kordes Söhne, Germany

BELFAST

HYBRID TEA

Gold Medal and Prize of the City of Belfast	'Peer Gynt'	Reimer Kordes, Germany
Certificates	'Timothy Eaton'	Sam McGredy, N. Ireland
	'Grand Amore'	Reimer Kordes, Germany
	'Bonsoir'	Pat Dickson, N. Ireland
The "Uladh" Award for fragrance	'Grand Amore'	Reimer Kordes, Germany

FLORIBUNDA

The "Golden Thorn" Award	'City of Belfast'	Sam McGredy, N. Ireland
Certificates	'Copper Pot'	Pat Dickson, N. Ireland
	'Taconis'	G. de Ruiter, Holland

CLIMBER

Certificates	'Bantry Bay'	Sam McGredy, N. Ireland
	'Benvenuto'	Alain Meilland, France

COPENHAGEN

Certificates	'Escapade' (flori.)	R. Harkness & Co. Ltd., England
	'Mullard Jubilee' (H.T.)	Sam McGredy, N. Ireland
	'National Trust' (H.T.)	Sam McGredy, N. Ireland
	'Red Parfum' (climber)	M. Robichon & A. Eve, France

NEW ZEALAND

"Gold Star" of the South Pacific and Certificate of Merit for the best hybrid tea	'Pania' (H.T.)	Sam McGredy, N. Ireland
"Gold Star" of the South Pacific and Certificate of Merit for the best floribunda	'City of Belfast' (flori.)	Sam McGredy, N. Ireland
Award for most fragrant rose and Certificate of Merit	'Happy Anniversary' (flori.)	G. Delbard, France
Certificates	'Gene Boerner' (flori.)	Jackson & Perkins, U.S.A.
	'Little Devil' (flori.)	G. Delbard, France
	'News' (flori.)	E. B. Le Grice, England
	'Superior' (flori.)	E. B. Le Grice, England
	'Petite Folie' (min.)	L. Meilland, France

Book Reviews

The Story of the Rose, by James McIntyre, 160 pp.
Published by Ward Lock Ltd. £2·10.

Mr McIntyre's book shows once again how the history, romance and beauty of the Rose catches the imagination and interest of flower lovers. The careful arrangement of the chapters goes from the supposed origin of the Rose through legend, religion, uses and evolution, up to notes on the rose trade and modern roses. Each chapter can be read as a separate article and this makes for light and easy reading as a bedside book. The printing and colour work is pleasant and the volume easy to hold. An undemanding book to fall asleep over.

The early part of the work is perhaps the most interesting; the later chapters on modern roses, rose personalities and gardens tend to be boring and indeed not always accurate. Although Mr McIntyre states in his introduction that his book is written for the experienced rose grower who knows little or nothing of the history of the Rose as few works are written on these lines, he lists in a later chapter a whole series of books already published on this theme. Many of his statements are bewildering and, as the knowledgeable rose grower progresses through the book, rather irritating.

Before accepting everything in this otherwise pleasantly readable book on roses, the amateur should check names and dates with The Royal National Rose Society.

ENA JEFFRIES
("ENA HARKNESS")

In Praise of Roses, by Harry Wheatcroft, 192 pp.
Published by Barrie & Jenkins Ltd. £2.

When I began to grow roses my enthusiasm soared like a swallow in the summer sky. I devoured every book that I could on the subject of rose growing. At that time I would have revelled in Harry Wheatcroft's book *In Praise of Roses.* I can still study it with avidity because it contains much of interest to the more experienced grower. Mr Wheatcroft is a figure in the rose world well known to gardeners, whether they be rose growers or turnip fanciers, and his views are worthy of some attention. He gives his opinion on roses grouped by colour and he considers in some detail the controversial question of blue roses. It is also interesting to note his choice of roses in every other colour.

The pictures in the book, although some suffer from poor colour rendering, especially those of the red roses—this colour scarcely ever reproduces satisfactorily—inspire flights of imagination based on the desire to grow the roses. They remind me of a Wheatcroft catalogue of the early 'fifties which I always studied assiduously. On the whole, for the tyro, they simulate a delicious wandering through a rose garden. However, I cannot enthuse about the illustration of 'Peace' facing page 32. This seems to me to be a travesty of a beautiful rose. It is deformed and does little credit to the original. Surely the introducer of this rose could have found a better photograph.

In contrast, the black and white picture of the same rose on page 118 is a sheer delight. After 'Peace' there are two photographs of 'Grand'mère Jenny' and 'Fragrant Cloud' which, except for the colour rendering of the latter, are perfect. I know there are few better judges of the perfect bloom than Harry Wheatcroft. Why spoil 'Peace'? The photograph of 'Anna Wheatcroft' is charming like the rose itself and recalls for me the moment of enchantment I experienced when it first came out. Some colour photographs suffer from being exposed in bright sunlight. This applies particularly to both illustrations of 'Super Star'.

I have always considered that there should be a chapter in a rose book devoted to a description of rose personalities. Here we have such a chapter and pleasant reading it makes. Although it is confined to Willi Kordes—the raiser of 'Perfecta' deserves to be remembered for ever—stories of Mathias Tantau, British, Dutch, French and American breeders are woven into the text throughout the book and these stories make fascinating reading.

The history, heredity and parentage of modern roses have always interested me. The story of 'Général Jacqueminot' was unknown to me and this has added to my knowledge of the older varieties. Mr Wheatcroft gives a comprehensive dissertation on parentage when he discusses hybridisation. I was happy to refresh my memory about 'Baby Château' and 'Independence', 'Lady Mary Fitzwilliam' and 'Crimson Rambler', 'Crimson Glory' and 'Mme. Caroline Testout'.

In his discussion about several roses which he groups under colour headings the author does not hesitate to indicate the faults of any variety. Nobody can blame him for having his favourites and he does not confine his praises to roses of his own introduction.

The chapter about the nursery is interesting. Mechanisation and mass production have kept prices lower than they might have been. They have also made roses more readily available.

Mr Wheatcroft informs us that he feels very proud to have been the introducer of 'Peace', 'Super Star', 'Queen Elizabeth' and 'Fragrant Cloud'. He fully deserves to feel this way and, if he had done no more, this should have assured him of the gratitude of rose lovers in this country.

The style of writing is easy, racy, and colloquial. Those who know Harry Wheatcroft the man will recognise him in his style.

J. H. WILDING

Powdery Mildew and Black Spot of Roses,
Ministry of Agriculture, Fisheries and Food Advisory Leaflet 569
(1969).

This six-page leaflet describes in detail the symptoms of Rose Powdery Mildew and Black Spot and useful information is given on methods of spread and overwintering. There are short lists of cultivars which are resistant to one or both of these two diseases and, although these lists are not intended to be comprehensive, it would seem that the floribunda 'Allgold' certainly merits an asterisk at the top of p. 5 as it is markedly resistant to both diseases.

In the notes on chemical control it is interesting to find that 'Volck', a proprietary summer white oil, has given more effective control of Powdery Mildew than has the well known dinocap.

No mention is made of the newer systemic fungicides which are perhaps still considered experimental: doubtless these will appear in a later edition. Perhaps the opportunity could then be taken to incorporate more information about Rose Rust in the light of research at Bath University.

This leaflet, which is primarily intended for the guidance of professional rose growers, is nevertheless a most valuable aid to the cultivation of healthy roses. Mr W. T. Dale, of the N.A.A.S., is to be congratulated on its publication.

E. F. A.

Plants for Ground Cover, by Graham Stuart Thomas, 273 pp.
Published by J. M. Dent & Sons Ltd., £3

The author of this book is so well known to rosarians and members of this Society, not only for his contributions to this Annual, but also for his authoritative books on *Old Shrub Roses, Shrub Roses of Today* and *Climbing Roses Old and New,* that they may be astonished to find him equally knowledgeable in a much wider field. Some years ago he wrote a book on *Colour in the Winter Garden* and now he has come right up to date with this very comprehensive book on plants for ground cover. In recent years labour for garden maintenance has become more and more precious and difficult to find, so that ground cover plants have come increasingly into the limelight. Originally this meant to some extent, at least as far as I am concerned, low growing plants which suppressed weeds, planted under choicer plants such as roses, but in no sense competing with them, rather complementing them in a pleasing manner.

Mr Thomas goes much farther than this, however, by advocating the use of some shrubs such as Forsythia, Fatshedera, Cytisus, Ceanothus and Lavender, which I would not regard as being any better as weed supressors than some roses, such as 'Lilli Marlene', 'Marlena' or 'The Fairy' which do not receive a mention. Roses are not forgotten however; several of the sprawlers such as R. × *paulii* and its pink form, R. × *paulii rosea* and R. *wichuraiana*; plants which require a fair amount of room in any garden. Several shrub roses, particularly *R. rugosa* and allied forms are advocated, quite rightly, for light soil and I am delighted to see *R. virginiana* recommended for autumn colour in addition to its weed suppressing virtues. Rose 'Nevada' also receives a mention, but its sport, 'Marguerite Hilling' does not; both are equally fine, not only for their magnificent garden performance, but also because their habit of growth discourages weeds underneath their branches.

A list of plants is given suitable for underplanting of roses of the Hybrid Tea and Floribunda classes. Many more could have been advocated, especially for the stronger growing cultivars. These have to be extracted from the shorter growing plants in the Alphabetical Tables, a reasonable exercise for winter evenings. These Alphabetical Tables make selection easier for those with special conditions, i.e. plants which require lime-free soils, those which tolerate chalk or clay, enjoy shade or hot sun, will stand wind and salt spray, thrive in town gardens and even deter small animals and presumably small boys! Comprehensive coverage indeed, which should be of great assistance as many of the plants recommended are worthy of cultivation for their flowering ability irrespective of their ground cover value.

No one of my generation will quarrel with the valuable advice given with regard to the thorough cultivation of the soil and adequate preparation of the site before going ahead with planting. Mr Thomas also recommends some of the chemicals which can be used in various circumstances which may arise to augment what may be considered as old fashioned, although well proven methods.

Mr Thomas argues the case for ground cover plants well and lucidly. This authoritative work should be particularly valuable to those concerned with maintenance and alterations in public parks and gardens, particularly where new landscaping schemes are being carried out. Not to the same extent, perhaps, will it be of benefit to those primarily interested in roses, but few will be disappointed who enjoy reading about plants and allied garden subjects. I certainly enjoyed it and its common-sense approach, even if I felt roses could have been given a slightly broader coverage, and Mr Thomas has without doubt enhanced his great reputation.

S. M. GAULT

Herbicides

Rosarians who own large gardens and who may have occasional difficulty in keeping the wilderness at bay will be interested to know that two years' trials by me of Casoron G, a granular formulation of dichlobenil, suggest that this weedkiller is safe on many rose cultivars and has considerable activity against Creeping Thistle, both Nettles, most annuals but not, unfortunately, against the Bindweeds. Couch is checked but not killed. This material, which is easy to spread, is applied at 1 lb/64 sq. yd.

E. F. ALLEN

The Rose Analysis

L. G. TURNER

In the Rose Analysis for 1961—just ten years ago—the first three places in the table for floribunda roses were held by 'Frensham', 'Masquerade', and 'Korona'. This year these three varieties—together with 'Scarlet Queen Elizabeth'—are omitted from the list for the first time. The susceptibility of 'Frensham' to Mildew is well known. 'Masquerade', being the first break in the multi-colour range, was a particular favourite but today's gardeners are not willing to wait so long for the second flush of flowers; 'Korona' was one of the forerunners of the orange-scarlet break, but it appears to be selective as to where it will thrive. These were all good varieties but I am not surprised to see them pass out of the list. The newcomers are 'Arthur Bell', 'Scented Air', 'Pernille Poulsen' and 'Apricot Nectar', all transferred from the Audit of Newer Floribundas, as they are no longer eligible for that list owing to date of introduction. 'Golden Treasure' and 'Charlotte Elizabeth' do not win a place in the main table. 'Molly McGredy', 'Orange Silk', 'News', 'Copper Pot', 'Lively Lady' and 'Stephen Langdon' make their début in the Audit of Newer Floribundas; all have received one of the Society's awards for new seedlings.

Newcomers to the Audit of Newer Hybrid Teas are 'City of Bath', 'Red Queen' (formerly 'Liebestraum'), 'Summer Holiday', 'Elizabeth Harkness' and 'Alec's Red'. 'Ernest H. Morse', 'Diorama', 'Brandenburg', 'Mister Lincoln' and 'Shannon' are omitted from the table owing to date of introduction, but the first three find places in other tables.

'Stella' does not seem to be quite so popular with the Northern exhibitors and 'Peace' is still continuing the inevitable descent. 'Fragrant Cloud' has taken over from 'Super Star' at the top in both North and South Tables for General Garden Cultivation, which is not surprising as the latter has become a slave to Mildew in so many parts of the country and the dry periods of the last two summers have provided ideal conditions for the disease.

Out go 'Eden Rose' and 'Sutter's Gold', while 'Ena Harkness' and 'My Choice' just manage to retain a place in one of the General Garden Cultivation tables. 'Sutter's Gold' is, however, still a favourite for use as indoor decoration.

The tables have been prepared using the same method as in the past, and although considerable thought has been given to improving this, no better procedure has been found. The system is to point each variety for merit in each voter's return, and also for popularity by taking into account the number of times a variety is mentioned. If any member can suggest a better method, not merely an alternative one, I shall be pleased to learn of it.

The thanks of the Editorial Board are extended to all those voters who participated, and without whose help the analysis could not have been presented. Any member growing over 400 rose trees, in thirty or more varieties, is welcome to vote and I shall be pleased to send the necessary forms.

THE ROSE ANALYSIS

AUDIT OF NEWER ROSES—FLORIBUNDAS

This table includes only varieties introduced in this country since 1 January 1966

Position	Number of points	NAME	Introduced	COLOUR
1	607	City of Leeds	1966	Rich salmon
2	489	City of Belfast	1968	Bright red
3	472	Irish Mist	1967	Orange salmon
4	468	Redgold	1967	Golden yellow edged cherry red
5	464	*Escapade	1967	Magenta with white centre
6	369	Sir Lancelot	1967	Apricot yellow
7	345	Princess Michiko	1966	Coppery orange
8	264	*Goldgleam	1966	Deep yellow
9	256	Molly McGredy	1969	Rose red, reverse silver
10	231	King Arthur	1967	Salmon pink
11	180	Orange Silk	1968	Orange-vermilion
12	160	News	1968	Beetroot red shading to purple
13	127	Copper Pot	1968	Copper-orange
14	90	Lively Lady	1969	Vermilion
15	85	Stephen Langdon	1969	Deep scarlet

* Most fragrant

FLORIBUNDA ROSES

This table includes only varieties introduced in this country before 1 January 1966

Position	Number of points	NAME	Introduced	COLOUR
1	1264	Iceberg	1958	Pure white, tinged pink in bud
2	1130	Evelyn Fison	1962	Vivid red with scarlet shading
3	1001	Queen Elizabeth	1955	Clear self pink
4	904	*Elizabeth of Glamis	1964	Light salmon
5	826	*Orange Sensation	1961	Light vermilion
6	778	Pink Parfait	1962	Medium pink, yellow base
7	712	Orangeade	1959	Bright orange vermilion
8	699	Europeana	1963	Deep crimson
9	681	Allgold	1956	Unfading golden yellow
10	624	Paddy McGredy	1962	Carmine, lighter reverse
11	618	*Dearest	1960	Rosy salmon
12	567	Sea Pearl	1964	Pale orange and pink with yellow
13	529	Violet Carson	1963	Soft pink, silvery reverse
14	494	Anna Wheatcroft	1959	Light vermilion
15	492	Lilli Marlene	1959	Scarlet red
16	489	*Arthur Bell	1965	Yellow to creamy yellow
17	417	Dorothy Wheatcroft	1960	Bright orient red
18	331	Woburn Abbey	1962	Orange with yellow
19	325	*Pernille Poulsen	1965	Light pink
20	311	*Scented Air	1965	Salmon pink
21	280	*Apricot Nectar	1965	Pale apricot, base golden
22	278	Chanelle	1958	Cream, overlaid peach pink
23	277	Circus	1955	Yellow, pink and salmon
24	245	Paprika	1958	Bright turkey red

AUDIT OF NEWER ROSES—HYBRID TEAS

This table includes only varieties introduced in this country since 1 January 1966

Position	Number of points	NAME	Introduced	COLOUR
1	692	Grandpa Dickson	1966	Yellow, fading to creamy yellow
2	609	*Red Devil	1967	Scarlet with lighter reverse
3	502	*Bonsoir	1968	Peach pink, deeper at base of petals
4	491	Fred Gibson	1968	Amber yellow to apricot
5	433	*Duke of Windsor	1967	Orange vermilion
6	410	*Red Lion	1966	Deep cerise pink
7	398	*Whisky Mac	1968	Coppery yellow and apricot
8	386	Peer Gynt	1968	Yellow, flushed pink on edges of petals
9	328	*Lady Seton	1966	Deep rose pink
10	250	*Alec's Red	1969	Cherry red
11	205	Santa Fé	1967	Salmon pink, lighter reverse
12	203	Elizabeth Harkness	1968	Off-white to creamy-buff
13	202	Summer Holiday	1967	Deep vermilion
14	172	Red Queen	1968	Cherry red
15	138	City of Bath	1969	Deep pink, paler reverse

* Most fragrant

HYBRID TEA ROSES PRODUCING LARGE SPECIMEN BLOOMS
SUITABLE FOR EXHIBITION

This table includes only varieties introduced in this country before 1 January 1966

Northern Counties

Position	Number of points	NAME	Introduced	COLOUR
1	332	Perfecta	1957	Cream, shaded rose red
2	320	Pink Favourite	1956	Deep rose pink
3	311	*Fragrant Cloud	1964	Geranium lake
4	306	*Wendy Cussons	1959	Cerise flushed scarlet
5	300	Stella	1958	Carmine shading to cream
6	294	Peace	1947	Light yellow edged pink
7	282	Memoriam	1960	White tinted pale pink
8	278	Gavotte	1963	Light pink with silvery reverse
9	272	*Royal Highness	1962	Soft light pink
10	239	Norman Hartnell	1964	Deep cerise
11	221	Isabel de Ortiz	1962	Deep pink, reverse silvery
12	202	Brilliant	1952	Rich scarlet
13	202	Princess	1964	Vermilion
14	197	*Ernest H. Morse	1965	Rich turkey red
15	185	*Super Star	1960	Pure light vermilion without shading
16	173	Chicago Peace	1962	Phlox pink, base canary yellow
17	150	Rose Gaujard	1958	White, flushed rich carmine
18	125	*Silver Lining	1958	Pale rose with silver reverse
19	120	Gail Borden	1956	Deep rose pink, reverse shaded creamy yellow
20	114	Christian Dior	1959	Velvety scarlet
21	114	Anne Letts	1953	Pale pink with paler reverse
22	82	Brandenburg	1965	Deep salmon, reverse darker
23	72	Margaret	1954	Pink with lighter reverse
24	67	Diorama	1965	Apricot yellow, flushed pink

SOME ROSES FOR INDOOR DECORATION

NAME	Introduced	COLOUR
*Super Star	1960	Pure light vermilion without shading
*Ernest H. Morse	1965	Rich turkey red
Mischief	1960	Coral salmon
*Wendy Cussons	1959	Cerise flushed scarlet
*Fragrant Cloud	1964	Geranium lake
Peace	1947	Light yellow edged pink
Queen Elizabeth	1955	Clear self pink
Pascali	1963	White
*Blue Moon	1964	Silvery Lilac
*Sutter's Gold	1950	Light orange shaded red
Mojave	1954	Deep orange and reddish flame
Virgo	1947	White

* Most fragrant

HYBRID TEA ROSES PRODUCING LARGE SPECIMEN BLOOMS
SUITABLE FOR EXHIBITION
This table includes only varieties introduced in this country before 1 January 1966

Southern Counties

Position	Number of points	NAME	Introduced	COLOUR
I	431	Pink Favourite	1956	Deep rose pink
2	380	*Fragrant Cloud	1964	Geranium lake
3	379	*Royal Highness	1962	Soft light pink
4	365	Perfecta	1957	Cream, shaded rose red
5	362	Gavotte	1963	Light pink with silvery reverse
6	297	Stella	1958	Carmine shading to cream
7	291	Memoriam	1960	White tinted pale pink
8	283	*Wendy Cussons	1959	Cerise flushed scarlet
9	283	Princess	1964	Vermilion
10	282	Isabel de Ortiz	1962	Deep pink with silver reverse
11	278	Peace	1947	Light yellow edged with pink
12	238	Rose Gaujard	1958	White, flushed rich carmine
13	210	Montezuma	1956	Deep salmon red
14	207	*Super Star	1960	Pure light vermilion without shading
15	200	*Silver Lining	1958	Pale rose with silver reverse
16	198	Norman Hartnell	1964	Deep cerise
17	193	Anne Letts	1953	Pale pink with paler reverse
18	190	*Ernest H. Morse	1965	Rich turkey red
19	189	Honey Favourite	1962	Yellowish pink, base yellow
20	151	Chicago Peace	1962	Phlox pink, base canary yellow
21	138	Brilliant	1952	Rich scarlet
22	126	Gail Borden	1956	Deep rose pink, reverse shaded creamy yellow
23	116	Karl Herbst	1950	Deep red with lighter reverse
24	89	Gold Crown	1960	Very deep yellow

REPEAT FLOWERING CLIMBERS

Position	Number of points	NAME	Introduced	COLOUR
I	493	*Golden Showers	1957	Golden yellow
2	421	Handel	1965	Cream edged rose pink
3	415	Danse du Feu	1954	Orange scarlet
4	412	Pink Perpetue	1965	Clear pink with carmine pink
5	394	*Zéphirine Drouhin	1868	Bright carmine pink
6	331	Mermaid	1917	Primrose yellow
7	328	Parkdirektor Riggers	1957	Blood red
8	314	*New Dawn	1930	Pale flesh pink
9	290	Schoolgirl	1964	Orange-apricot
10	284	Casino	1963	Soft yellow, deeper in bud
11	229	*Maigold	1953	Bronze yellow
12	198	Royal Gold	1957	Deep yellow

The following varieties may also be recommended: *'Aloha', 'Bantry Bay', *'Copenhagen', 'Dortmund', 'Galway Bay', 'Hamburger Phoenix', 'Parade', 'Raymond Chenault' and *'Sympathie'.

* Most fragrant

R.A.—13

HYBRID TEA ROSES FOR GENERAL GARDEN CULTIVATION

This table includes only varieties introduced in this country before 1 January 1966

Northern Counties

Position	Number of points	NAME	Introduced	COLOUR
1	429	*Fragrant Cloud	1964	Geranium lake
2	398	*Super Star	1960	Pure light vermilion without shading
3	385	*Wendy Cussons	1959	Cerise flushed scarlet
4	382	Peace	1947	Light yellow edged pink
5	371	Mischief	1960	Coral salmon
6	364	Pink Favourite	1956	Deep rose pink
7	330	Piccadilly	1960	Scarlet, yellow reverse
8	311	Rose Gaujard	1958	White flushed rich carmine
9	309	*Ernest H. Morse	1965	Rich turkey red
10	283	*Prima Ballerina	1958	Deep pink
11	278	Stella	1958	Carmine shading to cream
12	278	Chicago Peace	1962	Phlox pink, base yellow
13	196	King's Ransom	1961	Rich pure yellow
14	190	Pascali	1963	White
15	184	Perfecta	1957	Cream shaded rose red
16	182	Diorama	1965	Apricot yellow, flushed pink
17	165	Gail Borden	1956	Deep rose pink, reverse shaded creamy yellow
18	158	*Ena Harkness	1946	Bright crimson scarlet
19	157	*Silver Lining	1958	Pale rose with silver reverse
20	126	Gavotte	1963	Light pink with silvery reverse
21	117	*Josephine Bruce	1952	Deep velvety crimson scarlet
22	108	*Blue Moon	1964	Silvery lilac
23	94	Gold Crown	1960	Very deep yellow
24	93	Colour Wonder	1964	Orange salmon, reverse pale yellow

WICHURAIANA CLIMBING AND RAMBLING ROSES— SUMMER FLOWERING

Suitable for pergolas and fences

Position	Number of points	NAME	Introduced	COLOUR
1	484	*Albertine	1921	Salmon opening to coppery pink
2	410	Paul's Scarlet Climber	1915	Bright scarlet crimson
3	309	Emily Gray	1916	Rich golden buff
4	306	Excelsa	1909	Bright rosy crimson
5	302	American Pillar	1902	Bright rose with white eye
6	292	*Albéric Barbier	1900	Yellow to creamy white
7	245	Dorothy Perkins	1901	Rose pink
8	235	*Dr W. van Fleet	1910	Pale flesh pink
9	231	Crimson Shower	1951	Crimson
10	224	Chaplin's Pink Climber	1928	Bright pink
11	202	*Sanders' White	1915	White
12	100	Crimson Conquest	1931	Deep scarlet, white base

* Most fragrant

HYBRID TEA ROSES FOR GENERAL GARDEN CULTIVATION

This table includes only varieties introduced in this country before 1 January 1966

Southern Counties

Posi- tion	Number of points	NAME	Intro- duced	COLOUR
1	748	*Fragrant Cloud	1964	Geranium lake
2	662	*Super Star	1960	Pure light vermilion without shading
3	634	*Wendy Cussons	1959	Cerise flushed scarlet
4	622	Peace	1947	Light yellow edged pink
5	621	*Ernest H. Morse	1965	Rich turkey red
6	546	Pink Favourite	1956	Deep rose pink
7	524	Mischief	1960	Coral salmon
8	480	Stella	1958	Carmine shading to cream
9	451	Rose Gaujard	1958	White flushed rich carmine
10	450	Piccadilly	1960	Scarlet, yellow reverse
11	412	*Prima Ballerina	1958	Deep pink
12	355	Pascali	1963	White
13	321	Diorama	1965	Apricot yellow, flushed pink
14	316	*Silver Lining	1958	Pale rose with silver reverse
15	315	*My Choice	1958	Pink, reverse pale yellow
16	301	Perfecta	1957	Cream shaded rose red
17	298	Chicago Peace	1962	Phlox pink, base yellow
18	270	King's Ransom	1961	Rich pure yellow
19	264	Gavotte	1963	Light pink with silvery reverse
20	243	*Josephine Bruce	1952	Deep velvety crimson scarlet
21	227	Isabel de Ortiz	1962	Deep pink with silver reverse
22	176	Montezuma	1956	Deep salmon red
23	173	Gail Borden	1956	Deep rose pink, reverse shaded creamy yellow
24	152	*Blue Moon	1964	Silvery lilac

SHRUB ROSES—REPEAT FLOWERING

NAME	COLOUR	Height in feet
*Chinatown	Yellow, sometimes tinted pink	6
*Fred Loads	Vermilion orange	5-6
Nevada	Pale creamy white, sometimes with pink	6
Joseph's Coat	Yellow, orange and red	5-6
*Penelope	Creamy salmon	5
Heidelberg	Bright red	5-6
Bonn	Orange scarlet	6
Kassel	Scarlet red	6
*Cornelia	Pink, with yellow base	5-6
Elmshorn	Light crimson	5
*Blanc Double de Coubert	Pure white	6
*Felicia	Salmon pink, shaded yellow	6

* Most fragrant

CLIMBING AND RAMBLING ROSES FOR SPECIAL PURPOSES

Posi-tion	NAME	Intro-duced	COLOUR
	Suitable for walls or closeboard fencing		
1	Danse du Feu	1954	Orange scarlet
2	Mermaid	1917	Primrose yellow
3	★Albertine	1921	Salmon opening to coppery pink
4	★Maigold	1953	Bronze yellow
5	Parkdirektor Riggers	1957	Blood red
6	Pink Perpetue	1965	Clear pink with carmine pink reverse
7	Royal Gold	1957	Deep yellow
8	Cl. Mrs Sam McGredy	1937	Bright orange copper
9	★Cl. Shot Silk	1937	Light carmine shaded orange
	Suitable for open fences		
1	Danse du Feu	1954	Orange scarlet
2	★Albertine	1921	Salmon opening to coppery pink
3	★New Dawn	1930	Pale flesh pink
4	Parkdirektor Riggers	1957	Blood red
5	Paul's Scarlet Climber	1915	Bright scarlet crimson
6	American Pillar	1902	Bright rose with white eye
7	★Maigold	1953	Bronze yellow
8	Emily Gray	1916	Rich golden buff
9	Pink Perpetue	1965	Clear pink with carmine pink reverse
	Suitable for pillars		
1	★Golden Showers	1957	Golden yellow
2	Handel	1965	Cream edged rose pink
3	Danse du Feu	1954	Orange scarlet
4	Pink Perpetue	1965	Clear pink with carmine pink reverse
5	Casino	1963	Soft yellow, deeper in bud
6	★Zéphirine Drouhin	1868	Bright carmine pink
7	Royal Gold	1957	Deep yellow
8	Paul's Scarlet Climber	1915	Bright scarlet crimson
9	★Albertine	1921	Salmon opening to coppery pink

SHRUB ROSES—SUMMER FLOWERING ONLY

NAME	COLOUR	Height in feet
Canary Bird	Rich yellow	6
R. moyesii	Deep red	8–10
Frühlingsgold	Clear light yellow	6
R. rubrifolia	Pink, foliage tinted mauve and grey	6
R. hugonis	Yellow	5
Frühlingsmorgen	Deep pink to yellow, maroon stamens	6
★Mme. Hardy	White	6
★Celestial (Alba)	Pure pink	5
R. gallica versicolor	Crimson striped pink and white	4
★Maiden's Blush (Alba)	Warm pink shading to cream pink	5
R. cantabrigiensis	Yellow	8
R. highdownensis	Light red	8–10

★ Most fragrant

REPEAT FLOWERING ROSES FOR HEDGES
Up to 5 ft

Position	NAME	Introduced	COLOUR
1	Iceberg	1958	Pure white tinged pink in bud
2	Queen Elizabeth	1955	Clear self pink
3	Peace	1947	Light yellow edged pink
4	*Chinatown	1963	Yellow, sometimes tinted pink
5	Frensham	1946	Deep scarlet crimson
6	*Fred Loads	1967	Vermilion orange
7	Dorothy Wheatcroft	1960	Orient red with deeper shades
8	*Super Star	1960	Pure light vermilion without shading
9	Scarlet Queen Elizabeth	1963	Orange scarlet
10	Masquerade	1950	Yellow, pink and red
11	*Penelope	1924	Creamy salmon
12	Shepherd's Delight	1958	Flame, orange and yellow

REPEAT FLOWERING ROSES FOR HEDGES
Over 5 ft

Position	NAME	Introduced	COLOUR
1	Queen Elizabeth	1955	Clear self pink
2	*Chinatown	1963	Yellow, sometimes tinted pink
3	Nevada	1927	Pale creamy white, sometimes with pink
4	*Fred Loads	1967	Vermilion orange
5	Joseph's Coat	1963	Yellow, orange and red
6	Uncle Walter	1963	Scarlet with crimson shadings
7	*Golden Showers	1957	Golden yellow
8	*Zéphirine Drouhin	1868	Bright carmine pink
9	Bonn	1949	Orange scarlet
10	Heidelberg	1958	Bright red
11	Kassel	1958	Scarlet red
12	Frensham	1946	Deep scarlet crimson

WEATHER RESISTANT ROSES—HYBRID TEAS

NAME	Introduced	COLOUR
Peace	1947	Light yellow edged pink
*Super Star	1960	Light vermilion without shading
*Ernest H. Morse	1965	Rich turkey red
*Wendy Cussons	1959	Cerise flushed scarlet
Mischief	1960	Coral salmon
Stella	1958	Carmine shading to cream
Piccadilly	1960	Scarlet, yellow reverse
Grandpa Dickson	1966	Yellow, fading to creamy yellow
Rose Gaujard	1958	White flushed rich carmine
*Fragrant Cloud	1964	Geranium lake
Pink Favourite	1956	Deep rose pink
Chicago Peace	1962	Phlox pink, base canary yellow

* Most fragrant

WEATHER RESISTANT ROSES—FLORIBUNDAS

NAME	Intro-duced	COLOUR
Evelyn Fison	1962	Vivid red with scarlet shading
Queen Elizabeth	1955	Clear self pink
Iceberg	1958	Pure white, tinged pink in bud
Allgold	1956	Unfading golden yellow
Orangeade	1959	Bright orange vermilion
Lilli Marlene	1959	Scarlet red
*Elizabeth of Glamis	1964	Light salmon
*Orange Sensation	1961	Orange vermilion
Europeana	1963	Deep crimson
Paprika	1958	Bright turkey red
Paddy McGredy	1962	Carmine, lighter reverse
Frensham	1946	Deep scarlet crimson

MINIATURE ROSES
Mostly of about 6–9 in. in height, rarely more

Position	NAME	COLOUR
1	Baby Masquerade	Yellow and red
2	Coralin	Coral red to orange red
3	Rosina	Sunflower yellow
4	Pour Toi	White, tinted yellow at base
5	New Penny	Salmon, turning pink with age
6	Cinderella	White, tinted carmine
7	Colibri	Bright orange-yellow
8	Perla de Montserrat	Clear pink with deeper shadings
9	Baby Gold Star	Golden yellow

★ Most fragrant

International Rose Convention, New Zealand – November 1971

Many members of The Royal National Rose Society will already know that the next International Rose Convention will take place in New Zealand in November under the auspices of the New Zealand Rose Society.

The City of Hamilton, which has been chosen as the venue for the Convention, is one of the main centres in New Zealand and is situated in the heart of the country's most productive farming district. With a population of 70,000 it is New Zealand's fifth largest city and is renowned as one of the most beautiful and attractive cities throughout the two Islands.

The New Zealand Rose Society laid their initial plans for this Convention immediately following the International Rose Conference held in London during the summer of 1968. Their recently published Convention and tour brochures indicate that a wonderful programme of events has been arranged to cater for the interests of all visitors.

The official opening of the Convention takes place on Monday 8th November and a varied programme of activities, including national and local district rose shows, lectures by eminent international rosarians and visits to local places of interest, follows throughout the week up to the Convention banquet on the Saturday evening, and concluding with church services and farewells on Sunday 14th November.

The Royal National Rose Society has made arrangements for a special tour for the benefit of members wishing to visit New Zealand to attend the Convention. The tour will last four weeks and the tour party will leave London (Heathrow) on 23rd October and all air travel will be by International Air Transport Association air lines. The itinerary provides for stops at Bangkok, Sydney and at Melbourne where provision has been made for attendance at the Summer Show and annual luncheon of the National Rose Society of Victoria. Thence to New Zealand, arriving at Wellington on 31st October. The party will leave Hamilton on 14th November and proceed homewards by air with stops at Fiji and Mexico City, arriving back in London (Heathrow) on 20th November.

Arrangements for the tour include hotel accommodation and all meals, except that lunch and dinner will not be provided for the six days of the Convention as it is felt that members would wish to be left to make their own arrangements during this period. An attractive programme of sight-seeing tours has been arranged to cover the period to be spent in the North Island immediately prior to the Convention. It includes visits to the New Zealand Rose Society's trial grounds at Palmerston North, the astonishing Glow-worm Grotto at Waitomo Caves and the colourful hot springs and bubbling mud pools amid the renowned geysers of Rotorua. This facet of the tour will conclude with a visit to Auckland before proceeding to Hamilton on 7th November.

The cost of the tour will be about £628 and it is emphasised that in drawing up the itinerary every care has been taken to ensure the co-ordination of leisure time with overnight flying, in order to guard against the tour being conducted at too rapid a pace.

W. A. JAMES

Introducing

... a really outstanding new soft pink and white Floribunda — a must for all true rose-lovers — and another winner exclusively from Cants of Colchester.

Convince yourself — by seeing it in superb colour in our 1971 catalogue. Then order straight-away — supplies are limited, and demand is expected to be very heavy.

Order all your roses from our newly designed full-colour catalogue — offering a choice of nearly 400 carefully selected varieties, new and old — and including our three 1970 introductions, Solitaire, Red Dragon and Naughty Nancy.

It's the rose catalogue that sets the pace. Over 60 superb colour illustrations. Huge range of the best Hybrid Teas and Floribundas — every one chosen to give you lasting satisfaction. Wide range of Climbers, Standards, Miniatures, Old and Speciality Roses. Simple growing hints, too.

Our
1971 Introductions
(*Protected or Protection applied for)

*Agreement (Fl.–H.T.) type. Deep clear pink flowers in clusters on a 2/2½ feet bush at first flowering followed by strong, tall, upright, many flowered autumn growths 3/4 feet. Excellent for bedding and cutting.—50p

*Artistic (Fl.) An addition to the floral arranger's choice. Flowers golden brown fading salmon. Strong wiry stems, healthy in growth, free in flower.—50p

Harriny (H.T.) Clear salmon pink shapely blooms held erect. One of the sweetest perfumes of any rose. Foliage and growth very healthy and free.—50p

*Ripples (Fl.) A full flower with waved petals freely produced in a strong lilac shade.—50p

E. B. LeGrice (Roses) Limited
ROSELAND NURSERIES, NORTH WALSHAM, NORFOLK.

N E W S

Still in the news
Gold Medal Royal National Rose Society see page 175
* Trial Ground Certificate New Zealand
A new dimension in colour, health and continuity —50p

For these and many other excellent roses consult our illustrated catalogue with full descriptions, classified for colour, height and perfume.
A special section on Old Garden Roses.

We Concentrate on Growing Fragrant Roses

Why?

because we consider a rose, however new and beautiful, without fragrance is like a summer without sun.

Send now for our free colour catalogue of

Anderson's
Fragrant Scottish Roses

From Royal Deeside, the norths premier nursery
Devoted entirely to growing over one million rose bushes annually

Anderson's Rose Nursery 22 CULTS ABERDEEN

Britain's Number one Rose Grower

In 1970 Bees Roses won Gold Medals at Chelsea, Liverpool, Shrewsbury and Southport, plus a Large Gold Medal and the Coronation Trophy at the R.N.R.S. Summer Show. In addition to a Large Gold Medal at the R.N.R.S. Autumn Show, Bees were awarded the Autumn Roses Challenge Trophy for the best exhibit and the De Escofet Trophy for the third year in succession.

Only the best is good enough to gain the premier awards at shows.

Bees skill and experience, which brings success at shows, guarantees the high quality of Bees Hardy Plants, Shrubs and Fruit Trees.

Send now for Bees Free Catalogue to Bees Ltd., Sealand, Chester.

207

210

Why not be a Gregorys Agent?

C. Gregory & Son Ltd. are among the largest and most experienced of Britain's Rose Growers. Our Nurseries are ideally situated in the Midlands and have the largest rose test-garden in the country.

Gregory's market only top-quality well-tested rose-trees.

Everyone knows Gregory's consistent and unrivalled success in rose growing and thousands of rose lovers visit the Gregory nurseries at Stapleford, Nottingham every year.

WHY WE INVITE YOU TO REPRESENT US IN YOUR LOCALITY

As a keen rose grower you are recognised as an expert in such things as the varieties best suited to your local conditions. We have pleasure, therefore, in inviting you to represent Gregory's roses as an agent in your district. We feel that the valuable advice you can give and the quality of roses we supply would combine to provide a service second to none.

BE SOMEBODY SPECIAL

for full details, write now

OR PHONE 0602-39 5454

Agents are provided with full-colour catalogues for circulation among potential customers and a poster to advertise each Agency is also supplied.

Gregory agents are paid a generous commission in the £ for their services in obtaining orders, giving advice and maintaining (and developing) the Company's goodwill among rose-growers.

Agents are not involved in the collection of cash from, or the delivery of trees to clients.

The responsibility is entirely ours! We send your client top quality, fully guaranteed rose trees and submit our account. As soon as we receive the customer's remittance in settlement of this account, we credit the agent with his commission.

WHY NOT

... Share your rose-growing know-how with your friends, neighbours and colleagues?

... WHY NOT enjoy the pride and satisfaction in becoming known as the local rose expert?

... AND WHY NOT earn money at the same time?

213

ALEC'S RED
and ESCAPADE

 ALEC'S RED   H.T.

Raiser:	Jas. Cocker & Sons Ltd., Aberdeen.
Introduced:	1970
Parents:	Fragrant Cloud × Dame de Coeur
Awards:	RNRS President's International Trophy 1970
	RNRS Gold Medal 1970
	RNRS Edland Medal for Fragrance 1969
	RNRS Certificate of Merit 1969

This wonderful red Rose has sweet, rich perfume, large flowers of many petals, stiff flower stems, abundant foliage and strong growth. It is a remarkable triumph for Mr. Cocker to have bred not only the best Rose in the RNRS trials, but the only one which holds both the President's International Trophy and the Edland Medal for Fragrance. We are confident that in a very few years Alec's Red will be planted as widely as Super Star is today.   **50p**

ESCAPADE Flor.

Raiser:	R. Harkness & Co. Ltd., Hitchin.
Introduced:	1967
Parents:	Pink Parfait × Baby Faurax
Awards:	First Prize, Copenhagen 1970
	Golden Thorn, Belfast 1969
	Gold Medal, Baden-Baden 1969
	RNRS Certificate of Merit 1967

Of less immediate popular appeal than Alec's Red, Escapade is a fascinating example of hybrid vigour, and is having a remarkable international career, scooping the top awards from three different countries. It is also appearing to great effect on show benches about the country. The flowers are magenta rose, with a white eye, and there is something inexpressibly innocent and charming about them. The flowering period is long, the growth vigorous, and the fragrance sweet. Truly a connoisseur's item.   **50p**

Obtainable from us or from our licensees.

214

WE ANNOUNCE FOR 1971

SOME VERY DISTINCTIVE VARIETIES

ANNE COCKER

Vivid luminous vermilion. This is a new break, a strong growing plant which produces a bunch of Roses to a stem, each bloom on its individual shoot, several inches long. The flowers are small, neat as one can imagine, very brilliant, double—and they have a very long life in the vase. An outstanding variety. Cocker, 1971. Highlight × Colour Wonder. RNRS Certificate of Merit. **60p**

BUSY LIZZIE

Pink Floribunda. This is just about one of the best for freedom of flower; and not only that, but for the area of colour that a group of it will give well round the side of the plant as on the top. Fairly described as the modern Nathalie Nypels (a much loved variety we are still asked for). Harkness, 1971. (Pink Parfait × Masquerade) × Dearest. RNRS Trial Ground Certificate. **60p**

CURIOSITY

The extraordinary variegated Hybrid Tea. None other has foliage like this curiosity. The reddish young leaves are variegated with cream, and as the leaves change to green, the variegation becomes more pronounced. The flowers are red and gold. Cocker, 1971. **60p**

DEVOTION

Blush pink, with deeper flushes; large flowers, even for a Floribunda/H.T. type. A strong grower, well scented, producing heads of full and well formed blooms. A most interesting result from its cross. Harkness, 1971. Orange Sensation × Peace. RNRS Trial Ground Certificate. **60p**

NORTHERN LIGHTS

A classic Hybrid Tea, creamy yellow, with rich, sweet fragrance. This will produce exhibition flowers on a fine garden plant, and the scent in this colour is a marvellous bonus. The foliage is dark, glossy, abundant, the individual leaves being large. Cocker, 1971. Fragrant Cloud × Kingcup. **60p**

PRINCESS CHICHIBU

This is a smart little Floribunda, with double flowers of contrasting rose-red and creamy pink, very neatly made. It is an excellent variety to show, or cut for the house, as well as being an attractive garden plant. Dark green glossy foliage. Harkness, 1971. (Vera Dalton × Highlight) × Merlin. **60p**

ROB ROY

We can see we made a mistake in not saving this one up to bring out as an extra-speciality. It is the most superb bright crimson we have ever seen— the colour is Ena Harkness style, but deeper, and even more glowing. Classed as Floribunda/H.T. type, the flowers are large for the class, and shapely. Here is a red garden Rose which is bound to spread a great deal of pleasure and delight in the future. Cocker, 1971. Evelyn Fison × Wendy Cussons. RNRS Trial Ground Certificate. **60p**

James Cocker & Sons Ltd. Whitemyres, Lang Stracht, Aberdeen

R. Harkness & Co. Ltd. The Rose Gardens, Hitchin, Herts.

215

216

219

220

It's not only roses Sam McGredy gathers

To date he's won every major award there is!

It means you get the choicest blooms, the finest specimens whenever you order roses with the famous McGredy labels.

**Write to Samuel McGredy & Son Ltd.,
Dept R.A., Royal Nurseries, Portadown, Northern Ireland
and he'll send you some beautiful details.**

223

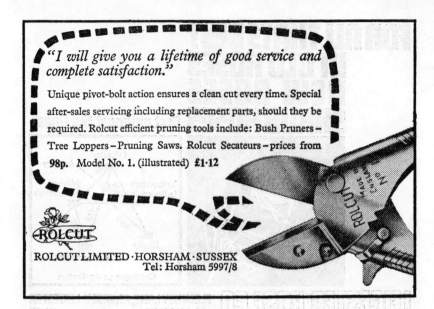

224

R.A.—15

225

Your beautiful, delicate, sensitive rose eats like a horse.

Roses are gross feeders. Most gardeners know that.
In fact, they require more food than you may have thought.
To satisfy their voracious appetites, there are any
number of formulations you could whip up yourself.
And it must be admitted that there are a few packaged
rose foods on the market in addition to ours.

So?

Well first of all, it's unlikely that anything you could
mix at home would be as good as Fisons Rose Food.
Honestly. Simply because we've had more practice
than you. And more roses to practise on. The same
applies if you're considering anyone else's rose food.

If you use Fisons Rose Food, you'll get more,
healthier, longer-lasting roses. It's as simple as that.

It all depends on what you want to breed.

Cart-horses or thoroughbreds.

▲FISONS·make gardening more like fun.

227

230

Tonk still cares

Edmund Tonk was a great Victorian authority on rose feeding. In 1889 he developed a formula for feeding roses properly. Since then, his well-proven formula has been regarded by great rose growers as the finest available rose fertilizer.

Toprose Fertilizer is based on Tonk's original formula and follows the same age-old principle that roses need a generous balanced feed every year. Toprose Fertilizer contains a slow-release form of nitrogen so that food is available for months rather than days. It also contains magnesium and iron for perfect blooms and gypsum for soil conditioning.

the modern name is Toprose

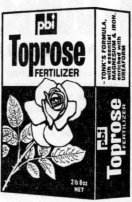

pbi Pan Britannica Industries Limited

232

235

237

238